NO MORE TOURIST TRAPS!

- A sprawling 1881 Victorian seaside guest house that makes it easy to go hawk watching by day, snuggle beneath a handmade quilt at night, and indulge in complimentary tea and finger sandwiches in the afternoon . . .

- A Howard Johnson's in Moncton, New Brunswick, Canada, which is not only near the magnificent tidal whirlpools and wildlife of the Bay of Fundy but located on Magnetic Hill—where if, at a certain point on the hill, you put your car in neutral, it seems to proceed uphill! . . .

- A winter trip to Kentucky to spot bald eagles in the Blue Mountains and to experience the phenomenon of a ghostly midnight moonbow at Cumberland Falls . . .

- A boat ride in Cape Cod's Dolphin Fleet to watch whales frolic, and later dine in town on exotic goosefish à l'orange . . .

Let John Thaxton be your guide to these and dozens more places to go, things to see, and ways to experience North America's wondrous . . .

NATURAL
ATTRACTIONS

NATURAL
ATTRACTIONS

JOHN THAXTON

WARNER BOOKS

A Warner Communications Company

W A Warner Communications Company

Printed in the United States of America
First Printing: May 1987
10 9 8 7 6 5 4 3 2 1

Cover design by Eileen Kramer
Cover illustration by Karen Bauman

Library of Congress Cataloging-in-Publication Data

Thaxton, John.
  Natural attractions.

  Includes index.
  1. Natural history—United States—Guide-books.
2. Natural history—Canada—Guide-books. 3. Natural
areas—United States—Guide-books. 4. Natural areas—
Canada—Guide-books. I. Title.
QH104.T464 1987   508.73   87-2102
ISBN 0-446-37021-5 (U.S.A.) (pbk.)
      0-446-37023-1 (Canada) (pbk.)

To Dylan Ross Williams,
who slept through his first bald eagle

CONTENTS

ACKNOWLEDGMENTS / *ix*

INTRODUCTION / *xi*

MAP / *xviii*

  1 HAWKS / *1*

  2 GLACIERS / *40*

  3 BEARS / *54*

  4 WATERFOWL / *75*

  5 ALLIGATORS / *108*

  6 THE MOONBOW / *125*

  7 WHALES / *131*

  8 METEOR SHOWERS / *183*

  9 WOLVES / *192*

10 LOONS / *204*

11 THE BAY OF FUNDY / *223*

12 ELK / *238*

13 NORTHERN LIGHTS / *245*

14 BISON / *253*

15 BATS / *263*

16 WHOOPING CRANES / *280*

INDEX / *291*

ACKNOWLEDGMENTS

I'd like to thank Jim Brett, curator of Hawk Mountain Sanctuary, for reviewing my chapter on hawks, and Phil Clapham, director of the Cetacean Research Program at the Provincetown Center for Coastal Studies, for going over my chapter on whales—both chapters are far the better for their suggestions, and any mistakes that may remain in either are entirely my own work.

I'd also like to thank Gene Barney, the Refuge Manager at Grays Lake National Wildlife Refuge, for taking the time to talk to me about whooping cranes. Nan Chadwick, of the National Audubon Society, and Paul Strong, of the Sigurd Olsen Environmental Institute, were generous with their time and knowledge of loon populations in, respectively, the Adirondacks and the Upper Peninsula of Michigan. Dan Faubert, of Parks Canada, helped me with logistics in Churchill, Manitoba; and Dr. Ian Stirling, of the Canadian Wildlife Service, answered several irksome questions I had about polar bears.

My thanks go as well to Alan Fish, of the Golden Gate National Recreation Area, for his insights into hawk migrations on the West Coast, particularly in the Bay Area, and to Jim Hainline, of the Klamath Basin National Wildlife Refuges, for his overall views of waterfowl population trends. Jim Housman, of Wood Buffalo National Park, shared his knowledge of a diverse range of subjects—buffalo, waterfowl, whooping cranes; and Jim Pisarowicz, of Wind Cave National

Park, answered several of my queries about buffalo. Don Strickland, superintendent of Algonquin Provincial Park, was more than generous with his time, enthusiasm, and knowledge of wolves; and for his thoughts on the nature of the moonbow, I thank Carey Tickner, of Cumberland Falls State Park. Dennis Trabant, of the Alaska Fish and Wildlife Service, answered some of my unresearchable questions about surging glaciers, and Dr. Merlin D. Tuttle, president of Bat Conservation International, answered a rataplan of my questions and deserves a thanks from anyone who cares about bats.

I feel especially indebted to Elmer Luke, my editor at Warner Books, who brought to bear on this project an infectious enthusiasm as well as a keen, sensitive, and flexible intelligence. Barney Karpfinger, my literary agent, nurtured this book from day one, and more than anyone else, it was he who guided it from an idea to a reality—his help at all stages was invaluable, and I couldn't thank him enough.

Lastly, I'd like to thank my wife, Pat, who loves.

INTRODUCTION

This book describes dramatic natural events—like a hundred thousand geese so thick in the sky they block the sun—and where and when to experience them.

Some animal, some mineral, some celestial, some terrestrial, the natural attractions in this book occur in a wide range of places. You can observe some of them from your backyard; others require a significant journey. If you want to see sixty shooting stars in an hour, you can do so from just about anyplace on the continent, providing it's dark. But if you want to see a glacier, or a loon, or a whooping crane, or a hundred eagles, you'll have to travel someplace. Unless you already live there.

Many of nature's most spectacular natural attractions are closer to home than most people realize. You don't have to buy special equipment, hire guides, and charter airplanes to witness a major natural event. All you have to do is show up, but before you do that you need to know where and when the event takes place. The majority of events and locations detailed in *Natural Attractions* are easily accessible, if not downright convenient. Many take place within easy day-trip range of major cities or population centers.

Natural Attractions is organized by event rather than place, by attraction rather than location. Each chapter consists of two parts. The first part, an essay, describes a particular natural attraction; and the second part details where and when the attraction takes place. The essay on whales, for example, is followed by descriptions of a dozen areas to see them, including an analysis of tours available and places to stay in the area. It's much easier to see whales than most people realize, and much more comfortable than they think as well. Ditto eagles, buffalo, glaciers, bats, and polar bears.

This book is directed at people who aren't necessarily outdoor types, who might never have camped out in their life. I don't include campgrounds in my descriptions of accommodations, largely because I'm sure that most campers realize that every location I mention has a campground nearby, if not right next door. The following remarks are for people with much curiosity about and little experience of the outdoors. The better part of the natural attractions detailed in this volume require no special equipment or precautions whatsoever, but some basic equipment and a sense of safety always enhance an outdoor experience.

EQUIPMENT

Approximately half of the events described in *Natural Attractions* can be experienced from the relative safety of an automobile. Through the windows of an automobile you can watch hundreds of thousands of waterfowl, thousands of hawks, a glacier, alligators. In street clothes you can board a very comfortable boat and go out whale watching, or board a helicopter for a cruise over the glaciers.

You could spend a fortune outfitting yourself for

the outdoors, but unless you plan to spend a lot of time there you would probably do better to outfit yourself as minimally as possible. If you have no outdoor equipment you probably never needed any. Most people never do. I believe in traveling light, in dragging along as little as possible. But I also believe in being comfortable, in always having something to eat or drink, in always being warm and dry.

If you've never spent a day in the wilderness, I suggest you consider acquiring the following items:

1. A daypack, preferably one with padded shoulder straps. An inexpensive daypack will hold everything you need for a day out of doors.

2. A pair of hiking shoes with a high ankle for support. It's incredible how many people sprain their ankles and experience considerable pain for no reason. An inexpensive pair of ankle-high boots, preferably waterproof ones, will make your life a lot easier. With a badly sprained ankle, walking across the living room can be excruciatingly painful; walking across a mountain ridge can be impossible.

3. A plastic water bottle or two. *Always carry water into the wilderness. No wilderness water source can be guaranteed to be safe.* There are two possible things to do: either carry your water with you, or boil water from a stream for a half hour. It's easier to carry water than to boil it. Increasing amounts of natural water sources have been found to be infected with *Giardia lamblia*, a nasty little parasite that can give you the runs for several years. Giardiasis, sometimes called "Beaver Fever," is a serious disease that's easily prevented—don't drink water even from the purest-looking of mountain streams.

4. An inexpensive waterproof poncho. When you get wet, you lose body heat about 200 times faster than you do when dry. In addition to causing serious discomfort, wet clothing can be downright dangerous in colder climates. Eight out of ten wilderness fatalities are caused by hypothermia, a drastic lowering of the body temperature. In northern or mountainous regions, where weather conditions can change suddenly, it is essential to keep yourself dry and warm. Waterproof rain gear takes up almost no room at all, and having some with you can make all the difference in the world.

5. Insect repellent. Much as I dislike the stuff, I've learned to carry insect repellent with me always. If you happen to show up someplace where the mosquitoes are thriving, they can drive you mad in no time flat. The only thing to do is liberally anoint yourself with insect repellent. I have found insect repellent creams to be more effective than aerosols.

6. A whistle. If you happen to get lost, or hurt, in the woods, a whistle can save your life. Hikers everywhere recognize three toots on a whistle as a distress call. The easiest way to summon help in the wilderness is to stay in the same place and signal with a whistle. Trying to shout for help will quickly render you hoarse.

7. A flashlight. Even experienced hikers occasionally misjudge how long it's going to take to get back. The scenario is classic: everybody's having a good time until someone realizes it's getting dark and there are no streetlights in the woods. Making your way through the woods in the dark is all but impossible, and very dangerous. With a flashlight it's easy. I always carry one.

8. A first-aid kit. It's a good idea to carry a small, basic first-aid kit. An alcohol swab to clean out a cut and a Band-Aid to cover it can make a big difference, psychologically as well as physically. I've seen extremely disoriented and agitated people calm down considerably after having a minor wound cleaned out and being given a couple of aspirins.

OTHER EQUIPMENT

In order fully to experience many of the events in *Natural Attractions*, you will need a pair of binoculars. I have read extremely long and complicated articles about which type of binoculars are best for what purposes. Dozens of manufacturers produce scores of different styles of binoculars, and evaluating them all would probably take you the better part of a year.

If you don't have a pair of binoculars and aren't sure if you want to invest in a high-quality pair, buy a cheap pair. Discount stores everywhere sell inexpensive binoculars for as little as $20, and if you don't drop them or leave them out in the rain they will probably last for years. Contemporary lens manufacturing technology is such that even low-quality binoculars are quite acceptable for most purposes.

Binoculars come in all sizes and powers, but the most popular size is 7×35. Relatively small and lightweight, 7×35 binoculars are versatile and readily available. Just about every binocular manufacturer makes a pair of 7×35 binoculars, which is also the size that tends to be offered on sale.

RESPECTING THE OUTDOORS

The wilderness areas described in *Natural Attractions* are as fragile as those who wander into them. Respecting the wilderness is, in a way, respecting your-self, as well as those who will come after you. Think of what remains of the wilderness as something we are obligated to pass on to our children, rather than something we inherited from our parents. Do us all the favor of following the rules of a particular wil-derness area.

THE ATTRACTIONS

As weather patterns change from one season to the next, one can only estimate when certain natural at-tractions take place. Some attractions, like glaciers, stay put; others, like peak flight days in the hawk migration, show up one day and disappear the next. It's always a good idea to check with a particular lo-cation before traveling there. Personnel at the wildlife refuges,.parks, and other locations described in this book tend to be more than willing to advise visitors.

RATES AND CREDIT CARD INFORMATION

I have used the following abbreviations for credit cards:
   AE—American Express
   CB—Carte Blanche
   DC—Diners Club
   MC—MasterCard
    V—Visa
  NCC—No Credit Cards
Rather than list rates in exact dollar terms, I have indicated instead their general range. Specific rate information can vary considerably even at the same place. The rate information is based on double occupancy—the cost for two persons per day—and I

indicate whether the rate includes any meals. I have used the following ranges:

Inexpensive—less than $45

Moderate—$45–$80

Expensive—$80 or more.

THE ORDER OF THINGS

I arranged the natural attractions described in this book in a sequence determined entirely by whim, for it was by whim that I first chanced to see most of them. I think we owe it to ourselves to notice more about us as we grow, to go out of our way a bit to witness the spectacular, however whimsical the detour may seem.

The sight of a skyful of hawks or a rainbow materializing in the spout of a whale works a magic on the soul, as surely as the eerie music of loons, or the elegiac howling of wolves. Part of the magic comes from watching others fall under the spell of powerful natural attractions, and part of it from falling under their spell yourself.

A brief whimsical detour can bring you in contact with profound natural forces, with sights and sounds that can change you forever.

Happy trails.

JOHN THAXTON
December 1986

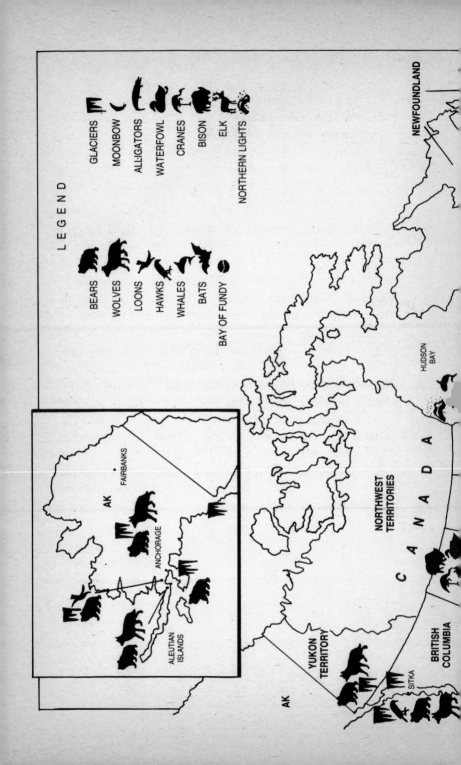

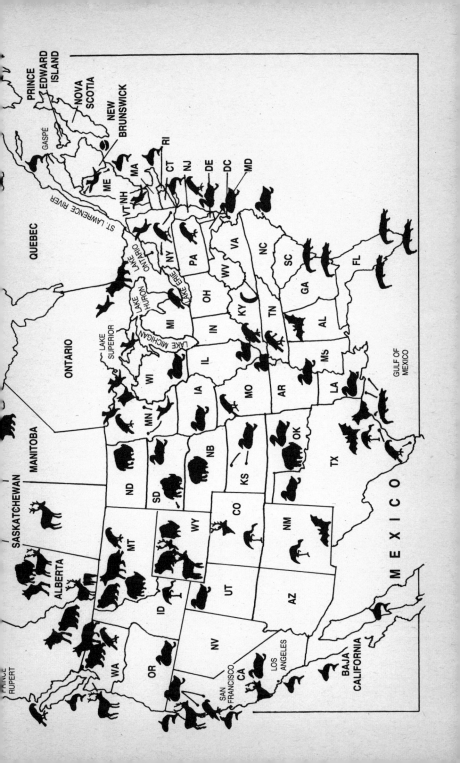

HAWKS

Members of the order Falconiformes, the thirty-eight species of hawk native to North America vary in size from small to enormous, in shape from thick to thin, in domestic habits from highly migratory to downright provincial, in color from brilliant to drab, in diet from crickets to antelopes, and in distribution from relatively common to extremely rare.

The American kestrel, a beautiful slate blue gray and apricot bird, with two prominent mustaches and tapered falcon wings on which it hovers, is the size of a robin and virtually cosmopolitan in range; whereas the California condor, a gruesome-looking creature with a bald orange and red head, has a wingspan of 9½ feet, enormous difficulty flying without the help of strong winds or thermals, and an entire species population of fewer than 30 individuals. I've seen American kestrels in the downtown sections of New York, Denver, and Seattle, but the only place to get a look at a California condor is within a 50–square mile section of southern California. Broad-winged hawks pack up twice annually and migrate between locations as distant as Nova Scotia and Brazil, gyrfalcons seldom stray below circumpolar latitudes, and snail-kites are unheard of north of Florida. Falcons are thin, buteos thick, accipiters and harriers and ospreys somewhere in between.

Differ though they do, most hawks have much in common: sharp talons for seizing and killing live prey; a powerful, stout, pointed beak for tearing it apart; incomprehensibly keen vision; ineffably graceful aeronautical skills; and a position at the very top of the food chain. Like humans and wolves, for example, hawks are high-order predators. They take mammals. They share among them, too, an enormous influence on the human imagination, with the result that over the centuries they have appeared continually as powerful symbols, representing everything from brutality to grace to swiftness to solitude to freedom. They have about them what W. B. Yeats called "a terrible beauty," a combination of ruthlessness and grace, and as we gasp in horror at the pitiable fate of the fleeing sparrow we lose our breath in awe of the dexterity of the sharp-shinned hawk snatching it out of thin air.

From an altitude of half a mile an osprey can spot a 6-inch fish swimming at eight knots a foot and a half below the surface of a choppy ocean, instantaneously plot its course and trajectory, plunge toward it at speeds upwards of 150 miles per hour, completely submerge itself as it grasps its prey, and then, as it flies off, water streaming down its wings, toss the fish in midair and catch it. Peregrine falcons, among the swiftest creatures on the planet, dive at speeds of up to 175 miles per hour, stun their prey with talons clenched like fists, and then catch it as it falls. Hanging in midair on motionless, extended wings, a red-tailed hawk can spot a small mouse a quarter mile away and capture it tens of seconds later. Ferruginous hawks sometimes hunt in groups so as to take larger prey than they could handle singly. Golden eagles have been observed turning lazy circles in the sky with caribou calves or coyotes in their talons.

As a serious avocation, hawk watching predates history itself. Some of the earliest attempts at recording history—cave paintings and primitive carvings—incorporate into their obscure mythological designs images of hawks. As history has progressed so has hawk watching, and one wonders what analogies might be drawn between the images of eagles on the walls of firelit caves and those on the walls of the White House. The complexities of history notwithstanding, it surely seems obvious that humankind, from the stone age through the atomic, has felt a strong affinity with birds of prey.

By an act of Congress in 1782, our founding fathers, with the notable exception of Benjamin Franklin, selected the bald eagle as the symbol of America, that proud, fierce, independent nation. Franklin tried to persuade his colleagues to choose instead the wild turkey, which he considered a more distinguished bird, instancing in his argument that bald eagles, magnificent as they are, eat carrion. Ironically enough, the bald eagle reestablished itself as our national symbol during the 1960s, when environmentalists discovered that the better part of the carrion they were eating was loaded with toxic levels of DDT. Another act of Congress eliminated the use of DDT, but not before the deadly pesticide had eliminated the bald as a breeding species in the contiguous United States. DDT had also eliminated the peregrine falcon as a breeding species and dramatically reduced the country's population of ospreys. Although environmentalists pressed the Congress with voluminous evidence about the dangers of DDT, it seems that it was the genocide of our most magnificent hawks, among them our national symbol, that finally stirred the indignation of Congress into action.

Fierce and proud and independent as they are, hawks can be delicate. Researchers discovered that ingesting a single DDT-contaminated duck could sterilize a peregrine falcon, and the effect of the pesticide on bald eagles and ospreys, which eat primarily fish, was to compromise their calcium-production systems so severely that newly laid eggs couldn't withstand the weight of their brooding parents. Massive and enormously expensive reintroduction programs have partially reestablished bald eagles and peregrine falcons as breeding species in the contiguous United States, but both birds are still highly endangered and require our strictest protection in order to survive.

Hawks have been persecuted for as long as they have been admired. Decades before the advent of DDT, hunters were shooting the birds right out of the sky—for target practice. Out of revenge for the loss of a moribund chicken, or because of sheer misinformation, poultry farmers have for as long as anyone can remember shot every hawk they had a chance to. The premier hawk-watching location in the country, Hawk Mountain Sanctuary, was at one time a target range for local sharpshooters, some of whom, of a Sunday afternoon, gunned down more than a hundred birds. The Endangered Species Act of 1972 markedly reduced the indiscriminate shooting of birds of prey, but their persecution goes on, albeit in a more sophisticated, more profitable fashion.

In October 1984, by way of commenting on the arrest of thirty-four individuals charged with illegally trafficking in endangered birds of prey, the United States Department of Agriculture estimated that a gyrfalcon sells for $50,000 or more in the Middle East. Operation Trophy Hunt, executed by the United States Fish and Wildlife Service and other federal and state agencies, involved three years of investigative work and revealed what was probably only a fraction of an enormously profitable industry—smuggling federally protected birds of prey. Six men, all of whom fly falcons for sport, pleaded guilty to receiving and trafficking in peregrine falcons, gyrfalcons, and goshawks. In exchange for suspended sentences and fines of as much as $10,000, the six gave federal agents information. The investigation unearthed such stuff as testimony by a young West German alleging that the pair of bald eagles presented as a Bicentennial gift by the people of West Germany to the people of the United States were not, in fact, raised in West Germany but smuggled there from Canada. The investigation also resulted in charges against an official of the Finnish Ministry of Agriculture, who, under the protection of diplomatic immunity, walked through United States Customs with a suitcase containing twenty-six goshawk eggs, which were destined for an illegal breeding project in California and, finally, for sale to the royal families of Saudi Arabia, one of which maintains 150 falcons in a mountaintop retreat. According to *The New York Times*, "The Saudis denied any knowledge of a smuggling scheme."

Funny thing is, if you ever saw a gyrfalcon fly you could understand why someone would pay $50,000 for such a bird, especially if that someone's backyard consists of 2000 square miles of the earth's richest oil reserves, with mountains that channel the wind.

They fly like nothing else, hawks. When you follow a moving hawk through a pair of binoculars, the rest of the world turns into a blur, a swirling panorama of forest or mountains or river or clouds or clear blue sky. At first they appear as specks on the horizon, tiny black floating things, but gradually their size, shape, pattern of flight, markings, and coloration become discernible—if you're lucky. If you're unlucky the bird flies directly across the sun and the only discernible phenomenon is a blinding intensity of light, or it dives below the tree line before you even get it in focus, or it rises so high on a thermal you lose sight of it somewhere in the firmament. The secret of watching hawks is learning how to be lucky at it. The science is learning where to look and when.

Between the 15th and 20th of October, with the highest concentrations usually on the 17th, as many as 21,000 broad-winged hawks soar and kettle over Hawk Mountain Sanctuary. A "kettle" is a lazy swarm of broad-winged hawks, as many as 10,000 of them, soaring in circles ever higher on a huge column of rising air. On September 20, 1981, 10,000 broad-wings passed over Hook Mountain, New York, in an hour. On September 14, 1978, 22,488 broad-wings passed over Hawk Mountain in six hours. On October 16, 1970, 25,000 American kestrels flew over Cape May Point, New Jersey. Every October and November thousands of bald eagles gather in the cottonwoods that overlook a series of gravel banks in the Chilkat River just above Haines, Alaska, where observers frequently see congregations of as many as 3000 bald eagles—in the same place at the same time.

Being in the same place at the same time as large numbers of hawks qualifies as something of a science, albeit luck plays a large role, as it does in all things natural. Hawks don't always cooperate, nor does the weather, but over the years we have managed to discover where they tend to show up and when. Most hawks migrate, and, like humans who go south for the winter and north for the summer, most of them travel along specific routes. We have I-95 and US 1, and the hawks have the Kittatinny Ridge and the Atlantic Coast. The Kittatinny Ridge, which runs from New York to Alabama and rises like a backbone separating the Coastal Plain from the Great Valley of the Appalachians, deflects the prevailing westerly winds upward, providing a continuous updraft of rising air, which to hawks designed for soaring is the equivalent of the superest of highways. For those who like to flap and take their leisure along dunes and beaches, the Atlantic Coast has all the stopping-off points of the most scenic routes.

You can see a hawk virtually anywhere. Next time you hear a bunch of crows or starlings making a racket, investigate the cause of their excitement, particularly if they're flying about chaotically. Study the flock of birds to see if one among them is larger than the others, or perhaps soaring instead of flapping. Often a group of hysterical birds indicates the presence of a hawk, which they are trying their best to harass out of their territory. I once saw what must have been a hundred snowy egrets simultaneously take flight from positions of rest in a huge eastern white pine, which at first glance I mistook for a gigantic cherry tree mysteriously blossoming in late September. Sure enough, a quick scan of the sky revealed a pair of northern harriers gliding toward the tree, their wings in a graceful dihedral, their bellies rusty brown. As exciting as chance spottings of individual hawks are, planned sightings of hundreds, or even thousands, of them are even more exciting, and more educational.

Educating yourself to identify hawks requires time, patience, and experience. Experience, I think, is the best teacher, and I daresay anyone who sees fifty individuals of a particular species in an afternoon will thereafter have little difficulty identifying it. Studying field guides and memorizing the characteristics of the continent's thirty-eight species of hawk will no doubt help you to tell them apart, but as often as not the effect of such a learning process is to turn the brain into mashed potatoes the moment a hawk actually appears. Appearing at the appropriate time at one of the continent's primary hawk-watching locations, or what the experts call "major concentration points of raptor migration," will not only bring you close to perhaps thousands of hawks but will also place you near experienced, indeed professional, hawk watchers.

Most of the hawk-watching locations described below are staffed with professional or semiprofessional hawk watchers, one of whose primary job is identifying and counting the birds of prey that pass overhead or, as the case often is, below. Professional hawk watchers tend to do things like scan the sky with their binoculars, stop suddenly, tilt their face forward three inches or so as if to get that much closer to the bird, and, out of the blue, announce to the crowd: "There's an osprey a glass and a half over the horizon, right at the top of that cumulo to the left of those hemlocks." The crowds tend to become somewhat skeptical after scanning the cumulo for a while and seeing zero, and then suddenly everyone starts shouting with excitement as they pick up the bird in their binoculars. One of the joys of watching hawks is noticing the transition from silence to a unanimous gasp of exhilaration as you and a crowd of strangers witness a bird of prey perform a breathtaking aerial maneuver, or simply float.

The best field guide is an experienced hawk watcher sitting or standing within earshot, and most of the locations will have one of those. The next best interpretative tool is knowing what to expect at a particular time and location. If you're watching for hawks in the Northeast there's no need to memorize the field marks of Aplomado falcons or snail-kites, and if you're in southern Texas you needn't worry about having to identify a rough-legged hawk or a gyrfalcon.

The following tips on identifying hawks are by no means intended as a substitute for a good field guide. They are, rather, a basic set of guidelines for beginners, a primer designed to complement rather than replace a comprehensive field guide to hawks. No field guide, regardless of its comprehensiveness, will enable novice or even intermediate-level hawk watchers to distinguish among certain birds of prey. A female sharp-shinned and a male Cooper's hawk, for example, look almost identical, and telling them apart requires a finely tuned eye; and when it comes to distinguishing among the various species, subspecies, races, and color phases of certain buteos, even seasoned experts sometimes give up.

The process of identification, whether it completes itself in microseconds or hours, most often proceeds from the general to the specific. Generally speaking, size, shape, and flight patterns are the most basic characteristics of hawks. When you see a hawk you see first a shape and a movement, even if the shape seems motionless. Coloration and diagnostic field marks (the tail of an eastern red-tailed hawk, for example, or that of a swallow-tailed kite) are more specific, more definitive features. The trouble is, you don't always get to see them. Unfavorable viewing conditions notwithstanding, you can usually notice at least one of a hawk's most general characteristics.

Frequently one can base a definitive identification of a hawk solely on very general characteristics. The size and shape of an osprey, for instance, are often all you need to see; a small, slender, hovering hawk is no doubt an American kestrel; a largish, thin one with broad wings and a long slim tail quartering low over a swamp is in all likelihood a northern harrier; a large, stocky one hanging motionless in air is probably a red-tail; and if you spot a small bird of prey with a long, thin tail and short, rounded wings flapping three or four times between glides you can rest moderately well assured it's a sharp-shinned hawk. If you see a group of thousands of hawks soaring together, they are doubtless broad-wings, and if you spot one with a long, forked tail it is a swallow-tailed kite.

Although thirty-eight species of hawk are native to North America, there are only three families within the order Falconiformes. One of them, New World Vultures, consists of just three species, and another, Caracaras and Falcons, embraces only eight. The remaining twenty-seven birds of prey resident on the continent belong to the diverse family Accipitridae, which includes kites, hawks (accipiters and buteos), eagles, harriers, and ospreys. It is not uncommon for an experienced hawk watcher to exclaim: "Falcon at four o'clock." Basic as it sounds, such an observation eliminates thirty of thirty-eight species of hawk, and, in a particular time and place, eliminates several species of falcon.

With the intention of aiding the complete novice, the following species descriptions focus on the most easily identified hawks, some of which are so distinctive as to be unmistakable if seen under reasonable conditions. Other birds can be virtually impossible to identify with certainty, and sorting them out goes beyond the scope of this book. If you can learn the essential characteristics of the most distinctive fifteen species of hawk you will have transcended the rank of novice.

NEW WORLD VULTURES

Large to extremely large, dark, soaring, carrion-eating birds with unusually small, featherless heads adapted to poking about in carcasses, vultures look magnificent in the air. On the ground they look ugly as sin, and if you approach one too closely, particularly near its nest site, it regurgitates in your direction, spreading one of nature's foulest odors. The three species of New World Vulture vary in distribution from cosmopolitan to southeastern to very southern Californian. Differences in their ranges make telling vultures apart relatively easy.

TURKEY VULTURE

The commonest and most widespread of vultures, these birds have a wingspan of 6 feet and a bald, conspicuously red head. They occur from Florida to Canada, from the Atlantic to the Pacific. They hold their wings in a distinct dihedral, or shallow V, and they rock back and forth as they soar, rather like slow, unsteady airplanes. From below, their wings look two-toned: their front feathers, coverts, appear black, and their rear flight feathers, primaries and secondaries, appear dark gray, light gray, or, in some light, white.

They have a longer, less square tail than black vultures.

BLACK VULTURES

Smaller than turkey vultures, black vultures are also more geographically restricted, occurring primarily in the Southeast. You probably will not see one north of New Jersey or the Ohio River, nor west of the Mississippi except in the southernmost parts of the Gulf States. They have wingspans of 5 feet, a small gray head, and conspicuous white patches on their wingtips. They soar less efficiently, though often higher, than turkey vultures, and frequently flap between glides with four or five rapid but laborious-looking strokes. Sometimes they hold their wings in a slight dihedral; at other times they hold them straight, like planks, after the fashion of eagles. You can easily distinguish black vultures from turkey vultures, but you can easily confuse one for an immature golden eagle, which will also have white patches near its wingtips. Immature golden eagles, however, have a large head, 7-foot wingspans, and a conspicuous white band on their tail. The black vulture has been expanding its range.

CALIFORNIA CONDOR

The continent's largest land bird, wingspan 9½ feet, the California condor exists now at the edge of extinction. Fewer than thirty individuals survive, and if the species prevails it will have done so because of the help given it by the California Condor Recovery Program, which has enjoyed admirable success at taking condor eggs from nests and incubating them elsewhere, feeding the newborn chicks with hand puppets that look like their parents, and then releasing the birds into the wild. The method relies on double-clutching, stimulating mature condors into breeding every year instead of every two: if they lay a fertilized egg and it is taken they will lay another the following year, otherwise they clutch biannually. In some instances, condors have triple-clutched.

Because southern California's indigenous people thought thunder came from the flapping of the condor's enormous wings, they called them thunderbirds. The only place you will see one is in southern California, along the Coast Range between Santa Barbara and Bakersfield. They have bald, orange, and red heads and a conspicuous, slender white triangle on the front part of their wings, thickest where they meet the torso and tapering into a thin line that disappears right before the end of their broad, fingered wings. Their huge size and limited range render them unmistakable.

CARACARAS AND FALCONS

Except for the crested caracara, an uncommon scavenger sometimes called the Mexican eagle, falcons are slender, long-tailed hawks with long, pointed, swallow-like wings. Their thin wings are adapted for rapid flight rather than for gliding and their aeronautical skills frequently dazzle observers. The spectacular high-speed dives, or stoops, of some species, particularly peregrines, defy description, as does their abuse by erstwhile and contemporary falconers. Several species (crested caracara, Aplomado falcon, gyrfalcon) appear infrequently in the contiguous United States. Variances in range help distinguish among the eight species.

AMERICAN KESTREL

The smallest, most numerous, most widespread falcon, the American kestrel resembles a parakeet, larger certainly, but similar of form and as brilliantly colored. Males have an apricot back, shoulders and crown, slate blue gray temples and wings, white cheeks with two prominent black mustaches, black bars on their back, black dots on their belly and wings, and a red tail with a black band and a white tip. Females look duller, with a barred rather than dotted belly and a chestnut red back and wings. Agile and colorful, robin-size hawks with wingspans of as much as two feet, kestrels hover frequently, and when they alight on a perch they tend to pump their tail like nervous squirrels. They eat primarily crickets and rodents, which they can spot a hundred yards away in a field of unmowed grass. They also partake of small birds, seizing them on the wing, and were at one time called sparrow hawks. They were also called windhovers, and students of English literature will recall Gerard Manley Hopkins's famous poem "The Windhover."

> I caught this morning morning's minion kingdom
> of daylight's dauphin, dapple-dawn-drawn Falcon
> . . .
> Stirred for a bird,—the achieve of, the
>   mastery of the thing!

PEREGRINE FALCON

Extirpated as a breeding species from the contiguous United States by DDT, which disturbs their sexual hormone balance, sterilizing them, peregrine falcons used to live in even the most urban areas, where they feasted on pigeons. Then they disappeared. Mercifully successful, a reintroduction program based at Cornell University continues to breed and release peregrines, which remain endangered even though they once again breed in the lower forty-eight states. A couple currently keeps house on the ledge of a bank building in Baltimore, and another pair seems to be making a go of it on the Whitestone Bridge in New York City. They look rather like extremely large, thin pigeons with a long tail and long, slender, pointed wings that flap rapidly and rhythmically. Their powerful downstrokes end suddenly and snap upward like whips. Mature birds have a slate blue tail, wings, back, nape, and crown; a beige belly with black bars; and a white chest and cheeks punctuated by a single, bold mustache. They look as though they are wearing skullcaps with long, droopy eye muffs. Young birds have brown upperparts, the adult's prominent mustache, and a heavily barred, beige chest and belly. Peregrines tend to migrate along coastlines—the Atlantic, the Pacific, and those of the Great Lakes—and appear frequently at barrier islands, such as Fire Island, New York, or over pieces of land that jut abruptly into the ocean, for example, Cape May and Cape Hatteras. In the West, one might easily confuse a prairie falcon for a peregrine. Their sizes overlap (wingspans vary from 3½ to 4 feet) and their shapes are very similar; the prairie falcon is less boldly marked than the peregrine and appears paler.

GYRFALCON

Hyperborean types seldom observed below the North American tree line, gyrfalcons fly deceptively faster than their languid-looking wingbeats suggest. A prize of falconers, these birds are at once large, fast, and powerful. A Canadian company, out of business since its principals were arrested, grossed $700,000 in a single year selling primarily gyrfalcons to clients they preferred going to jail for rather than identifying. Uniformly large, with 4½-foot wingspans, gyrfalcons come in numerous colors, ranging from an almost entirely black dark phase bird to ones virtually pure white but for a few black spots. They are thicker than peregrines and have less pointed wings, which give the impression, considering their range, of northern goshawks. You will probably see them only in the northern latitudes, in particular in areas with a healthy population of ptarmigans, which they pursue and overtake close to the ground.

HAWKS AND EAGLES

The diverse family Accipitridae encompasses twenty-seven species, which belong in turn to five subfamilies that consist of from one to twelve members. Two of these subfamilies, the osprey and the harrier, each distinctive and discussed below, embrace a single species. The subfamily, kites, consists of just five species, of which you will likely see only two, and although there are four species of eagle on the continent two of them show up so infrequently or in such remote places you needn't concern yourself with having to identify one. We are left with the subfamily hawks, which represents fifteen species that divide into two distinct genera, *Accipiter* and *Buteo*. Familiarize yourself with the most distinctive families first.

NORTHERN HARRIERS

Two feet from beak to tail, with 4½-foot wingspans, northern harriers are medium-size, slender, long-winged hawks. They have a disc-shaped face, like owls, and hunt by flying low, or quartering, over swamps and marshes, detecting their prey with an inordinately keen sense of hearing. They hold their wings in a distinct dihedral, and rock back and forth unsteadily like turkey vultures, even in slight winds. Young and mature birds both flash a prominent white rump patch, at the base of their tail and wings, and their typical flight style consists of laconic wingbeats followed by long, low glides. Adult males have blue or brown upperparts and appear white below except for seven or eight thin bands on their tail, and black wingtips. Mature females have a brownish back and cream belly, chest and underwings, which are barred with brown. Young birds resemble females but are a rich, rusty brown underneath, especially in the autumn. Their mating ritual consists of roller-coaster dives and startling upswoops ending in midair stalls.

OSPREYS

One of the more easily identified hawks, ospreys look rather like extremely large sea gulls, who have a similar bend, elbow, or crook in their wings and flash a lot of white from below. Their belly, chest, and head are white, their back brown, and a conspicuous brown bar runs from the base of their beak, through their eyes, and on to their brown shoulders. In large part white underneath, they sport brown wingtips and bold brown bars that curve inward from their elbows down to the base of their flight feathers near their feet, creating a large white area on their torso and inner wings. The overall effect is of a large, boldly patterned brown (in some light almost sepia-toned) and white bird. They have wingspans of 6 feet and can be easily mistaken for a large herring or great black-backed gull, especially an immature one. Unlike gulls, ospreys have a small head, and blunt and fingered rather than pointed wingtips. As ospreys and gulls tend to occur in the same coastal and riparian habitats, you can use gulls as an identification tool: constantly checking out the shapes of large gulls is the surest way to spot a large non-gull. If you have seen large gulls carrying fish in their feet, you have seen ospreys. They build huge nests woven of large sticks on the tops of dead trees, telephone poles, or channel buoys. During the breeding season they copulate frequently, the male balancing himself on the female's back with his long wings for a few seconds, and then typically going for a short fly around the nest.

EAGLES

> When thou seest an Eagle, thou seest a portion of Genius; lift up thy head!
>
> —WILLIAM BLAKE, *The Marriage of Heaven and Hell*

Winter brings most of the continent's eagles south, and they appear with regularity in significant numbers in places as diverse as Florida, New York, Tennessee, Kentucky, Oklahoma, and Massachusetts. You do, indeed, lift up your head when you watch one, for eagles tend to soar on motionless wings beyond the limits of vision, rather like William Blake did.

They weigh in at anywhere from 7 to 14 pounds, have body lengths of between 2½ and 3½ feet, and measure from wingtip to wingtip between 6 and 8 feet. In terms of identification, an eagle's most salient characteristic is its size. Eagles are huge, thick, heavy-bodied birds. Although two casual species of eagle occasionally appear on North America—the white-tailed eagle and steller's sea eagle—bald and golden eagles are the only two species you will in any likelihood see. There has been only one confirmed sighting of a steller's sea eagle (in extreme western Alaska), and only one of a white-tailed eagle since 1977, on Attu Island, the westernmost of the Aleutians. The last East Coast spotting of a white-tailed eagle was in 1914, off the coast of Nantucket, Massachusetts.

When mature, bald and golden eagles are easily distinguished from each other. The mature bald eagle is unmistakable: it has a large white head, almost a third of which consists of a conspicuous yellow beak, and prominent white tail feathers. Otherwise it is the darkest of browns, almost to black. From a distance these eagles look ebony and white. Immature birds vary considerably and with age. It takes them four to six years to develop the white crown and tail feathers, and before they do they appear as primarily dark brown with ungainly-looking blotches of white on their belly, wings, and back. They will often show distinct white bars running the length of their underwings, but only up front. The white bar under the wings of an immature bald eagle limits itself to the forward feathers, or coverts, and does not appear on either the primary or secondary, rear, flight feathers. The white patches near the wingtips of immature golden eagles, by contrast, appear only on flight feathers, not on the coverts.

Golden eagles have a smaller head than bald eagles, and their coloration differs significantly as well. Mature birds are almost completely dark, chestnut brown, with a subtle wash of gold on their nape and a barely perceptible area of white near the base of their tail.

Immature golden eagles are easily identified: they have a distinct patch of white near the tips of their wings and a broad, terminal black band at the end of a white tail.

The locations described below are prime eagle-spotting grounds, and although you will almost surely see a bald eagle at one of them, consider the sighting of a golden eagle as something rare, particularly in the East. Among eagle watchers, the truly lucky get to witness the spectacular mating ritual of the bald eagle. Some naturalists consider the behavior a play activity as well as a mating maneuver, but whether they're fooling around or breeding, the sight of them in action will change you forever.

At first the birds soar, one of them about 500 feet directly above the other, and then the bird on top dives as though to attack the one below, opening its talons and spreading its wings immediately before contact, just before which the bottom bird rolls over on its back and opens its talons so that they lock with the others. Then the birds go into a gyrating, downward spin, their talons locked, only to break apart before they hit the ground. Then they soar upward again, looking magisterially unruffled about the whole business, perhaps best described by Walt Whitman in "The Dalliance of the Eagles."

> Skirting the river road, (my forenoon walk, my rest),
> Skyward in the air a sudden muffled sound, the
>   dalliance of the eagles,
> The rushing amorous contact high in space together,
> The clinching interlocking claws, a living, fierce,
>   gyrating wheel,
> Four beating wings, two beaks, a swirling mass tight
>   grappling,

*In tumbling turning clustering loops, straight
    downward falling,
Till o'er the river poised, the twain yet one, a
    moment's lull,
A motionless still balance in the air, then parting,
    talons loosing,
Upward again on slow-firm pinions slanting, their
    separate diverse flight,
She hers, he his, pursuing.*

KITES

The subfamily Kites consists of five species, each of
which shares, generally speaking, two predominant
characteristics—a falcon-like shape and a southern
range. Once in a while someone spots a Mississippi or
swallow-tailed kite north of the Carolinas or Nevada,
but don't expect to see one other than in the South.
A sense of their range is the best identification tool
for prospective kite watchers. Two species, hook-billed
and snail kites, very rarely stray north of extreme
southern Texas and southern Florida, respectively.

AMERICAN SWALLOW-TAILED KITE

As beautiful as it is distinctive, the swallow-tail is unmistakable: it has a long, deeply forked tail that looks
at first glance like the branches of a compass extend-
ing from the bird's rump. Underneath their torso,
neck, head, and inner wings they are white in stark
contrast to their black flight feathers, wingtips, and
tail. Buoyantly graceful, swallow-tailed kites have
wingspans that can exceed 4 feet, and they appear
most often along the Louisiana and Florida gulf coasts,
making their way, rarely, as far north as coastal South

Carolina, Delaware, and New Jersey. During migration they frequently travel in small groups.

BLACK-SHOULDERED KITE

Observable primarily in southern California and southern Texas, black-shouldered kites look like a cross between a falcon and a gull. From below they flash a lot of white: their white, pointed, gull-like wings have dark tips, and their long, white tail appears square at its end and, up close, divided lengthwise by a thin, subtle line of gray. Perched black-shouldered kites look completely white but for a pale gray back and charcoal gray shoulders. They frequently hover.

HAWKS

The populous subfamily Hawks consists of two groups of species. One genus, *Accipiter*, has three members; the other, *Buteo*, accounts for twelve. Although telling buteos from accipiters is relatively easy even for beginners, distinguishing among the species that constitute the two genera can prove near impossible, even for experts, who have been known to grumble: "Prob'ly an immature red-tail, maybe a second year red-shoulder or a small ferruginous—let's just call that one a buteo." Despite these overall subtleties of uniqueness, certain species in this subfamily are unmistakable and may be so common as to demand consideration, however slightly it may prove of use. As a general rule, accipiters have a long, thin tail and short, rounded wings that they tend to flap three or four times between glides; whereas buteos have thick wings and a tail that they hold motionless as they glide or soar or hang motionless in the air. This is not to say that accipiters are not occasionally given to extended soars on motionless wings or that buteos do not hover.

ACCIPITERS

Sharp-Shinned Hawk

When sharp-shinned hawks get up speed and dive into the woods, it seems a foregone conclusion that they will crash immediately into any number of branches. Their agility dazzles. Sharp-shins feed primarily on small birds, such as sparrows and warblers, which they often capture after a daredevil chase through thickly wooded coniferous forests. Roughly the size of a jay, sharpies have wingspans of just under two feet and a long, thin, square or notched tail crossed by four dark bands. They are dark bluish-gray above, and pale and faintly streaked below. Visible during winter in a wide range of habitats as far south as the Caribbean, they breed in the northern United States and Canada. During migration they are frequently observed at numerous hawk-watching locations described below.

Cooper's Hawk

Twenty to 70 percent larger than sharp-shins, Cooper's hawks are more the size of a small crow than a jay. In the East, sharp-shins outnumber Cooper's hawks by a ratio of approximately ten to one; in the West, the birds appear in about equal numbers. Like sharp-shins, Cooper's hawks are dark bluish-gray above, pale and streaked below; although most observers cannot detect a difference under less than ideal viewing conditions, they have a rounded rather than square tail. Their tail has four dark and a white terminal band. They also have a faint suggestion of a hood on their heads.

BUTEOS

Red-Tailed Hawk

The most widespread and common bird of prey, often called a chicken hawk, the red-tailed hawk has a wingspan of 4½ to 5 feet, thick broad wings, a thick tail, and a mind-boggling assortment of coloration patterns. Immature and mature birds as well as eastern and western subspecies and color phases differ considerably, and to the inexperienced eye even distinctly marked birds bear confusingly strong resemblances to immature red-shouldered and ferruginous hawks. East of the Mississippi the adult bird's glaringly red tail is absolutely diagnostic and easily seen even at great distances when properly lit. I have watched red-tails for ten solid minutes and been able to discern only the soaring silhouette of a classic, large buteo, and then for an instant spotted a brilliant flash of auburn as they banked into the sun. No other hawk hangs motionless in the air, nor do many approach its size and bulk. It is smaller only than eagles, vultures, ospreys, and rough-legged and ferruginous hawks. Although not always the case, two field marks frequently appear on the undersides of red-tails—a dark belly band halfway between their feet and head, and a small dark band, rather like a comma, at their wrists. Red-shouldered hawks are slightly smaller than red-tails and lack their belly band, wrist marks, and red tail. They have washes of cinnamon on their shoulders and a finely barred tail.

Rough-Legged Hawk

A very large buteo with a 5-foot wingspan, rough-legged hawks breed in the Arctic and winter as far south as Tennessee and Arizona. Slightly larger than red-tails, they have a similar shape, but unlike red-tails they have a tendency to hover, keeping themselves aloft with laborious, slow wingbeats that look almost like the work of a puppeteer. They occur in two distinct color phases—dark and light. The dark phase rough-legged hawk is the only dark phase hawk you will see in the East, and it is boldly marked. From below it looks almost like an osprey in the negative, with a dark torso and dark upper wings surrounded by white flight feathers and wingtips, and a white tail with a broad, black terminal band. Light phase birds are entirely white below except for dark patches on their wrists, dark bands across their belly, and a dark terminal band on their tail. Out West you might confuse one for a ferruginous hawk, which also hovers but exhibits something of a faint, translucent crescent near the tip of each wing.

Other Buteos

The wide range of species that constitutes the genus *Buteo* presents formidable identification challenges, although the shape they share is distinctive, as is their tendency to soar. They are broad, thick-bodied birds, which range in size from the smallish broad-winged to the very large ferruginous hawk. One of nature's most dramatic migrations involves the broad-winged hawk population, which as a rule moves south almost simultaneously, filling the skies at certain times with thousands of birds. Readers are advised to consult field guides for further distinctions among buteos, and to consider the range information in the location descriptions below as an identification tool.

DESTINATIONS AND ACCOMMODATIONS

CAPE MAY, NEW JERSEY

CAPE MAY POINT STATE PARK

As Delaware Bay widens, its northern coastline runs southeast until Maurice River Cove, where it begins proceeding almost due east and forms, near the mouths of West and East and Dennis creeks, the widest part of the bay. Then the coastline makes a 90-degree turn to the south and becomes the western coast of Cape May Peninsula, which encloses, roughly, the northern third of Delaware Bay. The southern coastline also runs southeast and then south as the bay widens, but then it turns sharply north at Cape Henlopen, Delaware. Eighteen miles of water separate Cape Henlopen and Cape May Point, which look on a map rather like the two open tips of a giant caliper that widens to the west before narrowing again.

Birds migrating south on the Atlantic flyway tend to hug the coasts of the Atlantic Ocean and Delaware Bay, with the result that great numbers of them follow the contours of Cape May Peninsula and arrive, as though the narrow strip of land were a funnel, at its southern extreme, Cape May Point. Eighteen miles of open water represent a formidable challenge to many species of birds. Unfavorable winds could blow them out to sea, and even under ideal weather conditions running out of energy over open water invariably proves fatal. Fortunately for migrators along the flyway, Cape May Point State Park provides 300 acres of varied habitat—dunes, marshes, ponds, thickets, hardwood forests—where migrating birds can feed and rest before attempting the flight across Delaware Bay.

Three hundred sixty-three species of birds have been identified here, and annual Christmas counts average 140 species. Autumn is spectacular: swans, geese, ducks, egrets, and ibises litter the place; song-birds rustle in every thicket; the sun sets directly into the bay's open water; New York asters, white sweet clover, forget-me-nots, and toadflax bloom; and thousands of hawks pass overhead. Sporadic counts over the years indicated that Cape May Point was perhaps the continent's foremost concentration point of raptor migration, and in 1976 the New Jersey Audubon Society initiated thorough counts of migrating hawks. A viewing platform was erected tall enough to provide spectators with a view over scores of acres of phragmites punctuated by brackish ponds, and on a reasonable day upwards of seventy people, binoculars or spotting scopes to their eyes, watch for birds of prey. On a good day 5000 to 10,000 hawks pass over, on mediocre days perhaps 500. The best hawk-watching days here traditionally occur after a cold front passes over New England and clear skies with strong northwest winds prevail.

Cape May is an excellent place to look for falcons: 230 peregrines were sighted one year, and observers record an annual average of 12,000 American kestrels. Sharp-shinned hawks outnumber all other species, having tipped the scales with a record of 48,447 sharpies passing through one season. Among the buteos, red-tailed and red-shouldered hawks are fairly common, as are ospreys and northern harriers. Bald and golden eagles pass through in small numbers, averaging perhaps twenty per season. The peak season here is from late September through early November.

Nearby natural areas of interest include Barnegat

and Brigantine National Wildlife Refuges, 40 and 60 miles, respectively, north along the Atlantic Coast; Stone Harbor, 15 miles north and rife with glossy ibises; and the New Jersey Pine Barrens, a vast undeveloped tract of pine forest that occupies almost a third of New Jersey. Seekers of unnatural attractions will find Atlantic City 40 miles north on the coast, and history enthusiasts will delight in the town of Cape May, a large part of which is a National Historic Landmark District containing over 600 historic structures. The historic district has the largest concentration of Victorian architecture in the country, and right at the peak of hawk-watching season the town sponsors Victoriana Weekend, which focuses on guided tours of the district's plethora of meticulously restored Victorian houses.

Driving Instructions: From points north take the Garden State Parkway south to its terminus, Route 109, which passes over a bridge into Cape May and becomes Lafayette Street; bear right on to Perry Street, which becomes Sunset Boulevard; follow Sunset for 2 miles and turn left (through the stone pillars) on to Cape Avenue; proceed perhaps 50 yards and turn left again; then go right on Lighthouse Avenue for .7 miles: the park entrance is on your left, immediately at the base of the lighthouse.

The Queen Victoria
102 Ocean Street
Cape May, NJ 08204
Telephone: (609) 884-8702
Open all year.

A sprawling 1881 Victorian, the Queen Victoria features period antique furnishings, a handmade quilt on each bed, fresh flowers in every room, a generous complimentary breakfast, and complimentary tea and finger sandwiches in the afternoon. Of the twelve rooms, four have private baths; none have a television or telephone.

Rates: moderate to expensive; MC,V

The Dormer House International
800 Columbia Avenue
Cape May, NJ 08204
Telephone: (609) 884-7446
Open all year.

The Dormer House consists of eight apartments with housekeeping facilities in an 1895 Colonial Revival building. Public areas include a wicker-furnished glassed-in porch, and a central staircase area sprinkled with antiques and an unusually fine stained-glass window. The comfortably furnished apartments also feature some antiques, and vary in size from small units to large suites with private porches.

Rates: inexpensive to moderate; MC,V

Marquis de Lafayette
591 Beach Drive
Cape May, NJ 08204
Telephone: (609) 884-3431

This modern, six-story motor hotel has seventy-three rooms, forty-three of which have kitchens. Some rooms have balconies overlooking the ocean, every room has a television, and the building has a pool, sauna, restaurant, cocktail lounge featuring live entertainment, valet service, bellhops, coin laundry, golf privileges, and a package store. A sixth-floor restaurant overlooks the ocean.

Rates: expensive; AE,CB,DC,MC,V

NYACK, NEW YORK

HOOK MOUNTAIN STATE PARK

Three miles long and a half mile wide, Hook Mountain State Park consists of some 661 acres that front the Hudson River just north of the Tappan Zee Bridge. The park's facilities include a manicured gravel trail that runs right along the river and an unmanicured rock trail that ascends to the summit of Hook Mountain, at 758 feet the highest point for some distance. The view from the top of Hook Mountain encompasses 360 degrees, and on a clear day one can easily see the Manhattan skyline, 30 miles distant.

Although from the air the mountain looks exactly like a hook, its name comes from a Dutch expression, Verdrietige Hoogte, that suggests the mountain created treacherous winds for sailors trying to navigate up the Hudson River. Indeed, the nature of the mountain is such that winds from all directions deflect off it, with the result that migrating hawks looking for an updraft of air to ride on head for the mountain. Observers at Hook Mountain have counted more than 10,000 hawks in a single day.

The migration here begins in late August and continues through November, but the optimum times to appear are in September and October. Broad-winged hawks migrate over the mountain in great numbers, with several thousand on a good day not being uncommon. Other species that pass overhead in significant numbers include sharp-shins, red-tails, ospreys, northern harriers, red shoulders, and American kestrels. Now and again, an eagle passes by.

The trail to the top of Hook Mountain is steep and rugged, but only about three-quarters of a mile in distance. Good shoes are a must, and a little bit of determination helps. On a clear day, the view alone is worth the trip, especially in autumn when the Hudson Valley turns yellow and orange, and the great blue river flashes in the sun. Hook Mountain is one of the places where the hawks come extremely close to the hawk watchers; I have felt the breeze from a sharp-shin's wings here.

Bed and Breakfast USA, Ltd.
PO Box 606
Croton-on-Hudson, NY 10520
Telephone: (914) 271-6228

Bed and Breakfast USA represents scores of B&Bs in the Rockland/Westchester County area. The accommodations available range from modest homes to luxurious estates, and the rates vary accordingly.

Holiday Inn
329 Route 303
Orangeburg, NY 10962
Telephone: (914) 359-7000

The Nyack Holiday Inn is a 120-room motel with a restaurant, pool, and health club.

Rates: moderate to expensive; AE,CB,DC,MC,V

Bear Mountain Inn & Cabins
Bear Mountain State Park
Bear Mountain, NY 10911
Telephone: (914) 786-2731

A series of buildings, the oldest of them a 1910 stone and wood lodge, Bear Mountain Inn & Cabins has about seventy-five rooms available, some in lodges with shared fireplaces, others in the main building. The facilities include a restaurant and a bar. The inn and cabins are located in Bear Mountain/Harriman State Park, a 55,000-acre preserve roughly an hour north of Hook Mountain. Hawk watchers who stay here have a lot of park to explore, including the summit of Bear Mountain, which is accessible by car and flown past by hawks.

Rates: moderate; AE,MC,V

KEMPTON, PENNSYLVANIA

Perhaps the premier hawk-watching spot on the continent, Hawk Mountain Sanctuary consists of 2200 acres in southeastern Pennsylvania, roughly 30 miles west of Allentown. The sanctuary sits atop the Kittatinny Ridge, the easternmost ridge of the Appalachian ridge and valley system, and when conditions are right, wind striking the ridge causes powerful updrafts of air that represent to migrating hawks the ideal superhighway.

The sanctuary has two lookouts, one facing north and the other facing south. The south lookout is easily accessible, a short walk from the parking area, and produces the best results when the winds are from the south. (Although not officially wheelchair-accessible, the south lookout can be accessed by people in wheelchairs or on crutches.) The north lookout, elevation 1521 feet, produces the best results when northwest winds blow, particularly after a few days of overcast weather. Access to the north lookout involves a hike of about two-thirds of a mile; the trail is well-groomed and people with street shoes do not seem to have too much difficulty climbing it. The north lookout is also reachable via an escarpment trail, which is a little on the rough and steep side but endowed with the best views.

The north lookout consists, more or less, of a boulder field wooded at its peripheries with hemlock and mountain ash, and on a clear day the view alone is worth the climb. The sanctuary itself as well as the surrounding terrain exhibits an almost textbook example of fall foliage—oaks, maples, and birches predominate; conifers break up the reds and oranges with a sprinkling of green, and neat Amish farm fields trail off into the distance of the valleys.

The best time to appear at Hawk Mountain is from mid-August through mid-September, and from late September through Thanksgiving. The facilities here include a visitors center that also serves as a museum, ample parking, and restrooms.

Hawk Mountain Sanctuary is a people-oriented kind of place, where staff members greet you at the end of your hike and the director of the place calls hawks and converses while leaning against a tree at the top of the boulder field. The sanctuary has a fascinating history that involves ghosts as well as hawks, and the spirit of the place as well as the nature of its transient raptors is authoritatively discussed in *The Mountain and the Migration*, by James J. Brett, the curator of the sanctuary.

Hawk Mountain Sanctuary is situated in Pennsylvania Dutch country, where a rich cultural tradition endures. Visitors here might want to investigate the Pennsylvania Dutch Folk Cultural Center, telphone: (215) 562-4803, in Hamburg, or the Kempton Farm Museum, telephone: (215) 683-7130, in Kempton. Kutztown is the site of Kutztown University, which specializes in art and media programs.

Bed & Breakfast of Southeast Pennsylvania
Joyce Stevenson
PO Box 278, RD 1
Barto, PA 19504
Telephone: (215) 845-3526

Bed & Breakfast of Southeast Pennsylvania offers a
wide range of lodging possibilities in the Hawk Mountain area. The accommodations vary from inexpensive rooms with shared baths to suites in historic
farmhouses. Joyce has a knack for finding people just
the right place to stay.

Dusselfink Motel and Restaurant
Route 61 (1 mile south of Schuylkill Haven)
Pottsville, PA 17901
Telephone: (717) 385-2407 or toll-free 1-800-847-3465 (in PA);
** 1-800-843-3465 (outside PA)**

The Dusselfink is a hundred-room motel with a large
restaurant, and a lounge with entertainment. Each
room has a color television, telephone, and private
bath. The rooms vary from economy singles to spa-
cious suites. Hawk Mountain is fifteen minutes from
here.

Rates: inexpensive; AE,CB,DC,MC,V

TIPTONVILLE, TENNESSEE

Reelfoot Lake State Park Resort
Route 1
Box 296
Tiptonville, TN 38079
Telephone: (901) 253-7756

Situated in the northwest corner of Tennessee, a little
southeast of where the Mississippi makes a 359-degree
turn at the Kentucky border, Reelfoot Lake State Park
Resort consists of about 19,000 acres, 18,000 of them

water, along the south shore of Reelfoot Lake. Formed by the New Madrid earthquakes of 1811–12, the lake is laced with huge expanses of lily pads and giant, submerged cypresses that, during winter, serve as perches for bald and golden eagles, which winter here in significant numbers. Eighteen miles long and three miles wide, Reelfoot Lake hosts a winter population of upwards of 300 eagles, and from December through March park naturalists lead tours of popular eagle habitats.

The dense forest surrounding the lake is also home to any number of wintering birds from farther north, and the lake itself hosts, during winter, more than 200,000 waterfowl.

The park facilities include a marina where visitors can rent boats, a museum with Indian and Civil War relics, a restaurant, tennis courts, and a swimming pool.

Reelfoot National Wildlife Refuge is next door.

Driving Instructions: Reelfoot Lake State Park is on Tennessee Route 21, about five miles east of Tiptonville.

Airpark Inn & Restaurant
Route 1
Box 296
Tiptonville, TN 38079
Telephone: (901) 253-7756

Located in the park, Airpark Inn & Restaurant has twenty-five rooms, all of them with color television, telephone, and private bath. The rooms have balconies overlooking a willow swamp rife with wildflowers and ferns, and the modern inn also has a restaurant. Some of the rooms have kitchenettes, and the inn has an airstrip for those inclined to fly in.

Rates: inexpensive to moderate; AE,MC,V

Eagle Nest
Box 8
Tiptonville, TN 38079
Telephone: (901) 538-2143

Outside the park but on Reelfoot Lake, the Eagle Nest is a fourteen-room motel with kitchenettes. The facilities include a casual restaurant, playground, and pool. The rooms have color television and telephone. Guests can rent boats, motors, and guides.

Rates: inexpensive; NCC

ROCKPORT, WASHINGTON
SKAGIT RIVER BALD EAGLE NATURAL AREA

Jointly managed by the Nature Conservancy and the Washington State Department of Game, Skagit River Bald Eagle Natural Area consists of 1500 acres of prime bald eagle wintering habitat along the banks of the Skagit River, which rises in British Columbia and flows south and then west through Washington, emptying, finally, into Puget Sound. The river runs through the Ross Lake National Recreation Area section of North Cascades National Park, a stunningly beautiful area completely surrounded by national forests, and it attracts eagles because spawning chum salmon come to the end of their life cycle here, stranding on the river's many gravel bars, or in its shallow waters, where the eagles can get at them.

Eagles begin arriving here in early December and remain in residence until mid-March, but the peak of eagle attendance occurs in January, when 300 or more birds gather along the river. For the sake of the eagles, the preserve's shoreline is off limits to foot traffic, but several viewing areas provide excellent opportunities for eagle watching. One lookout is located a mile east of Rockport at Washington Eddy; and another lookout is a few miles farther east. Boaters here are asked not to beach, on the shore or the gravel bars, between Marblemount and Rockport, and to be as silent as possible while plying the river.

Driving Instructions: From points west take Highway 20 to Rockport.

Cascade Mountain Inn
3840 Pioneer Lane
Concrete-Birdview, WA 98237
Telephone: (206) 826-4333

Situated on 10 acres, Cascade Mountain Inn is a gambrel-roofed cedar structure with six rooms, all of them with private bath. The decor includes many antiques and curios, and the rates include a full breakfast. Two lakes immediately north of the inn (Shannon and Baker) have high concentrations of ospreys.

Rates: moderate; MC,V

Northwest Bed & Breakfast, Inc.
Laine Friedman and Gloria Shaich
7707 SW Locust Street
Portland, OR 97223
Telephone: (503) 246-8366

Northwest Bed & Breakfast represents upwards of 250 host homes in the Northwest. Many are in Washington, and the accommodations range from the rustic to the regal, with prices varying accordingly.

Town & Country Motor Inn
2009 Riverside Drive (Old 99)
Mount Vernon, WA 98273
Telephone: (206) 424-4141

Thirty miles from the Skagit River Bald Eagle Natural Area, Town & Country Motor Inn is an eighty-room motel. Each room has a color television, telephone, and private bath. Facilities include a pool, sauna, restaurant, and bar.

Rates: inexpensive to moderate; AE,DC,MC,V

HAINES, ALASKA

Alaska Chilkat Bald Eagle Preserve
Box 518-TD
Haines, AK 99827
Telephone: (907) 766-2202

From mid-October through December, bald eagles from southeast Alaska, and from as far as Washington State, gather at the Chilkat River to feed on spawning chum salmon. Geothermal activity under the river prevents it from freezing, and the result is an unusually late salmon run. And an unusually large congregation of eagles. Even conservative estimates of peak concentrations count more than 3000 eagles in November. They gather along a four-mile stretch of river known as the Chilkat Bald Eagle Council Grounds. Hundreds feed on salmon on gravel bars in the river, as hundreds more roost in the cottonwoods along its banks. Fifty or sixty birds roosting in the same tree is common.

Access to the Council Grounds is easy. The Haines Highway runs along the river, with several pullouts for viewing. The Council Grounds is located between miles 19 and 23 on the highway. Cars can be rented in Haines and tours to the Council Grounds are usually available (check the visitor center). Haines, situated at the northern end of Lynn Canal, a fjord lined with glaciers and waterfalls, marks the end of the Inside Passage (Alaska's Marine Highway) and the beginning of roads to the interior. The area is spectacularly scenic.

Alaska Private Lodgings
P.O. Box 10135
Anchorage, AK 99502
Telephone: (907) 345-2222

Alaska Private Lodgings is a bed and breakfast reservation service that offers a wide variety of lodging—from basic to luxurious, with appropriate prices.

Halsingland Hotel
P.O. Box 158
Haines, AK 99827
Telephone: (907) 766-2000

Formerly the Officers' Quarters at Fort William Seward, Halsingland Hotel has 60 rooms, some furnished with antiques, some overlooking the fjord. Facilities include a restaurant and bar.

Rates: inexpensive to moderate; AE,MC,V

OTHER PLACES TO OBSERVE HAWKS

Braddock Bay State Park   *(spring)*
Greece, NY 14420

Glacier Bay National Park   *(see "Glaciers")*
Gustavus, AK 99826

Glacier National Park   *(see "Bears")*
West Glacier, MT 59936

Lake Barkley State Resort Park   *(wintering eagles)*
PO Box 790
Cadiz, KY 42211

Squaw Creek National Wildlife   *(wintering eagles)*
  Refuge
Box 101
Mound City, MO 64470

GLACIERS

"Where are the snows of yesteryear?"
—FRANÇOIS VILLON, *Le Grand Testament*

Glaciers are rocks—solid, plastic, crystalline masses of the mineral ice—that form when more snow falls than melts. The very snows of yesteryear, they begin as airy and delicate hexagonal crystals that as they accumulate weigh more and more heavily upon themselves, until time and pressure change them.

At first the lacelike crystals float down to earth and lay there unchanged, loose and fluffy and blown about by the wind, perfect for making snowballs. But after a few weeks or months, the crystals start shrinking and deforming, changing from frilly to crudely shaped hexagons, with less and less air between them. This dense and compacted mass of crystals, called granular snow, eventually gets buried by more accumulation, which compresses it further, squeezing out even more air and creating, finally, an extremely dense form of snow called firn. After a decade or two of continuing accumulation, the increasing pressure from above transforms firn into solid glacial ice, an incredibly dense mosaic of spheroid crystals containing very little air. By the time loose snow metamorphoses into solid glacial ice, the percentage of air among the crystals falls from ninety to ten.

But glacial ice alone does not a glacier make. Masses of glacial ice, however tiny or enormous, do not officially become glaciers until they move, or until we determine that they at one time did. Glaciers move constantly. Although we think of them as slowness itself, they are active, dynamic forces that shape the landscape even as we watch. The nature of glacial movement depends on many factors, and while some glaciers seem never to move, others "gallop," advancing hundreds of feet a day. In August 1986, Valerie Glacier, a tributary of Hubbard Glacier, made news all across the United States when it "surged" and blocked Russell Fjord, turning it into Russell Lake. Seals and porpoises were stranded in the newly formed lake. Attempts to rescue them were mounted, only to be abandoned when the weather turned outrageously foul. Finally, during the wee hours of October 8, the dam broke and Russell Lake, which had risen more than 80 feet above sea level, poured into Disenchantment Bay.

Though many people were surprised by the surge of the Hubbard Glacier, which has been surging since 1974, glaciologists in Alaska were not. There are approximately 2900 square miles of glaciers in Alaska, and hundreds of glacier-bound lakes fill and empty in cycles as surging glaciers here advance and retreat dramatically. One of the more notorious of these, the Knik Glacier, continually impounds Lake George, near Anchorage.

Scientific interest in surging glaciers began in 1906,

when Alaska's Variegated Glacier began moving at a hundred times its normal rate, covering about 165 feet a day. Scientists have since recorded surging glaciers moving at rates of almost four miles a year—a formidable rate of flow indeed. Damage from surging glaciers has been significant. In sections of the Alps, advancing ice sheets in the late sixteenth century dammed tributary valleys and drowned entire settlements. And Norwegian farms, established in the twelfth century, disappeared under advancing glaciers in the eighteenth.

Surges seem to result from a redistribution of ice within the glacier, from a movement of its plastic mass from its upper to its lower layers, and a buildup of water pressure at its base, where rising heat from radioactivity deep in the earth's core melts the basal layers of ice. These forces combine to make the glacier slide, sort of, on a lubricating layer of water, and during a dramatic surge one can almost think of the glacier as floating.

Some scientists suspect that the great ice ages might well have been precipitated by a surging of the antarctic ice sheet. This massive ice sheet, which covers slightly less than 5 million square miles and gets as thick as 10,000 feet, is at the melting point at its base. The rapid surge of an ice sheet so large, the theory goes, would reflect so much solar energy back into space that earth's atmosphere would cool significantly, and a new ice age could begin.

Geologists don't really have a tidy explanation of why the planet periodically experiences an ice age, but all manner of interesting theories have been proposed. A Yugoslavian geophysicist, Milutin Milankovitch, suggested in the 1920s that ice ages resulted from irregularities in the earth's orbit and its axis of rotation. Over the course of 90,000 years, the earth's orbit around the sun varies from an ellipse to an almost perfect circle, with the result that the planet is sometimes closer and sometimes farther from the sun. Similarly, but over a period of 41,000 years, the earth's angle of tilt differs by as much as 3 degrees. Meanwhile, the planet's direction of tilt in space wobbles, completely reversing itself every 21,000 years or so, like a giant top. Some combination of these factors, said Milankovitch, affects the amount of solar radiation reaching the earth and causes major fluctuations in global climate. If these little wobbles, angles, and orbits seem too insignificant to cause an ice age, consider how in the temperate climates the angle of the earth to the sun makes the difference between summer and winter.

Although the amount of data Milankovitch needed to prove his theories did not exist during his lifetime, scientists working on the international CLIMAP (Climate: Long-Range Investigation, Mapping and Prediction) project verified many of his findings in 1976. As much of a revelation as it eventually became, Milankovitch's theory does not by any means provide the entire picture. Geologists tend to consider it alongside several other schemes, which could easily complement each other and intensify their effects.

Studies of glacial ice reveal that during the last ice age the earth's atmosphere contained low levels of carbon dioxide, a gas responsible for the "greenhouse" effect, whereby solar radiation entering the atmosphere stays there rather than dissipates back into space. When the great glaciers melted, carbon dioxide in the atmosphere increased substantially.

Analyses of deep-sea core samples seem to support the possibility that the ice ages occurred during periods when the earth's magnetic field was most intense, the inference being that a strong magnetic field would somehow shield the planet from solar radiation. Other possible factors include nuclear winter-like clouds of volcanic ash that blocked out the sun, fluctuations in the sun's output of heat, and the movements of earth's continents relative to the poles.

We don't know what caused the great ice ages, nor for that matter what caused them to end. We are living now in an interglacial period, called the Holocene, or Recent, epoch, which began about 15,000 years ago when the temperature of the earth started rising and the Laurentide ice sheet began retreating. Since then, the mean temperature of the atmosphere has fluctuated, and although we're not expecting another ice age, glacial activity since the fourteenth century has been so significant that many geologists think of it as the beginning of the Little Ice Age. During the past five hundred years, several warming and cooling trends have affected glacial activity. A warming trend in the mid-nineteenth century generated a widespread retreat of the world's glaciers, and a cooling trend began sometime around 1945.

Unless you act truly recklessly, you needn't fear either advancing or retreating glaciers. Even when they gallop you can get out of their way. When it is quiet you can hear them, or at least I think so, groaning away with precisely the sound one would expect countless billions of crystals to make. In the right light, glaciers can assume absolutely surreal colors—pale and electric shades of blue, deep purple tints—that can seem to glow as though from within. From the air they look like exactly what they are: mind-bogglingly massive rivers of ice moving slowly toward their terminus, with rugged mountains all around them.

Most glaciers have a flow rate of about 200 yards a year. This *does not* mean that in winter they advance 200 yards down the valley and by late summer retreat 200 yards up it. Even though a glacier moves 200 yards in a year, it may for all intents and purposes not advance or retreat at all. It may, in short, stay almost exactly where it was. In such a situation, the 200 yards of flow rate represents a movement within the glacier itself, an internal flow of crystals.

Even though the antarctic ice sheet formed 10 million years ago, core samples from its base date back only about 30,000 years. The snow that falls and turns into glacial ice eventually travels the length of the glacier and melts at its terminus. From here it might flow right into a stream or, as in the case of tidewater glaciers, it might become part of an iceberg that breaks off.

Crystals of glacial ice flow because of the enormous pressure that constantly deforms them. Indeed, the internal flow of glacial ice can be thought of as a constant shifting of deforming crystals. The same stress that squeezes the air out of snowflakes and compresses them into crystals of glacial ice, compresses glacial ice crystals until they slip and shift position. Sometimes they melt under the pressure and then reform a millionth of an inch downstream. Like many geological processes, the flow of glaciers represents a movement made up of billions of smaller movements. It is an enormous momentum caused by microscopic crystals sliding and shifting under stress.

In addition to a glacier's internal flow of crystals, other factors, such as gravity and the glacier's temperature, affect its movement. Cold as they look, many glaciers have internal temperatures that hover at the melting point. The condition often generates passageways of water within the glacier as well as a liquid layer at its base. When this condition prevails, as it does during a dramatic surge, the glacier's overall movement becomes a combination of internal flow and basal sliding. Naturally, glaciers move more quickly down steep grades than across gradual slopes.

There are two types of glaciers: valley glaciers, such as those in North America and Europe; and continental glaciers, which cover approximately 80 percent of Greenland and 90 percent of Antarctica. Valley glaciers form in mountain amphitheaters called cirques, and flow downward, cutting U-shaped valleys. In many cases, as in that of Alaska's Harvard Glacier, numerous tributary glaciers flow into the main glacier, just as so many tributary streams flow into a river.

Continental glaciers flow somewhat differently, and in a manner of speaking, they create their own gravity. If we could lift one off the ground and look at it from the side, a continental glacier would look like a somewhat flattened bell, or a convex lens, with most of its mass at the center and its peripheries attenuated. The major accumulations of snow that form continental glaciers fall near their center, where the ice reaches thicknesses of two miles and moves, primarily through the molecular motions of deforming ice crystals, downward and outward to the sea.

Like most of us, glaciers have a budget, and their annual growth is simply the difference between the amount of snow that falls (accumulation) and the amount that melts (ablation). When accumulation and ablation are more or less equal, and the budget balances, glaciers achieve something of a steady state, an equilibrium. Generally speaking, most of the planet's glaciers (and we estimate as many as 200,000 currently exist) have been in a steady state during the past few thousand years. If from the deck of a boat in Glacier Bay, however, you watch as a chunk of ice the size of a building breaks away from a tidewater glacier, cracking like thunder and generating 30-foot waves in the ice-choked water, the concept of a steady state seems truly remote.

OBSERVING GLACIERS

If you want to see glaciers, you want to go to Alaska. Observing them can be as simple or as complicated an activity as you care to make it. You can drive right up to the Mendenhall Glacier outside Juneau, or the Worthington Glacier outside Valdez, or you can hire helicopters to look at them from above, or land on them. You can watch tidewater glaciers from elegant cruise ships, sipping drinks cooled off with 10,000-year-old glacial ice, or from kayaks low and quiet in the water. Even the truly jaded get excited about glaciers, which are such popular attractions that access to them does not require major logistics. If there's a glacier nearby, there's a tried and true way of going to see it.

DESTINATIONS AND ACCOMMODATIONS

GLACIER BAY NATIONAL PARK, ALASKA

Two hundred years ago a glacier 4000 feet thick covered what is now Glacier Bay, and scientists still wonder, as they did a hundred years ago, why the ice in this area retreated so rapidly. A glacial retreat as sudden as that which occurred here remains unheard of elsewhere on the planet. At the moment, sixteen tidewater glaciers front Glacier Bay. When they calve, a sound like thunder travels through the air as a huge iceberg, or several, crash into the water. One of the tidewater glaciers here, Johns Hopkins Glacier, calves such enormous blocks of ice that even the largest cruise ships stay a good mile or two from its face. No matter how big a boat is, a 200-foot-high iceberg can spell disaster.

The sixteen tidewater glaciers in Glacier Bay represent more than half of the tidewater glaciers in the world. Those on the bay's east and southwest sides continue to retreat as those on the west side advance. Wildlife in the area includes humpback, minke, and killer whales, as well as porpoises, bears, and eagles. Habitats range from snow-covered mountains, including Mount Fairweather, at 15,320 feet the highest summit in southeastern Alaska, to rain forests.

Glacier Bay National Park embraces more than 3 million acres of ruggedly beautiful terrain, and activities here include everything from backcountry hiking and camping to gourmet dining on sleek, luxurious cruise ships. Mixed drinks in the Glacier Bay area usually contain 10,000-year-old ice cubes, which some people swear by. Planning a trip to Glacier Bay requires knowing well in advance what kind of experience you want, for most of the tours and accommodations in the area tend to be booked well in advance.

For information, contact Glacier Bay National Park, Gustavus, AK 99826, telephone: (907) 697-3341.

Glacier Bay Lodge and Cabins
PO Box 31
Gustavus, AK 99826
Telephone: (907) 697-3221 or, off-season, (206) 624-8551
Open late May through late September.

Situated in the lush rain forest at Bartlett Cove, Glacier Bay Lodge consists of a huge, cathedral-ceilinged main building with all kinds of glass, and fifty-four cabins. The main lodge building has a large stone fireplace, restaurant, bar, meeting rooms, and, upstairs, the National Park Ranger information station. Boardwalks lead through stands of Sitka spruce to the cabins, which are built along a hillside that affords views of the bay or the rain forest.

The lodge is the focal point for any number of activities, including a simple walk along one of the trails that emanate from the lodge and follow the beach along the cove. Information about organized activities and tours is readily available at the lodge.

Rates: inexpensive to moderate; AE,MC,V

Gustavus Inn
Box 31
Gustavus, AK 99826
Telephone: (907) 697-2254 or, in winter, (907) 586-2006
Open late May through mid-September.

A genuine Alaska homestead operated by the second generation of homesteaders, Gustavus Inn is located in Glacier Bay National Park, about a mile from the airport. The inn, which accommodates no more than sixteen guests, has shared baths and emphasizes Glacier Bay activities, which the hosts are more than happy to arrange for guests. The food here is home-cooked and plentiful, with herbs coming from the root cellar and fish from the bay. The inn has a small bar and a well-stocked library. Rates here include all meals, and numerous organized tours and activities emanate from the lodge.

Rates: expensive; NCC

Alaska Discovery
Box 26
Gustavus, AK 99826
Telephone: (907) 697-2257

The oldest expedition company in Alaska, Alaska Discovery offers a plethora of wilderness excursions, several of them in conjunction with the University of Alaska. Most of the tours last from four to seven days and take place on the water. Alaska Discovery offers several kayak trips that bring you right up to the edge of the glaciers, as well as journeys in diesel cabin cruisers and raft trips on the Tatshenshini/Alsek River.

Rates: Four-day trips run around $700; seven-day trips around $900.

Gray Line of Alaska
300 Elliott Avenue West
Seattle, WA 98119
Telephone: 1-800-544-2206

The Gray Line of Alaska offers several short trips (two days) to Glacier Bay from Juneau. They include a stay at Glacier Bay Lodge, a park naturalist's talk, and a cruise past Casement, McBride, Riggs, and, weather permitting, Muir Glacier. The tours leave from Juneau. The Gray Line also offers tours to the Columbia, Mendenhall, and Portage glaciers.

Rates: The two-day, one-night Glacier Bay tour costs approximately $275 per person.

MENDENHALL GLACIER, ALASKA

The state capital of Alaska, Juneau is accessible only by boat or aircraft. As the city has grown, its 28,000 residents have pushed farther and farther into the suburbs, and the only reason they have been able to do so is because the Mendenhall Glacier has been graciously receding up its valley. Billed throughout Alaska as the original "drive-up" glacier, the Mendenhall is a 200-foot-tall, mile-and-a-half-wide glacier a little less than 13 miles from downtown Juneau.

The Mendenhall Glacier originates in the Juneau ice field, a 1500–square mile ice cap that feeds thirty-six glaciers and flows for 12 miles to its face outside Juneau. Municipal buses and taxis make access to the glacier easy, and a visitors center at its face offers free films and interpretive exhibits. The Mendenhall Glacier feeds the Mendenhall River, a popular thoroughfare for relaxed float trips, and several hiking trails affording views of the glacier fan out from the visitors center.

The best way to see the Mendenhall Glacier is from the air. Just about every air taxi company in town is more than willing to accommodate individuals or groups who want to fly over, or land on, the glacier. Magnificent though it looks on sunny, clear days, the Mendenhall, like most glaciers, takes on an almost supernatural beauty under cloudy, overcast skies, which emphasize the electric blues and psychedelic purples of glacial ice. Helicopter tours to the Juneau ice field leave frequently and usually last about forty-five minutes, although longer trips are easily arranged, and are more expensive. Forty-five-minute helicopter trips to the ice field cost about $100 per person; hour-and-a-half trips about $175.

For information about helicopter trips to the ice field, contact The Gray Line, Baranof Hotel, Juneau, AK 99801, telephone: (907) 586-3773; or, Temsco Helicopters, Inc., 1873 Shell Simmons Drive, Suite 111, Juneau, AK 99801, telephone: (907) 789-9501.

Alaska Bed & Breakfast Association
526 Seward Street
Juneau, AK 99801
Telephone: (907) 586-2959

Alaska Bed & Breakfast Association represents B&B host homes in southeastern Alaska, particularly in Juneau. Accommodations vary considerably—some are modest, some fancy—and prices range accordingly from inexpensive to moderate.

Alaskan Hotel
167 S. Franklin Street
Juneau, AK 99801
Telephone: (907) 586-1000

Listed in the National Register of Historic Sites, Alaskan Hotel is located in downtown Juneau. The hotel has forty rooms, some of them with private bath and some with kitchenette. The facilities include a bar, sauna, and Laundromat.

Rates: inexpensive to moderate; AE,DC,MC,V

Baranof Hotel
127 N. Franklin Street
Juneau, AK 99801
Telephone: (907) 586-2660; 1-800-544-0970

The fanciest place in town, the Baranof is a large, imposing structure with 225 rooms. The rooms have color television, some have antiques, and some have a kitchenette. Suites are also available. The facilities here include a coffee shop, restaurant, and meeting and banquet rooms.

Rates: expensive; AE,DC,MC,V

OTHER PLACES TO OBSERVE GLACIERS

Banff National Park
Box 900
Banff, Alberta TOL OCO
CANADA

Glacier/Mount Revelstoke National Parks
Box 350
Revelstoke, British Columbia VOE 2SO
CANADA

Jasper National Park
Box 10
Jasper, Alberta TOE 1EO
CANADA

Kenai Fjords National Park
Box 1727
Seward, AK 99664

Kluane National Park
Haines Junction, Yukon Territories YOB 1LO
CANADA

Lake Clark National Park
701 C Street
Anchorage, AK 99513

Wrangell-St. Elias National Park and Preserve
PO Box 29
Glenallen, AK 99588

BEARS

Be scared. You cant help that. But dont be afraid. Aint nothing in the woods going to hurt you if you dont corner it or it dont smell that you are afraid. A bear or a deer has got to be scared of a coward the same as a brave man has got to be.

—WILLIAM FAULKNER, *The Bear*

I also believe that bears are very formal. I think that protocol is a comfort to them. Glacier Park recommends that hikers in bear country use bear bells—bells worn to jingle at each step, to let the bears know that someone's coming.

—IAN FRAZIER, *Bear News*

If during your travels you chance to encounter a bear, you might as well take Faulkner's advice and stand your ground with dignity, scared but not afraid, whatever that means. A brochure about bears published by one of the state parks lists fifteen things to do if a bear confronts you in the wild, and although for the life of me I cannot recall the second through four-teenth recommended actions, I remember clearly the first: "FREEZE."

The official bear confrontation advice published by the Canadian Ministry of the Environment always sounded to me like something right out of Faulkner: "Remember that a bear rearing on its hind legs is not always aggressive. Remain still and speak in low tones to indicate to the animal that you mean no harm." The Canadian publication goes on to assure the reader: "Be aware that bears sometimes bluff their way out of a threatening situation by charging and then veer-ing away at the last second."

Ambiguous as it sounds, Faulkner's concept of being scared but not afraid somehow rings true, for al-though you should fear bears in no uncertain terms you should never panic in their presence. Like wolves, bears instinctively charge animals that flee from them, and though they may look like big, lazy, roly-poly creatures, they can easily outrun any human. Re-searchers have clocked 700-pound grizzlies galloping at just under 40 miles per hour, a speed no human runner has ever come close to. If you encounter a bear in the wild, you have nothing going for you other than your wits: the fight or flight mechanism, in such a situation, has no meaning. A bear can kill a human with one swat. Be scared but not afraid.

The locations described below all distribute litera-ture about what to do if you encounter a bear, but for the sake of those who might run into one in the parking lot of the ranger station, perhaps a few basic rules bear repeating:

1. If you confront a bear, freeze. Try to act as calm and relaxed as possible, and speak soothingly and reassuringly to the animal, in low tones, on any subject that seems appropriate.
2. Do not run, nor for that matter make any sudden moves.
3. Slowly remove your backpack if you have one, and toss it toward the bear by way of distracting it.
4. Slowly retreat, giving the animal as wide a berth as possible.
5. If the bear confronting you is a grizzly, attempt as nonchalantly as possible to climb a tree if one is available, but only if you're sure you can get at least 15 feet up the tree by the time the grizzly gets to it. If you're dealing with a black bear, don't bother trying to climb a tree. If you have enough time to identify the kind of bear confronting you, you're probably out of danger.
6. If the bear attacks, play dead. Get into a fetal position with your hands clasped behind your neck and hope for the best.

Your chances of getting attacked by a bear are virtually nil, but if you venture into bear country you should acquaint yourself to some degree with the nature of the animals. The best way to avoid an untoward confrontation with a bear is to announce your presence as you wander through the wilderness. The gentle tingle of a bear bell will warn the animals of your approach, and they will avoid you. If you don't have a bear bell, try singing, reciting Augustan poetry or, if sympathetic ears present themselves, the good old expedient of sweet discourse. Don't slink silently through the woods, for surprised bears represent perhaps the greatest threat to humans. Be formal. Don't sneak up on bears.

Members of the family Ursidae, the three species of bears native to North America vary in height from 7 to 14 feet tall, in weight from just under 200 to just under 2000 pounds, in color from black to white to cinnamon to blue, in habitat from subtropical to arctic, in diet from garbage to narwhals, and in ecological status from abundant to endangered.

The black bear, smallest of the three species, thrives throughout most of Canada and Alaska as well as in perhaps thirty-five of the lower forty-eight states, as far south as Florida and Louisiana. In many states the hunting of black bears is permitted, but the species continues to flourish nevertheless, with populations in most areas rising, in some quite dramatically. The Northeast has seen a marked increase in the number of black bears of late, and in the upper Midwest people can't stop talking about the 1985 black bear invasion of Duluth, Minnesota. Probably because of a poor nut and berry crop, hundreds of Minnesota's more than 8000 black bears took turns wandering into downtown Duluth, breaking into station wagons to get the groceries, slinking down alleyways dragging trash cans noisily, entering houses and eating all the porridge, terrifying everybody.

The invasion generated hundreds of distress calls a day, and from midsummer to early fall the police had no choice but to kill upwards of 200 bears. Between the Minnesota and Michigan hunting seasons that year, and the sporadic but ubiquitous dispatching of nuisance animals, 2000 black bears bought it. Not knowing how properly to respond, the Duluth Convention and Visitors Bureau, which one imagines meeting semiannually at most, rushed into action and set up a twenty-four-hour-a-day bear watchers' hotline. Rumor had it that one could obtain an extended bear forecast. Cold weather, mercifully, finally drove the animals back to their dens.

In addition to enormous Alaskan and Canadian populations, black bears exist in considerable numbers along the northern tier of the contiguous states, as well as all the way down the Cascades and the Sierra Nevada, the Rockies, and the Appalachians. I saw one in the Everglades, loping down the road like it was nobody's business. As their invasion of Duluth suggests, black bears aren't endangered in the lower forty-eight states, where they prevail as prolifically as they do because humans tolerate them. We tolerate them because they tolerate us, which is to say, essentially, that they tend not to kill us when our ranges overlap, and vice versa. When a black bear raids the garbage in Pennsylvania, people joke about it. Often they will tell exaggerated stories about their dachshunds treeing the animals for hours. When a grizzly bear raids the garbage in Montana, however, people do not joke about it, nor do their dogs survive.

Not called *Ursus arctos horribilis* for nothing, grizzlies can wax truly ugly when hungry, surprised, provoked, frightened, or otherwise inspired to rage with tooth and claw. Their power defies description. They can kill a 1000-pound moose with a single blow from one of their 30-pound paws, eat 50 pounds of it in as many minutes, and in half that time excavate a pit in root-gnarled soil large enough to bury the carcass. They can outrun a horse and catch an airborne sockeye salmon in jaws strong enough to bite through a lodge-pole pine 6 inches in diameter, at chest height. They fear nothing, and as a result they live only on the fringes of polite society. We don't tolerate them because they don't tolerate us, and who could blame them? Or us?

Fewer than a thousand grizzlies prevail now, and only in the most rugged, remote, northwestern sections of the lower forty-eight states. They used to roam much of the West, especially California, which at one point had a population of grizzlies surpassed only by that of southeastern coastal Alaska, where the animals still thrive. At one time considered a separate species, the Alaska brown bear (*Ursus arctos middendorffi*) represents a large, northwestern coastal strain of the grizzly. With some individuals standing 14 feet and weighing in at 1700 pounds, the Alaska brown bear qualifies as the planet's largest terrestrial carnivore.

The polar bear, at half a ton the middleweight of the three North American ursine species, occurs only above the tree line. Indeed, except for an isolated population along the western shore of Hudson Bay, polar bears exist only above the Arctic Circle. They are an endangered species, so much so that countries incapable of agreeing on all manner of ecological issues, such as what species of whales to spare, unanimously signed a treaty outlawing the taking of polar bears other than by subsistence Eskimo hunters. Astonishingly enough, the Soviet Union, which could care less about the ecology of whales, initiated the international agreement protecting polar bears. Signed by all the "polar bear" countries—the Soviet Union, United States, Canada, Norway, and Denmark—the agreement acknowledges the fragile existence of a creature that no longer lives beyond the pale of oil fields and whose pelt would easily fetch $20,000 in Paris or New York.

Though far more endangered than either grizzly or black bears, polar bears are perhaps the most easily observed of the three species. One has, of course, to go out of one's way to observe them, but they appear like clockwork along the western shore of Hudson Bay during October and November, and a significant tourism industry follows them around, in specialized vehicles with balloon tires that don't damage the tundra. The situation is not as vulgar as it sounds. In its own way, it represents something of a model of bear management, in stark contrast, say, to the exploitation of grizzly and black bears in Yellowstone National Park during the first half of this century.

From about 1920 through the beginning of the Second World War, visitors to Yellowstone could take a seat in the bleachers and watch, on a good night, upwards of fifty bears—some grizzlies, some blacks —feeding in felicitous harmony. The bleachers overlooked a garbage dump, which park rangers, under orders from the Department of the Interior, had arranged like a dining room—with platforms instead of tables, and no chairs. Rather than dumping it higgledy-piggledy in a pile, park personnel spread the garbage across the platforms, buffet style. Hundreds of people sat and cheered as the bears feasted. When the war came and attendance at the park dropped, so did the amount of garbage.

After several people were killed by bears with a large appetite for garbage and no fear of humans, the powers that be at Yellowstone did an about-face and closed the garbage dumps, in effect exposing the bears to a cold-turkey garbage withdrawal. This action, which took place in the sixties when increasing numbers of people began utilizing the country's national parks, was in direct defiance of advice offered by America's two most imperious bear experts, John and Frank Craighead. Sure enough, after one of the major dumps closed, bear incidents at the campgrounds doubled. As the Craigheads had predicted, some of the grizzlies couldn't make the transition from a garbage-filled to a garbage-free environment, so they appeared at campgrounds. Because they couldn't stay away from garbage and people, two hundred grizzlies died at the hands of park personnel between the late sixties and the mid-seventies.

Fewer than two hundred grizzlies remain in the greater Yellowstone ecosystem, which consists of 5.5 million acres in and around the park. The Yellowstone population seems to be in trouble. The healthiest grizzly population in the lower forty-eight states, about six hundred animals, resides in the Continental Divide ecosystem, another 5.5 million acres, which embraces Glacier National Park and several wilderness areas—Great Bear, Bob Marshall, Scapegoat, Mission Mountains. Other than in these two areas, grizzlies in the lower forty-eight states exist only in small pockets in Idaho and Washington, where we allow them to. Because they have a low reproductive rate, the killing of a single bear, particularly a female, has a significant impact on a particular population.

Poaching has become a significant problem. Alaska, in December 1984, outlawed the selling of bear parts, which constitutes a small industry in areas heavily populated with any species of bear. It seems that buyers in the Orient, particularly Korea, willingly pay $3000 for a frozen two-pound bear gallbladder, from which they extract a cup or so of bile. As surely as Western scientists wonder about the efficacy of bile as a medicine, its use in the Orient, Western gourmands wonder about the palatability of bear paws.

These can either be baked whole and served with a sweet-and-sour sauce or filleted (there's a thin layer of meat between the pads and the foot) and poached in plum wine with ginger. As an entree, baked bear paws run about $40 in upscale Korean restaurants. Oriental buyers, apparently, do business as far afield as Maine and Wisconsin, and the temptation to harvest bear gallbladders and paws is sufficiently powerful that several states now have laws prohibiting the sale of bear parts.

Curiously enough, recent research indicates that the gallbladder of a bear does, in fact, have serious medical potential. While studying the physiology of hibernating bears, scientists discovered that the bears' bile contains a specialized acid, ursodeoxycholic acid, that dissolves gallstones. One might well expect this ursodeoxycholic acid to see increasing use as a nonsurgical treatment for human gallstones.

The physiology of hibernating bears differs significantly from that of all other hibernating mammals. A true hibernator's body temperature drops almost to freezing and its pulse rate almost disappears. A hibernating bear, on the other hand, experiences a relatively small drop in temperature, and though the bear's pulse rate falls by 80 percent it also rises back almost to normal once a day. As a consequence, hibernating bears do not fall into as deep a sleep as other hibernating mammals, but they sustain their sleep for far longer.

Other hibernators fall into a profound sleep from which they cannot be awakened. Nonetheless, during this period, their body wakes them up every few days so the animals can defecate and eat; then they fall back to sleep and there's no waking them up. Bears, however, go out for the count, and if nothing disturbs them they can sleep for months. They can wake up relatively quickly, though they seldom do so. While asleep, female bears give birth and even nurse their young.

The ability to sleep for months without awakening requires a unique biology, a series of bodily systems that resemble nothing else in nature. Even though hibernating bears burn up enormous amounts of fat while they sleep (4000 to 8000 calories depending on size) and their cholesterol levels go sky high, they do not develop problems with hardening arteries any more than they develop gallstones. Nor do they develop kidney stones.

The kidneys of bears, in fact, shut down while they hibernate, and yet they experience no toxic effects of their own metabolism. Other mammals with dysfunctional kidneys have a few days to live, because urea, a waste product filtered by the kidneys, is extremely poisonous. It seems that bears break down toxic urea into nitrogen molecules, which they resorb right through the walls of their gallbladders and utilize in the manufacture of new protein. A nifty system indeed, the hibernation mechanism of bears represents a singular biological phenomenon, an almost mystical form of self-reliance. One thinks of the serpent with its tail in its mouth. The only bears that do not hibernate are male polar bears, who spend the winter out on the pack ice.

OBSERVING BEARS

The locations below focus on grizzly and polar bears, which are far less numerous than black bears. You can observe black bears in perhaps thirty-five of the lower forty-eight states. In many natural areas, such as Yosemite National Park, the black bears may well come over to observe you, especially if you have some good food around. Very generally speaking, black bears are relatively unaggressive and far less of a threat than grizzly or polar bears. Nevertheless, black bears should be respected because, simply, if they choose to they can kill you.

DENALI NATIONAL PARK AND PRESERVE, ALASKA

Larger than the state of Massachusetts, Denali National Park and Preserve embraces some 6 million acres. The landscape here varies from expansive stretches of taiga and tundra to the tallest peak in North America. Mount McKinley rises 20,320 feet. The summit of the mountain, however, remains hidden by clouds 75 percent of the time in summer, but you can usually see glaciers creeping down the base.

Because of the vast expanses of taiga and tundra, you can see for miles here. Thus, much of the wildlife that would remain hidden in a forested area presents itself as nowhere else. The catalogue of species inhabiting the park is exhaustive, with everything from Dall sheep to wolves to grizzlies to golden eagles disporting about. Visitors here are almost certain to see grizzly bears, and those who get lucky spot a wolf. Eagles are everywhere, and the almost twenty-four hours of summer daylight generates profusions of wildflowers that look like seas of color stretching toward the mountains.

Although you can drive to Denali, as well as fly or take the train, vehicles are not permitted on the road that runs into the park. Rather, the Park Service operates a fleet of free shuttle buses that you can get on to and off of at will, stopping at this location or that for a hike or lunch, and catching a later bus back to Mount McKinley Village, the gateway to the park.

Denali National Park Hotel
McKinley Park, AK 99755
Telephone: (907) 278-1122
Open late May through mid-September.

Denali National Park Hotel is a complex of buildings with 140 guest rooms, 100 of them with private bath. The rooms are in several structures (including converted railroad cars), and the range of furnishings—as well as cost—is from economy to luxury. The facilities include a dining room, gift shop, and cocktail lounge. The Park Service presents lectures in an auditorium here, and information about special tours is readily available. Popular tours include flightseeing trips around McKinley and the glaciers.

Rates: inexpensive to expensive; MC,V

McKinley Chalets
McKinley Park, AK 99755
Telephone: (907) 683-2215
Open late May through mid-September.

The Denali Park Hotel also administers the McKinley Chalets, which consist of 144 two-room suites in Bavarian-style cedar structures. The facilities include a restaurant, snack bar, cocktail lounge, and gift shop.

Rates: moderate; MC,V

KODIAK NATIONAL WILDLIFE REFUGE, ALASKA

The 2 million–acre, 3000–square mile Kodiak National Wildlife Refuge has 800 miles of coastline, hundreds of nesting bald eagles, and a couple of thousand Kodiak bears. *Ursus arctos middendorffi*, the Kodiak, or Alaska brown, bear is actually a large, coastal strain of grizzly, *Ursus arctos horribilis*. These enormous animals can stand 14 feet tall and weigh in at 1700 pounds, making them the world's largest terrestrial carnivore. The bears and the eagles both feast on the tens of thousands of salmon that swim up Kodiak's streams to spawn, only to die on the way to the spot where they were born, or on the way back.

Though as a rule not particularly social, Kodiak bears can congregate in relatively large groups of, say, six to twelve, and work a salmon stream in relative harmony. Visitors here often see the bears playing, sliding into the streams like otters. Although they can make a truly adorable sight, they should, like all bears, be considered a potential danger of the first order. The surest way of seeing them is from one of the many flightseeing planes that tour the refuge.

Kodiak National Wildlife Refuge is on Kodiak Island, which is accessible from Homer by the Alaska Marine Highway (the ferry system) or by air. The town, which has a population of almost 5000, was the first permanent Russian settlement in America, and several historic structures, including a 1794 church (rebuilt several times), attest to the Russian presence in Kodiak. The town suffered a major setback in 1964, when the Good Friday earthquake sent a tidal wave through downtown, killing seventy people and destroying 158 homes. The town has been rebuilt and now boasts an unusually scenic harbor, which hosts some 2000 boats and ranks as the nation's fourth largest fishing port.

In addition to Kodiak bears, the island boasts another prodigious inhabitant, the Alaskan king crab, which can measure 4 feet from one claw to the other.

Kodiak Sheffield House
324 South Benson
Kodiak, AK 99615
Telephone: (907) 486-5712
Open all year.

Situated across from the harbor, of which several rooms have a view, Kodiak Sheffield House has eighty-eight rooms with private bath, color cable television, and telephone. Several suites are also available. The facilities include a snack bar, dining room, and cocktail lounge.

Rates: expensive; AE,DC,MC,V

Kodiak Star Motel
119 Brooklyn Terrace
Box 553
Kodiak, AK 99615
Telephone: (907) 486-5657
Open all year.

The Kodiak Star Motel has twenty-eight rooms with private bath, telephone, and television. Some of the rooms have kitchenettes, and four suites are available. The facilities, located in two different buildings, include a Laundromat.

Rates: moderate; AE,DC,MC,V

CHURCHILL, MANITOBA

Situated on the western coast of Hudson Bay, on the east side of the Churchill River estuary, Churchill is Canada's most northerly deep-water port. Settled way back in 1700 B.C., Churchill became one of the main outpost for the Hudson Bay Company, which constructed Fort Prince of Wales in an effort to protect its trading interests. Fort Prince of Wales is now a National Historic Park. Its walls are 17 feet tall and 40 feet thick, and with its forty enormous cannons, the fort seems totally out of place on the rugged coast of Hudson Bay. The fort's history is as curious as its appearance, for the only time it came under attack it surrendered before a single shot was fired. The railroad to Churchill was completed in 1929, and in 1931 the first grain shipments were made from the port.

Churchill is located right at the edge of the tree line, which gives way to tundra and muskeg that run down to a rocky coast. The black spruce, arctic fir, and tamarack around Churchill are skinny, no taller than 9 feet, branchless for the wind on their northwest side and, surprisingly, 200 or more years old. Along the river, the area is more wooded, primarily with stunted willows. The landscape may strike some as forbidding in autumn and winter, but summer sees a profusion of wildflowers along the tundra.

Churchill serves as the backdrop for any number of spectacular natural attractions. In July and August, beluga whales feed in the Churchill River estuary. From mid-October to mid-November, polar bears are everywhere along the coast. Moreover, because of its geophysical position, Churchill is probably the best place in the Northern Hemisphere to watch for the aurora borealis, or northern lights.

The polar bears in Churchill have the highest reproduction rate of any known polar bear population, and the care taken to preserve the 1500 or so bears that frequent the area is something of a model of wildlife management. Organized tours leave regularly in tundra buggies—balloon-tired vehicles that don't damage the tundra—to see the polar bears. Signs everywhere keep visitors and residents well aware of the bears' presence. Now and then a problem bear wanders into town, but Churchill has a polar bear–alert hotline and qualified people respond to calls. The town has, in fact, a cement jail for locking up problem bears, which they release as soon as the bay freezes over. During summer when the ice breaks up, polar bears get stranded on the shores of Hudson Bay. Their recourse is to head for Churchill because it is one of the places where the ice in autumn freezes first to the land.

Whether you come here in spring, summer, or autumn, birding is excellent. Thousands of snow and Canada geese fly down the coast in autumn. Common species at most times include peregrine falcons, gyrfalcons, and rough-legged hawks.

Though remote, Churchill offers year-round services, including an indoor Civic Center that houses just about everything—government offices, health services, a pool and recreational facilities, a movie theater, exhibits of native art, and a cafeteria. The Civic Center also overlooks Hudson Bay.

Churchill is accessible only by plane or train. For transportation information, contact Pacific Western Airlines, telephone: 1-800-592-7303; or VIA Rail, (204) 949-7477. Other sources of travel information include Travel Manitoba, telephone: 1-800-665-0040; and the Churchill Chamber of Commerce (sometimes National Park Service people answer this phone), (204) 675-2022.

At any time of year except winter, reservations are a must in Churchill: individuals and tours frequently book a year in advance.

The Tundra Inn
PO Box 999
32/34 Franklin Street
Churchill, Manitoba ROB OEO
CANADA
Telephone: 1-800-661-1460 and (204) 675-8831

A 1977, two-story motel-style structure in downtown Churchill, The Tundra Inn has thirty-one rooms with television and telephone, a central whirlpool, laundry facilities, and a kitchenette facility. Across the street, the inn's dining room serves steaks, ribs, chicken, veal, and arctic char (rather like salmon). Eighty-five percent of the tour groups in town eat here, and Pat and Bob Penwarden, the hosts, make sure that guests know what's going on in town.

Rates: moderate; AE,MC,V

Seaport Hotel
PO Box 939
Churchill, Manitoba ROB OEO
CANADA
Telephone: (204) 675-8807

The Seaport Hotel has twenty-one rooms, five rooms with microwaves and refrigerators, sixteen rooms with refrigerators only. The rooms have a color television and telephone, and the facilities include a laundry, coffee shop, dining room, and cocktail lounge.

Rates: moderate; AE,MC,V

GLACIER NATIONAL PARK, MONTANA

A spectacular wilderness area, Glacier National Park consists of over a million acres of rugged—very rugged—beautiful country. It adjoins another third of a million acres of similar rugged beauty across the border in Canada. The two wilderness areas together, both of them National Parks, are called Waterton-Glacier International Peace Park. They constitute a million and a half acres of relatively pristine terrain, and to the south and west of them lie an additional several million acres of National Forest.

Glacier hosts the largest population of grizzlies in the contiguous United States, with an estimated 600 individuals in residence. As you will discover as soon as you arrive here, bears are quite a subject in the park: posters and brochures appear everywhere, and rangers tend to introduce them into just about every conversation.

In addition to bears (black as well as grizzly), Glacier also hosts a large population of bald eagles from mid-October to early December. Peak times are mid-October to mid-November, when 300 or so eagles show up at Lower McDonald Creek to feed on kokanee salmon. Two eagle-viewing sites on bridges are located right near the Apgar Information Center at the West Glacier park entrance. Rangers at both the information center and the viewing sites are on duty to answer questions.

For information, contact Glacier National Park, West Glacier, MT 59936, telephone: (406) 888-5441.

Glacier National Park offers a wide range of accommodations possibilities, from the palatial 155-room Glacier Park Lodge to the rustic Granite Park and Sperry Chalets, which are lit by kerosene lamps and accessible only by trail. In between these two extremes are economy to luxury motel rooms in structures at different locations in the park. All of these accommodations, except for the Granite Park and Sperry Chalets, are operated by Glacier Park, Inc., Grey-

hound Tower, Station 5185, Phoenix, AZ 85077, telephone: (406) 226-5551, mid-May to mid-September,
and (602) 248-2600, mid-September to mid-May. All
reservations are made through Glacier Park, Inc.

The Granite Park and Sperry Chalets are operated
by Belton Chalets, Inc., Box 188, West Glacier, MT
59936, telephone: (406) 888-5511.

Reservations for these accommodations, especially
the chalets, should be made as far in advance as possible. Though they vary somewhat, most open in early
June and close by mid-September. For eagle viewing
in October and November, accommodations are available outside the park.

Glacier Highlands Motel
PO Box 397
West Glacier, MT 59936
Telephone: (406) 888-5427
Open all year.

A hundred yards from the Amtrak station and a mile
from the park entrance, Glacier Highlands Motel has
thirty-three rooms with private bath; some have telephones, some have televisions. The facilities here
include a restaurant, gift shop, gas station, and sauna
and Jacuzzi whirlpool bath for the use of the guests.

Rates: inexpensive; MC,V

Izaak Walton Inn
Essex, MT 59916
Telephone: (406) 888-5700
Open all year.

A large half-timber, chalet-style structure built in the
1930s by the Great Northern Railroad Company, Izaak
Walton Inn has pine paneling throughout and a huge
lobby with a stone hearth. An annex houses a sauna

and Laundromat facilities. Of the thirty rooms, nine have private baths; the others have sinks and a shared bath down the hall. Many furnishings original to the inn are still here.

Rates: inexpensive; MC,V

OTHER PLACES TO OBSERVE BEARS

Mount Revelstoke/Glacier
   National Parks
Box 350
Revelstoke, British Columbia
   VOE 2SO
CANADA

Glacier Bay National Park   *(see "Glaciers")*
Gustavus, AK 99826

Jasper National Park
Box 10
Jasper, Alberta TOE 1EO
CANADA

Katmai National Park
Box 7
King Salmon, AK 99613

Kluane National Park Preserve
Haines Junction, Yukon
   Territories YOB 1LO
CANADA

Kootenay National Park
Box 220
Radium Hot Springs,
   British Columbia VOA 1MO
CANADA

North Cascades National Park
800 State Street
Sedro Woolley, WA 98284

Yellowstone National Park
Box 168
Yellowstone National Park, WY
 82190

WATERFOWL

As the clarion notes float downward on the still night air, who can resist the temptation to rush out of doors and peer into the darkness for a possible glimpse of the passing flock, as the shadowy forms glide over our roofs on their long journey? Or, even in daylight, what man so busy that he will not pause and look upward at the serried ranks of our grandest waterfowl, as their well-known honking notes announce their coming and their going, he knows not whence or whither?

—ARTHUR CLEVELAND BENT, *Life Histories of North American Waterfowl*

Twice a year they pass over, sometimes in the dead of night, sometimes at noon, forming and reforming enormous Vs in the sky, honking riotously. At once cacophonous and resonantly musical, the sound of a flock of Canada geese creeps up on you, especially if you haven't heard it for half a year. And it always comes as something of a surprise, as if it were new each time, like the seasons it heralds, or as if you had never heard it before. From a distance the sound falls faintly on the ear, just barely getting its attention, and even a gentle autumn wind, or your footfalls, can drown it out in the leaves. As it moves closer, perhaps fading in and out with the wind, the sound grabs your attention completely.

Even when I expect it, the sound of an approaching skein of Canada geese invariably catches me unaware. Whether it stops me dead in my tracks in the woods or causes me to pause while brushing my teeth before retiring, the sound at first confuses me. Nine times out of ten I mistake it for a pack of barking beagles engaged in an hysterical hunt, but eventually it occurs to me that nobody around here hunts and that beagles don't fly. Recognition, the old ah-ha reaction, finally arrives when the sound comes into its unmistakable own, when the loud clear notes fill the air completely, overpowering all other noise but the whirring of wings. And I smile.

As the season progresses, the sound of honking Canadas becomes a ubiquitous part of the scene, a constant music one learns to recognize instantly, even in one's dreams. They oftentimes rouse me from my sleep, and no matter how tired I feel I sit up immediately in bed, determine the music's direction, and head for the appropriate window. On clear nights you can watch them fly in front of the moon. If you know the heavens, you can draw a bead on their sound and watch the invisible flock as it eclipses stars.

Watching geese and other migrating birds fly across the moon stirred the imaginations of ancient peoples, who down through the ages offered all kinds of theories as to why they fly at night, and where. The most memorable of the ancient theories—and one, incidentally, subscribed to by Aristotle—hypothesized that all those birds flew across the moon at night and then disappeared for the winter because, obviously, they wintered on the moon. The ancients figured the journey took the birds about six weeks. These days we know quite well the whence and the whither of geese and other waterfowl, and naturalists continually gather data about the nature and locations of breeding grounds, wintering grounds, and migratory routes.

Though they never go to the moon, increasing numbers of waterfowl might as well, for some of their traditional habitats have deteriorated so badly as to be just as inhospitable as the lunar surface. People and waterfowl like the same kinds of areas, and although they're not building condominiums along the eastern shore of Hudson Bay, they're building them on the eastern shore of the United States, and in the central valley of California, and all along the Gulf Coast. Originally blessed with 127 million acres of wetlands, the contiguous United States had fewer than 82 million in the late 1950s. Wetlands continue to vanish at a rate of about a half million acres per year. Today the lower forty-eight states probably embrace fewer than 70 million acres of productive waterfowl habitat. Estimates vary.

Managing this habitat is a full-time job for thousands of people. Local, state, and federal government agencies, conservation organizations, hunting organizations, volunteers, and unclassifiable others spend considerable time, energy, and money laboring to protect what remains of our wetlands. The wetlands used almost to protect themselves, as before the advent of extremely efficient and not prohibitively expensive earth-moving equipment, draining a marsh was simply too much work. For a farmer whose land contained both forest and marsh, it took less time to clear trees than to dig a drainage ditch, and you got some firewood thrown in as a bonus. Nowadays, you can dig a drainage ditch in no time flat, while smoking a cigarette and listening to the stereo in an air-conditioned cab.

Since the advent of modern agricultural equipment, farmers rearrange their land quickly and efficiently. The situation has thus become a major threat to the primary waterfowl breeding area on the continent— the prairie pothole region. The work of receding glaciers, the prairie pothole region is a poorly drained, 300,000-square-mile swath of land that runs in a giant arc from Alberta, Canada, southeast to Minnesota, the Dakotas, and Montana. Though it represents just 10 percent of the continent's waterfowl breeding area, the region produces more than 50 percent of North America's ducks. In both the United States and Canada, agricultural reclamation projects have been draining this vital habitat rapidly and, in the opinion of many, foolishly. In North Dakota, for example, farmers already burdened with surplus crops continue to drain prairie pothole wetlands for no sane reason.

Most people do not realize that the vast majority of waterfowl migrate, some of them thousands of miles. The local mallards on the lake across town or the Canada geese grazing on the golf course represent a fraction of the continent's waterfowl population, perhaps 5 percent. The other 95 percent pass by on their way north and south, with the result that at the peaks of migratory movement a golf game can be impossible. A golfer friend tells the story of a canceled tournament, which never got off the ground because an estimated 5000 Canada geese landed on the fairways and refused to move. The club brought in a few tractor trailers, and with enormous effort managed to relocate only a fraction of the geese, who in no time flat were cruising over the golf course, making almost as much of a racket as their colleagues still grazing on the fairways.

The migration of waterfowl, as well as that of other birds, continues to fascinate, and in many cases baffle, ornithologists and other scientists who study this behavior. Research into the mechanisms that stimulate and sustain migration has turned up facts that seem more like fiction. The primary factor that stimulates the migratory urge, or migratory restlessness, is the length of the day—that is, the amount of light that falls on the bird's environment. As the day shortens during early autumn or lengthens during early spring, changes in the level of light affect the pituitary and pineal glands of birds, and they grow restless. This biological mechanism, photoperiodism, probably affects all species of birds, but other systems that are triggered subsequently differ radically among various species. Some birds fly at night and navigate by the stars, others orient themselves by sensing the earth's magnetic poles, and others follow landmarks they recognize.

On the journey from their breeding grounds, which biologists call duck factories, to their wintering grounds, the vast majority of waterfowl follow traditional routes, or flyways. Some species, apparently, learn their migratory route from their elders, who have traveled it before. Others, it seems, innately know the way to go. Whether by instinct or experience, migrating waterfowl stick to the flyways, which follow the predominant contours of the continent. These ancient, biological flyways now serve as waterfowl management zones, as vital migratory corridors that offer the traveling birds food and shelter, for the whole winter if need be. The major National Wildlife Refuges are situated along the flyways, and during the peak of the migration season several refuges boast waterfowl populations in the hundreds of thousands.

North America has four major flyways—the Atlantic, Mississippi, Central, and Pacific.

Shaped rather like an irregular funnel, the Atlantic flyway attracts waterfowl from as far east as the western coast of Greenland and as far west as the Northwest Territories and into Alaska. Waterfowl from the Far West fly almost due southeast across Canada and the Great Lakes, pass over the Appalachians, and hit the coast somewhere between New Jersey and Virginia (greater scaups raised on Alaska's Seward Peninsula winter in southern New England or the northern mid-Atlantic). Birds from the North and Northeast fly almost due south. Many of them follow the extremely irregular Atlantic coastline, which though only 1800 miles long from Maine to Florida, as the crow flies, provides, as the duck paddles, more than 7000 miles of islands, bays, swamps, marshes, and estuaries. Though it embraces more than a third of the wetlands in the contiguous United States, the Atlantic flyway hosts only about a fifth of the waterfowl that winter here.

Shaped almost like a perfect funnel, the Mississippi flyway follows the course of the great river from the Gulf Coast north, fanning out to the north and east at the top of Tennessee, and to the north and west right above Missouri. The upper reaches of the funnel extend into northern Quebec, follow the east coast of Hudson Bay, and extend to Baffin Island. To the west, the flyway extends through the Dakotas, Alberta, and into Alaska. Within the lower forty-eight states, the flyway embraces 750,000 square miles and more than half the viable waterfowl wetlands in the contiguous states. Human residents along the flyway purchase about 40 percent of the duck stamps sold in the country, and they take about the same percentage of ducks. The Mississippi Valley is enormously fertile. Between what grows naturally and what the farmers grow, plenty of food exists for migrating waterfowl. Birds that travel the length of the funnel fan out along the Gulf Coast in a semicircle that extends from northwestern Florida to southeastern Texas.

Shaped like a broad, diagonal band that runs from northeast Alaska to the Gulf Coast of Texas, the Central flyway runs along the east face of the Rocky Mountains and through the prairie pothole region and the Great Plains. The flyway embraces more than a million square miles within the contiguous United States, and thus represents more than a third of the area of all four flyways combined. But the populations of waterfowl using it vary considerably. During dry years in the prairie pothole region, the number of waterfowl using the flyway drops radically. When it is wet up north, enormous "bumper" crops of ducks follow the corridor down to the Texas coast, an extremely important waterfowl wintering area.

A large, broad band that runs from northern Alaska and western Canada right through Mexico, the Pacific flyway occupies the space between the crest of the Rocky Mountains and the Pacific Coast. Though the area embraces more than a quarter of the contiguous United States, only a few percent of it represents good waterfowl habitat. Development in the area proceeds at breakneck speed, especially in California and its central valley, where the interests of waterfowl and people clash constantly. Nevertheless, several refuges along the flyway play host to mind-boggling concentrations of waterfowl. The refuges in the Klamath Basin, for example, attain peak populations of 700,000 birds. If you show up at the right time, you can catch a glimpse of a quarter million snow geese flashing brilliantly white in the sky against the backdrop of Mount Shasta, or see and hear 20,000 whistling swans, or a few of the 700 eagles that winter there.

IDENTIFYING WATERFOWL

Members of the family Anatidae, the forty-eight species of ducks, swans, and geese native to North America vary in length from 12 to 72 inches, in weight from 1½ to almost 40 pounds, in coloration from pure white to dazzling patterns of iridescent greens and reds and electric blues, in range from circumpolar to subtropical, and in ecological status from stable to endangered.

As any beginning birdwatcher will tell you, distinguishing among the various species of waterfowl takes considerable time and practice, especially if you don't know what to expect in a particular spot. At the locations described below, however, you will know what to expect, and I daresay that even the complete novice can identify a duck if he or she can observe thousands of them at the same time. The remarks below are by no means a substitute for a good field guide. They are, rather, a series of identification aids intended to give the complete novice something of a grip on this widely diverse family of birds.

SWANS

Because of their enormous size, swans are easy to distinguish from other waterfowl, but making distinctions among different species of swan might, at times, prove difficult. There is, however, a relatively safe identification rule: the swan you see is probably a whistling swan. Three other species of swan occur in North America, but all three have limited ranges.

The whooper swan breeds in Eurasia above the Arctic Circle and winters on the central and western Aleutian Islands, so unless you're an intrepid traveler you probably won't see one. The mute swan, an introduced species that arrived here in the middle of the nineteenth century, occurs almost exclusively along the East Coast between Massachusetts and New Jersey.

The trumpeter swan, whose name could scarcely be more apt, can be observed, and attended, in Yellowstone National Park and Red Rock National Wildlife Refuge. The trumpeter swan almost passed into extinction in the nineteenth century when early fur traders on the continent slaughtered them in sufficient numbers to afford the Hudson Bay Company to sell more than 100,000 trumpeter swan skins. Rigid protection policies have, fortunately, succeeded in saving the species as well as increasing its population.

Whistling swans, which spend half the year in the Arctic, did not overlap in range with fur traders.

People like swans, which have about them an air of grace, romance, and purity. The most beautiful woman in the world, Helen of Troy, was born to Leda after Zeus, in the form of a swan, raped her. Swans mate for life, and although they take another mate if mortality claims their first one, they do so, some say, only after a period of intense grief.

WHISTLING SWAN

Also called tundra swans, whistling swans are far and away the most common, numerous, and widespread species of swan on the continent. As their name suggests, they nest in the far north on the tundra, from which they migrate to wintering grounds along both coasts of the lower forty-eight states. Of the estimated 100,000 whistling swans on the continent, half of them winter along the Atlantic Coast in the Chesapeake Bay/Currituck Sound area. During fall and early winter spectacular congregations of them are easily observed. Ten thousand of them in the same place can make serious amounts of noise.

Pure white, whistling swans measure about 5 feet from bill to tail. While swimming, standing, or resting, they hold their neck straight, a posture that distinguishes them from mute swans, which hold their neck in a graceful S-curve. They have a black bill. Under ideal conditions, you might see a yellow or orange oblong spot immediately in front of their eye; this spot can be absent.

MUTE SWAN

Commonly found in parks and wildlife areas in southern New England and the mid-Atlantic, the mute swan cuts an elegant figure indeed. Mute swans hold their neck in a sinuous S-curve, and when they display, they fan up their wing feathers and lean back, further accentuating the curve in their neck. They have a large, conspicuously orange bill that has a large black knob at its base, near the eyes. They seldom make any noise, but if you approach them, especially when they're with their young, they can hiss quite noisily. One should never approach their nest, for they protect their young or eggs against all comers, including people. They are extremely powerful and capable of inflicting harm, particularly to a child. When they fly by, you can hear their wingbeats at a hundred yards.

TRUMPETER SWAN

So named because of its incredibly loud, trumpet-like call, the trumpeter swan measures almost 6 feet from beak to tail. It is the largest swan on the continent. Trumpeter swans look like whistling swans but lack the yellow spot in front of their eyes, and they are conspicuously larger. If the birds are calling there is no mistaking them for anything else. You will not see one other than in the northwestern states, southeastern Alaska, British Columbia, Alberta, and Saskatchewan. The resident populations at Yellowstone National Park and Red Rock National Wildlife Refuge generate all kinds of excitement, even among non-birdwatchers. These two populations are a refreshing conservation success story.

GEESE

The eight species of geese native to North America vary considerably, in some cases even within the same species. Ornithologists generally accept eleven subspecies of Canada goose, which at the same time qualifies as the smallest and the largest goose on the continent. Somehow that distinction seems appropriate for the Canada goose. Among snow geese one finds two distinct races, and in one of them a blue color phase. The bean goose and the emperor goose rarely appear farther south or east than southwestern Alaska, and the Ross goose, once rare, seems increasingly common and likely to be hybridizing with "Lesser" snow geese. Nobody ever sees barnacle geese in the wild, and if you go to the beach in the winter you will probably see brant.

Some flocks of snow geese take off in the Arctic, fly up about 6000 feet, get into a rhythmic 60-mile-per-hour pace, and land in coastal Louisiana, not having stopped for a few days. Flocks of Canada geese proceeding north sometimes make only 25 or 30 miles a day as they follow with uncanny accuracy the 35-degree isotherm, below which they can always find open water.

Geese have been studied extensively by everyone from psychologists to gourmets, and over the years we have learned quite a bit about them. They are extremely social creatures that breed in large colonies. They mate for life, and their social structure rotates around a strong family bond. If a nesting pair of Canada geese loses their eggs or their hatchlings, their young from the previous year come back to stay with them. Babysitting among geese seems fairly common, and researchers frequently observe scores of young geese being attended by just a few mature individuals, who protect the young fiercely. Konrad Lorenz, the distinguished ethologist, describes as well the activities of homosexual geese, pairs of ganders that, though anatomically incapable of copulation, perform all the usual male/female rituals.

Whether they look majestic as they fly overhead in a huge formation, or clownish as they stand in the middle of the road blocking traffic, geese are fun to watch. One should stay away from their nest and their goslings, as an angry goose can inflict quite a bite. I once watched a German shepherd run in terror from an angry Canada goose.

For purposes of identification, I describe two species, the Canada goose and the snow goose.

CANADA GOOSE

A tough, adaptable species, the Canada goose occurs across most of North America, and you're likely to see one just about anyplace. The eleven subspecies of Canada goose vary in size. When they congregate at a popular wintering spot, observers frequently note size differences. Regardless of size, though, Canada geese all look alike, and their distinctive markings render them easily identifiable. They have a black neck and head boldly punctuated by a conspicuous white cheek patch, which is visible even at a considerable distance. Their body is brown, and their undertail covert is white. Their call is a rich, bugle-like, musical sound that can carry quite a distance—from far off, it sounds like barking dogs—and they fly in a classic V formation. Though totally at home in the water, Canada geese walk quite well on land and spend a good deal of time grazing. The symbol on the National Wildlife Refuge signs is a Canada goose.

SNOW GOOSE

Though there are, technically, two races of snow geese, the "Greater" and "Lesser," for purposes of basic identification I will consider them as one. They are very close in size and, except for the blue phase of the lesser snow goose, identical in appearance. The birds are pure white with black wingtips: it looks, indeed, as if the birds dipped their wingtips into a black inkwell. They have a pink bill and pink feet. Blue phase lesser snow geese, usually called blue geese, are dark, slate blue to brown birds with a white head and upper neck. The easiest way to distinguish between the snow geese is by their range. Greater snow geese winter exclusively along the Atlantic Coast, generally no farther south than the Carolinas. Lesser snow geese winter in the Midwest, along the Gulf Coast, which is where you will find most of the blue phase birds, and in the central valley of California.

Snow geese breed in the Far North. When they head south, they can form enormous flocks that make non-stop flights between locations as distant as Hudson Bay and coastal Louisiana. They fly in loose formations, long wavy lines, and highly irregular Vs that form and re-form constantly. Their call is a high-pitch bark or yap. They can be extremely noisy, and large congregations of them can drown out virtually all other sound. At their wintering grounds, tens of thousands of them might decide to take to the air and fly around for a bit, a sight one never forgets.

DUCKS

The thirty-some-odd species of ducks native to the continent can pose formidable identification problems for beginners. Even experienced birders sometimes have difficulty identifying ducks, particularly females, which can look extremely similar. A female mallard, for example, looks almost exactly like a black duck; in many cases, a positive identification is all but impossible until the bird flies and displays the trailing edges of its wings. The bird might not, of course, display its trailing edges at all, or the light might not cooperate. Even though I spend a lot of time looking at ducks, I often have trouble identifying them, even though I've seen them many times before. It's almost as if I have to begin again each year by getting out the field guides and memorizing, yet once more, the field marks of the ducks I'm likely to see in a particular spot.

The best way to learn how to identify ducks is to go someplace where there are tens of thousands of them, such as the locations described below. A large congregation of ducks offers the advantage of multiple angles of view, so that one can see this duck from the front, that one from the side, and another one from the back. Some ducks are boldly marked and instantly recognizable, while others display only extremely subtle field marks. Learning to distinguish among them requires practice, but as a general rule even complete novices can learn to identify a few species almost immediately.

The following species of ducks are, in my opinion, among the easiest to identify. A basic familiarity with their field marks should enable even the inexperienced to identify them.

MALLARD

The most common and widespread duck on the continent, mallards show up everywhere, from remote wilderness lakes to inner-city parks to dining tables. The domestic duck descended from mallards, which are so comfortable in the presence of humans it's no wonder they've been domesticated for centuries. I have always thought it ironic that something so beautiful could be so common, and although I can't prove it, I suspect that even the most jaded of birders can't help but smile, if only in their mind's eye, at the sight of the ubiquitous mallard and the sound of its comical quack.

Males have an iridescent, metallic green head and neck separated from a deep chestnut-colored breast by a conspicuous white band, which looks rather like a necklace, or a white collar. Their bill is bright yellow, and their body gray. When they fly they exhibit an electric purple speculum on the trailing edge of their wings. They have pink feet. Females are a dull, mottled brown, about as indistinct as you can get, but they, too, flash an electric purple speculum on the trailing edge of their wings. The purple speculum on both males and females can sometimes be seen when the birds are at rest.

Mallards belong to a group of ducks referred to as dabblers, or puddle ducks, which is to say ducks that feed in shallow water by sticking their head underwater while projecting their rump above the surface. Like other dabblers, they take off vertically, requiring absolutely no runway.

NORTHERN PINTAIL

A slender, elegantly shaped duck, the northern pintail has the widest breeding range of any duck on the continent, with the result that it qualifies as one of the three most abundant ducks. Males in breeding plumage are all but unmistakable. Their most imperious field mark is their incredibly long, slender, pointed tail, which appears as long as their neck. They have a chocolate brown head and a gray back and sides; their chest is white, and a thin white line extends from their chest up the sides of their head. Viewed from the side, the bird appears to be wearing a bib, or an apron, that does not quite reach completely around its head. Also from the side, especially in dim light or if you squint, the colors and curves of the male pintail's head, neck, and chest resemble a question mark. Females are mottled dark brown with a less conspicuous tail. Under good lighting conditions they will flash an iridescent brown speculum with a trailing edge of white when they fly.

WOOD DUCK

Hunted almost to extinction by the beginning of the twentieth century, the wood duck, with a little help from its friends, has come back strongly and is now quite abundant. The bird had to be protected from hunters because it nested in, rather than merely migrated through, heavily gunned areas. And they taste good. But everyone rallied to the cause and saved the imperiled woodies, even as schoolchildren today build boxes for them to nest in. They nest in tree cavities, and have adapted readily to artificial nesting boxes— so readily that their numbers are increasing dramatically. In the East alone, naturalists estimate the wood duck's population at upwards of 5 million.

They are, in the opinion of many, myself included, the most beautiful species of waterfowl. The first time I saw one I thought my eyes were deceiving me, for the beauty of the wood duck seems not of this world. I daresay their startling beauty is their most telling field mark.

Small ducks, woodies ride high in the water, their tail, as a rule, raked upward at a 45-degree angle. Males have a crested, iridescent green head with sinuous white stripes running back from the bill and the eyes. They have a white throat that forms two white bars, one of them running back along the neck and outlining the head, the other running up to just below and behind the eyes. They have brilliantly red eyes and a red beak. Their chest is colored a rich burgundy, sort of stippled with white and separated from their creamy buff sides by a bold vertical white and black bar. Their back is dark. The overall impression is one of surreal beauty: the red eye seems almost to pop out at you, and the bold white bars intensify the iridescent green head. You cannot mistake a male wood duck for anything else.

Females are duller. Colored uniformly grayish brown, they also have a crested head, and a conspicuous white oval patch surrounds their eyes.

GREEN-WINGED TEAL

A small duck, the green-winged teal has simple but dramatic markings that render it easily identifiable. Males are dark gray on their sides and back, and they have a slightly crested, rich chestnut head with an electric green bar running back from the eyes to the base of the neck. A thin, crescent-shaped vertical white line separates their breast from their sides, and their speculum, like their face bar, is an iridescent electric green. In the right type of light, the electric green markings of the green-winged teal shine as though illuminated from within. In late afternoon light, I once watched a flock of about a hundred green-winged teal coming in for a landing. As they approached I couldn't tell what type of ducks they were, but suddenly they banked right over the water. Instead of seeing ducks, I saw a simultaneous flash of electric green lights, and then another as more birds caught the sun.

The female green-winged teal is mottled a uniform grayish brown. Although it lacks the male's face bar, it also has the brilliant green speculum. As it happens, wintering males and females sometimes form separate flocks, so identifying the females can be quite difficult if you don't get a reasonable look at the speculum.

GREATER SCAUP

A common winter visitor from the north, greater scaups gather in huge "rafts" along both coasts and on large lakes. It is not uncommon to see 5000 floating together out beyond the breakers. They are, with one hitch, pretty easy to identify, especially as one tends to see thousands of them at once. The hitch has to do with lesser scaups, which look almost identical: to tell the two apart requires significant experience, keen eyes, and ideal conditions. Even serious birders sometimes leave out the adjectives and say simply, "Scaups!"

Males have a white to pale gray back and sides, a black rump, a black chest, and a black head. Under ideal lighting conditions, the head exhibits a faint dark green sheen. They have a pale, dusty blue bill (many people call them bluebills) and conspicuous yellow eyes. The overall impression is of a white duck with a black front and rear. In flight they display a long white stripe along the trailing edge of their wings.

Females appear uniformly brown. They are easily identified by a small, white oval patch that extends from the base of their blue bill almost to their yellow eyes. Females in flight also exhibit the long white stripe along the trailing edge of their wings.

AMERICAN WIGEON

A medium-size, fairly common duck, the male American wigeon, from a distance, looks as though it has on a helmet. Sometimes called baldpates, American wigeons have a white crown that runs from the base of their bill to the top of their head. They have a pale blue bill that from a distance seems a continuation of the white crown bar. This appears in bold contrast to the dark brown sides of the head. Under reasonable conditions, one can see an iridescent green bar that begins just in front of the eyes and runs back through the ears and onto the neck. Uniformly brown on their sides and back, they have black tail feathers and, a little up from them, a white patch. In flight they exhibit a distinctive white rectangular patch on their upper wings, and if they're making noise they're really easy to identify.

Their call is an amazingly clear, high-pitched whistle that sounds almost exactly like a child's squeak toy, and if their call wasn't the inspiration for squeak toys it should have been. It has a faint resemblance to the call of a greater yellowlegs, and American wigeons deliver it in three fast notes. A small flock of calling males make a truly delightful sound, an unforgettable ethereal squeaking.

Mottled brown with a grayish head, females are difficult to identify when by themselves, but they do have the same pale blue bill and white rectangular shoulder patch. Unlike the male's whistle, their call is a low quack.

SOME BIRDS OF THE FEATHER

One of the joys of watching waterfowl is watching all the other birds that gravitate, as it were, to the same habitats, especially during the height of migration season, when the birds seem to come through in waves. If you show up at a major concentration point of waterfowl migration, or a major wintering ground, you will encounter more species of birds than you can shake a pair of binoculars at. A beginner determined to identify every bird seen in such a habitat will surely encounter major frustration. Even the experts wonder what kind of plover emerged for a second from among the bulrushes, or what kind of warbler just flew by.

Even the beginner, however, should know how to identify three species that frequent the same habitats as waterfowl—snowy egrets, great egrets, and great blue herons. At one time almost completely eliminated by the burgeoning plume trade, these elegant, graceful birds have made a significant comeback. They are now quite common. When they gather in large congregations, and a strong wind ruffles their feathers, they impress even the most jaded of viewers with their beauty. I know at least two serious birdwatchers who had no interest in birds whatever until they spent some time in an area full of herons and egrets.

A friend of a friend telephoned one evening to introduce himself and ask a question about birds. "Whadya wanna know?" I asked, expecting some baroque question about the mating rituals of the wedge-rumped storm petrel. It turned out that he had just moved to Greenwich, Connecticut, and he wanted to know if I had ever heard of a 5-foot-tall, pure white bird with long, downy feathers trailing from it in all directions. He wanted to know if he should call the local Audubon Society. I told him not to worry, that the bird, a great egret, was seen regularly in his area. He asked where else in his area he could go to see one. I told him. We have never spoken since, but twice a year he sends me postcards from exotic birdwatching places.

GREAT EGRET/SNOWY EGRET

Four feet tall, with a 5-foot wingspan, the great egret is a large, pure white bird. It has an extremely long, thin, sinuous neck that bends every which way while the bird stalks its prey, and it has a conspicuous yellow bill that's visible even at a great distance. The bird has long, black legs, and it hunts in a solitary fashion, catching frogs and crayfish in shallow waters. Extremely patient while hunting, the great egret often gives the impression that it is not so much hunting as posing. In flight, it folds its neck in an S-curve onto its back, plying its way with slow, measured wingbeats.

In breeding plumage, the bird looks nothing less than spectacular—long, lacelike feathers drip down its back. The call is a deep croak.

The snowy egret looks like a miniature version of the great egret, but on closer inspection shows different markings other than size. It has a black bill, black legs, and conspicuous yellow feet. Like the great egret it hunts its prey in shallow waters, but the stalking style differs considerably. Rather than relaxedly standing around waiting for some food to pass, a snowy egret frequently dashes about frenetically, half running and half flying.

The breeding plumage of the snowy egret used to be the mainstay of the millinery industry, and plume hunters could scarcely keep themselves away from these birds. In full breeding plumage, long, lace-like plumes trail down their back and chest, and a crest of lacy plumes fans up on the top of their head. When the wind catches their breeding plumage and fans it out in all directions, the snowy egret looks decidedly otherworldly.

GREAT BLUE HERON

Our largest heron, the great blue is also our most widespread. Though common, great blues never fail to excite most observers. They are enormous, graceful birds, with a wingspan of 7 feet. In the air they look as large as eagles, and could possibly even be mistaken for them, but the great blue heron's legs stick out when it flies. Like all herons, great blues fold their neck back when they fly, and their call is a deep croak or squawk. They have a large, yellowish bill and a white head with black stripes over the eyes; a few short feathers trail off the back of the head, like a cowlick. Their long, thin neck is grayish and their body uniformly slate blue gray.

In some light the slate blue gray color of these birds takes on a luminous quality, a brightness that seems almost unnatural. Even when strongly backlit, the plumage of the great blue manages to gather the light, to glow. Great blues often stand around with their neck tucked in, and they are solitary hunters. Like great egrets they stalk their prey in the shallows. They can stand motionless for some time, only to strike out suddenly, in the blink of an eye, at a passing fish.

DESTINATIONS AND ACCOMMODATIONS

KLAMATH BASIN NATIONAL WILDLIFE REFUGES, CALIFORNIA/OREGON

Situated at a key point on the Pacific flyway, Klamath Basin hosts the largest concentrations of migratory waterfowl that gather in North America. At peak times during migration, 750,000 birds inhabit the area, which straddles the border of California and Oregon and consists of six different National Wildlife Refuges, all managed as one.

A huge wetland area reclaimed except for the refuges, the basin is surrounded by mountains. The perennially snow-covered peak of Mount Shasta rises imperiously to 14,162 feet, 50 miles southwest of the refuge system. There are 6000- to 8000-feet mountains everywhere. When the light is right, you can glimpse a couple hundred thousand snow geese flying around, catching the sun, and looking like confetti against the dark greens and grays of the mountains behind them. From December through February, congregations of 15,000 whistling swans put in an appearance here, as does the largest gathering of bald eagles outside Alaska. Wintering here are 500 to 700 bald eagles, and summer nesting species include golden as well as bald eagles. A healthy population of white pelicans also nests in the area, as do tens of thousands of ducks and an estimated 150 or so other species of birds.

Doubtless because they attract the largest congregations of waterfowl on the continent, the Klamath refuges represent something of an index of the environment, a barometer of change. Spectacular as they are, the three-quarter million birds that gather in the basin represent only a fraction of the number that flocked here thirty years ago. During the late fifties and early sixties, congregations of 7 million birds littered the refuges. Although it taxes the imagination, ten times as many birds as now once visited the place. Waterfowl population trends in the Klamath Basin have declined significantly, some say because Eskimos harvest eggs in the Far North or because droughts and reclamation have devastated the prairie pothole regions. Yet others blame it on development in California's Central Valley, and along the coasts of Alaska, which has proceeded at breakneck speed.

The Klamath refuges are worth the trip at any time of year, but the peak time, in terms of sheer numbers, usually occurs around the first week in November.

The Klamath refuges are located north and south of Klamath Falls, a town of about 16,000 people located about 50 miles south of Crater Lake National Park and approximately 40 miles north of Lava Beds National Monument. The town is contiguous with the Tule Lake National Wildlife Refuge.

For information, contact Klamath Basin National Wildlife Refuges, Route 1, Box 74, Tulelake, CA 96134, telephone: (916) 667-2231.

Driving Instructions: Take Oregon Route 39 or California Route 139 to Tulelake, California. Then go west for 6 miles on East-West Road to Hill Road. Turn south and proceed a couple of hundred yards to the Klamath Basin Headquarters.

Northwest Bed & Breakfast, Inc.
7707 SW Locust Street
Portland, OR 97223
Telephone: (503) 246-8366

Northwest Bed & Breakfast represents over 250 B&B homes in the Northwest. The accommodations range from the simple to the luxurious, and the prices vary accordingly.

Molatore's
100 Main Street
Klamath Falls, OR 97601
Telephone: (503) 882-4666

Molatore's is a ninety-eight-room motel with a heated pool, Laundromat, restaurant, and bar. All the rooms have color cable television and telephone, and the restaurant does all its own baking.

Rates: inexpensive; AE,MC,V

LACASSINE NATIONAL WILDLIFE REFUGE, LOUISIANA

The coastal marshes of Louisiana attract millions of wintering waterfowl, which share the area with everything from alligators to hawks. Lacassine National Wildlife Refuge, about 20 miles from the Gulf Coast, embraces more than 30,000 acres of prime waterfowl habitat, and at times of peak concentration, November through January, close to a million birds gather here.

The location of the refuge is such that birds from the Mississippi and Central flyways make their way here. Major species include snow geese, 100,000 of which might well be in attendance, having arrived here after a non-stop flight from Hudson Bay. White-fronted geese winter here in significant concentrations as well. Moreover, the refuge hosts the country's largest migratory populations of fulvous whistling ducks, a bizarre-looking, aptly named duck with incredibly long legs.

Wading birds as well as ducks and geese utilize the refuge, and egrets, herons, gallinules, ibises, bitterns, and rails are everywhere. Bald eagles are fairly common during winter, as are several other raptor species. Alligators, too, are here in large numbers.

The refuge has an auto route, several walkways, and miles of channels. Natural attractions close by include Sabine National Wildlife Refuge, which has an alligator population of about 8000, about 75 miles distant on the other side of Calcasieu Lake; and Sam

Houston Jones State Park, a thousand-acre preserve
of dense woods and lagoons (the park has cabins available; telephone: [318] 855-2665). The town of Lake
Charles has an extensive historic district with scores
of restored Victorian houses.

For information, contact Lacassine National Wildlife Refuge, Route 1, Box 186, Lake Arthur, LA 70549,
telephone: (318) 774-2750.

Driving Instructions: Call for specific driving instructions.

Hilton Lake Charles
505 North Lakeshore Drive
Lake Charles, LA 70602
Telephone: (318) 433-7121
Open all year.

The Hilton Lake Charles has 269 rooms, all with color
cable television, telephone, and private bath. The facilities include a pool, restaurant, free airport and bus
terminal pickup, and bar with entertainment and
dancing. Suites, with refrigerators, are also available.

Rates: moderate to expensive; AE,CD,DC,MC,V

BRIGANTINE NATIONAL WILDLIFE REFUGE, NEW JERSEY

Ten miles north of Atlantic City, Brigantine National
Wildlife Refuge consists of more than 22,000 acres of
prime waterfowl habitat. Located on a barrier island
in the Atlantic Ocean, the refuge is immediately south
of Great Bay, into which the Mullica River empties.
The refuge is, essentially, an expansive wetland system of fresh and saltwater impoundments, with an 8-
mile auto route running through them.

At the height of migration, 50,000 to 60,000 black ducks stop at Brigantine. In a good year, thousands of brant will show up as well. From mid- to late November, 30,000 to 40,000 snow geese visit the refuge, bringing its peak population of waterfowl to more than 150,000 birds. One of the area's great sights is an enormous flock of snow geese taking to the air, totally obscuring views of Atlantic City casinos across the water in the distance.

Two hundred sixty-nine species of birds have been recorded here. The refuge's location on the Atlantic flyway is such that it enjoys a particularly long migration season. Some species come through as early as mid-August and others not until late December.

Brigantine is located near several natural areas worth a visit, including the Pine Barrens of New Jersey, a vast undeveloped tract of land with several large State Forests in it. The 108,000-acre Wharton State Forest is about twenty minutes from Brigantine, the 30,000-acre Lebanon State Forest is perhaps an hour away, and the Bass River State Forest is about a forty-minute drive. In the other direction, an hour's drive will get you to Cape May, which boasts the densest concentration of Victorian houses in the country as well as one of the finest hawk-watching locations.

For information, contact Brigantine National Wildlife Refuge, Box 72, Oceanville, NJ 08231, telephone: (609) 652-1665.

Driving Instructions: From points north take the Garden State Parkway to Route 9 south to the Oceanville Post Office and turn left on to Great Creek Road.

See Cape May ("Hawks") for accommodations suggestions.

CHINCOTEAGUE NATIONAL WILDLIFE REFUGE, VIRGINIA

Chincoteague National Wildlife Refuge embraces approximately 10,000 acres of Assateague Island, the 37-mile-long barrier island off the coasts of Virginia and Maryland. The part of the island in Maryland constitutes the Assateague Island National Seashore; at the Virginia border it becomes the Chincoteague refuge; and then, right at the end of Assateague Island, it becomes national seashore again for a small stretch. The island has miles and miles of unspoiled beach and dunes on the ocean, and as one moves inland the terrain becomes an almost pure stand of loblolly pine.

An extremely accessible refuge, Chincoteague has a well-paved 3.5-mile loop that winds through ponds and marshes. The loop opens for autos at 3 p.m.; before then, cyclists and walkers have the run of the place. The refuge is extremely wheelchair-accessible, and two visitors centers dispense information. During summer naturalists conduct land and boat tours of the refuge, and during autumn and winter tens of thousands of waterfowl put in their appearance.

More than 250 species of birds have been identified at Chincoteague, and several species show up in significant numbers. From late November through early December 10,000 to 15,000 snow geese litter the refuge's ponds, which 25,000 to 30,000 ducks also utilize. Whistling swans winter at the refuge, and during late fall through winter upwards of 3000 swans are here. The swans and snow geese can, at times, generate almost deafening amounts of noise. All kinds of ducks and wading birds also winter here, and early in the fall peregrine falcons and kestrels zoom through.

Other wildlife at the refuge includes everything from Sitka deer to Delmarva fox squirrels, and, of course, the famous wild ponies of Chincoteague. The children's story "Misty of Chincoteague" is about one of these wild ponies, which are actually small horses believed to have swum to the island from a sinking Spanish galleon in the fifteenth century. Actually stunted horses, the ponies of Chincoteague, graze throughout the refuge and occasionally go galloping through the surf.

For information, contact Chincoteague National Wildlife Refuge, PO Box 62, Chincoteague, VA 23336, telephone: (804) 336-6122.

Driving Instructions: Take US 13 to Route 175, then go east to Chincoteague Island; once there, go east on Maddox Boulevard to the refuge.

Year of the Horse Inn
600 South Main Street
Chincoteague, VA 23336
Telephone: (804) 336-3221
Open all year.

Overlooking Chincoteague Bay, Year of the Horse Inn is a bed and breakfast with three rooms, each of which has a private balcony and view of the bay. The rooms feature some antiques, one has a kitchenette, and another has two bedrooms. A complimentary continental breakfast, which one takes back to one's room, is included in the rates.

Rates: moderate to expensive; MC,V

Channel Bass Inn
100 Church Street
Chincoteague, VA 23336
Telephone: (804) 336-6148
Closed December and January.

Furnished entirely with period antiques, Channel Bass Inn is an historic Colonial structure with eleven elegant guest rooms, some of them suites. The facilities include a restaurant, bar, and room service.

Rates: moderate to expensive; AE,DC,MC,V

Island Motor Inn
711 North Main Street
Chincoteague, VA 23336
Telephone: (804) 336-3141
Open all year.

Island Motor Inn has forty-eight rooms with air-conditioning, color cable television, telephone, and private bath. Each room has a private balcony that overlooks Chincoteague Bay. The "Executive Level," or third floor, has more poshly decorated rooms than the first two levels. The facilities include a pool.

Rates: expensive; AE,DC,MC,V

OTHER PLACES TO OBSERVE WATERFOWL

Bear River Migratory Bird Refuge
Box 459
Brigham City, UT 84302

Buffalo Lake National Wildlife Refuge
Box 228
Umbarger, TX 79091

Crab Orchard National Wildlife Refuge
Box J
Carterville, IL 62918

DeSota National Wildlife Refuge
Route 1, Box 114
Missouri Valley, IA 51555

Horicon National Wildlife Refuge
Route 2
Mayville, WI 53050

Humboldt Bay National Wildlife Refuge
San Francisco Bay
Box 524
Newark, CA 94560

Kirwin National Wildlife Refuge
Kirwin, KS 67644

Malheur National Wildlife Refuge
PO Box 113
Burns, OR 97720

Mattumuskeet National Wildlife Refuge
Route 1, Box N-2
Swanquarter, NC 27885

Mingo National Wildlife Refuge
Route 1, Box 103
Puxico, MO 63960

Quivira National Wildlife Refuge
Box G
Stafford, KS 67578

Sacramento National Wildlife Refuge
Sacramento Valley Refuges
Route 1, Box 311
Willows, CA 95988

Salt Plains National Wildlife Refuge
Route 1, Box 76
Jet, OK 73749

San Luis National Wildlife Refuge
Box 2176
Los Banos, CA 93635

White River National Wildlife Refuge
Box 308
706 S. Jefferson Street
DeWitt, AK 72042

Yazoo National Wildlife Refuge
Route 1, Box 286
Hollandale, MS 38748

ALLIGATORS

Did he remember the baby alligators? Last
year, or maybe the year before, kids all
over Nueva York bought these little
alligators for pets. Macy's was selling them
for fifty cents, every child, it seemed, had
to have one. But soon the children grew
bored with them. Some set them loose in
the streets, but most flushed them down
the toilets. And these had grown and
reproduced, had fed off rats and sewage,
so that now they moved big, blind, albino,
all over the sewer system. Down there, God
knew how many there were.

—THOMAS PYNCHON, *V*

Although native Manhattanites grow up with very few
myths, we grow up with the myth of the alligator. As
children we were told never to cross the street near
a sewer, for the steam rising from the manhole covers
was, in fact, the breath of ferocious alligators, lurking
below the streets, waiting to nail an unsuspecting child.
I know of no native New Yorker who didn't at one
time, invariably in his or her youth, have a pet alli-

gator. And yet I know of no one who recalls the precise fate of their alligator. Most, to my knowledge, were last seen spiraling helplessly into the porcelain abyss, that offal fate.

So it came as no surprise to hear, in August 1977, that the most serious blackout in the city's history was caused, you guessed it, by albino alligators. Spokespeople for the Consolidated Edison Company, the utility that supplies New York City with electricity, explained at a press conference that tens of thousands of people were stranded underground in subways and overhead in skyscrapers because albino alligators had chewed through the main power cables leading to Big Bertha, the massive generator that supplies the better part of the city's power.

Other municipalities have had their troubles with alligators, too. The severe drought the Southeast suffered in 1986 drove who knows how many alligators living in the Okefenokee Swamp into the sewer systems of bordering towns. Although all the facts have yet to come in, it seems likely as well that alligators all over the Southeast, having very little choice, migrated from the parched land to the wet sewers of civilization. In August 1986 a swimmer in an Alabama lake encountered an 11-foot alligator, which bit off one of his arms. The man, understandably upset, claimed he was extremely pleased not to have drowned during the incident. Some wildlife people consequently killed the alligator.

On Hilton Head Island, South Carolina, a rather exclusive resort and retirement area, toy poodles and Yorkshire terriers disappear with ominous regularity. When residents hear the cowlike bellowing of the alligators in spring, they shoo their pets inside. A banker friend who arranges mortgages for condominiums on

Hilton Head related perhaps the classic alligator anecdote. While attending a cocktail party one balmy July afternoon he and several other guests found themselves intruded upon by the sound of an explosion—which turned out to have come from a 12-gauge shotgun fired not 20 feet away. The host of the party, as it happened, had gone out back to check on his dogs—a pair of champion German shepherds that roamed about on a quarter acre of lawn surrounded by a wire fence 5 feet tall—and discovered an alligator scaling the backyard fence. The two dogs, each of which weighed upwards of 90 pounds, were huddled together and shaking with fear, their tails between their legs. Their master appeared in time and killed the alligator, which clung to the wire fence even in death.

Beware of alligators. Though they look like laziness itself, they can move with uncanny speed and agility, even on land, where they frequently lunge in attempts, often successful, to capture prey. Like bears, alligators become dangerous when they lose their fear of people, when excited tourists or foolish locals feed them, trying to coax them closer. In a Florida state park, authorities found the arm of a missing four-year-old boy in the stomach of a "tame" alligator.

Stopping to check out a lake along a road in the Everglades, my wife and I once chanced upon a young couple tossing potato chips to an alligator no less than 6 feet long, in an attempt to lure the 'gator close enough for a picture in which they hoped to include their daughter, an adorable blonde of three, maybe four years of age. Intuitively intelligent as well as adorable, the young girl screamed at the top of her lungs as she hid behind her mother, who also screamed when the alligator hissed and took a few very quick steps forward.

Alligators lose their fear of people when people feed them, which, for reasons I cannot fathom, people continue to do despite signs and educational brochures admonishing them not to. The reason many people cannot resist feeding these enormously powerful, primordial-looking creatures has to do, I think, with the habits of the alligator. During daylight hours, alligators tend to remain motionless for extended periods of time, as often as not sunning themselves for hours at a stretch, or floating motionless in water as still as they. People observing them for the first time almost can't help but try to get a rise out of them, to make them move or do something. Insensitive dullards from all walks of life have been known to do things like throw rocks or empty bottles at the alligators, which by their nature spend the daylight hours resting and relaxing. They hunt at night, and if they score a large meal, they may not look for another one for a week or more.

Alligators can go for extended periods of time without food, probably because they have such low metabolic rates and require so much less food than they consume. During winter periods of temperatures below 68 degrees Fahrenheit, your average alligator languishes for weeks or months at a time, its interest in food as negligible as its need for it. Cold-blooded, alligators assume the temperature of their environment, an adaptation that allows their caloric energy to dedicate itself to growth rather than to maintaining body temperature. Alligators don't grow to lengths of 19 feet because they lack nutrients or burn up their available energy carrying on for no reason. Conditions being equal, a 200-pound alligator burns roughly 5 percent of the oxygen a human being of the same weight consumes.

Members of the order Loricata, alligators belong to the genus *Crocodylus*, which embraces some twenty-two species of alligators, crocodiles, and caimans worldwide. Only two species, the American crocodile and the American alligator, inhabit North America, although fossil records indicate that other species at one time inhabited the continent. Indeed, a primitive form of alligator, the Montana alligator, lived as far afield as Montana and China, a curious coincidence considering the only two extant species of this alligator live today in China and the United States, though far south of Montana. In those days a huge swamp covered much of the planet, which consisted, give or take a few hundred million years, of one huge continent, Pangaea, surrounded by one huge ocean, Panthalassa. Hundred-ton dinosaurs, 40-foot ferns, 30-foot flying reptiles, and 12-foot alligators thrived. Twelve-foot alligators still thrive, and their amazing biology and durability strike scientists as something of a postcard from the volcano, an atavistic presence from a world long ago gone.

Perhaps because they can survive without food for six months, or maybe because they know how to take it easy and lie low, alligators managed to survive beyond the threshold that eliminated the dinosaurs and the countless other species of reptile that up until about 65 million years ago dominated the planet. The border between the Cretaceous and the Tertiary periods of geologic time marks the demise of the reptiles and the rise of the mammals, which had scarcely just begun to evolve at that time.

The sudden disappearance of the enormous Cretaceous reptiles has always fascinated scientists, who over the years have held forth with all manner of theories explaining the abrupt Armageddon that wiped out the thunder lizards. The most credible theory to date hypothesizes that a huge comet or asteroid collided with the earth. The response to this colossal impact was huge tsunami (tidal waves) and widespread volcanic eruptions that spewed so much dust, ash, and gas into the atmosphere that an impenetrable cloud blocked the sunlight for months at a time, killing all green plants and hundreds of animal species in the process. The scenario closely resembles what mammals at all costs should avoid—nuclear winter.

Though alligators made it through the apocalypse of the Cretaceous/Tertiary transition, they came quite close to extinction during the last few decades of the nineteenth and the first half of the twentieth centuries, when they were hunted relentlessly. The major assault on alligators took place during the Victorian era, when smart continental ladies wore corsets made of whalebone and shoes fashioned of lizard. As it happens, Queen Elizabeth II still wears riding boots fashioned of American alligator, but her foundation garments, surely, no longer come from whales. Tanning industry records indicate that some 2.5 million alligator hides were harvested between 1880 and 1890, and that up until the 1950s the toll of crocodilians harvested in the United States approached 10 million.

By the 1960s, alligator populations had dwindled to negligible levels, and throughout most of the Southeast they became classified as endangered, likely to pass out of existence. Even though protected by federal law, alligators still fell prey in considerable numbers to poachers. Alligators were harvested in places like the Everglades and the Okefenokee and sold illegally. The poaching finally slowed down after 1969, when New York State passed the Mason-Smith Act, which prohibits the sale of products made from endangered species. Many states followed suit with similar statutes, which, taken together, proved quite effective. Alligator populations began to recover, and today sufficient numbers of them prevail to allow for a limited harvest.

In 1985 about 25,000 alligators were taken in closely regulated hunts, which became permissible after the species' classification changed from endangered to threatened. This new classification also spurred something of an alligator farming industry, which supplies the skins for Queen Elizabeth II's riding boots and discovered, sometime during the past five years, that the temperature at which an alligator egg is incubated determines the sex of the about-to-hatch alligators.

One study proved that alligator eggs incubated at 86 degrees Fahrenheit produced exclusively females, whereas those incubated at 93 degrees Fahrenheit resulted exclusively in males. Alligators, apparently, lack those chromosomes that determine their sex. Instead, gender owes itself to temperature, that is, whether or not the temperature falls low enough to produce estrogenic hormones, which result in female offspring. Female alligators (the males have nothing to do with nesting or rearing the young) do not incubate their eggs like birds, for example. Rather, they deposit them in a nest that they cover with vegetation, packed lightly over the eggs. This earthen incubator retains moisture, creating a highly humid atmosphere, and its position relative to sunlight or shadow probably determines its temperature, hence the sex of the baby alligators that finally emerge from it.

When baby alligators hatch, they grunt and head

for the water, where their mother usually awaits them. Females lay between twenty and eighty eggs, averaging thirty or so, and the 9-inch-long babies stay with their mother for as long as two years, climbing onto her back for a better spot in the sun or hiding behind her from such predators as great blue herons and great egrets, which love baby alligators just a little less than they fear mature ones.

During winter, a dry season throughout most of their range, alligators congregate at water holes, many of them built by alligators themselves, and, sure enough, wading birds of all varieties coexist with the alligators at such places. One wonders what kind of ballet goes on between a great blue heron and a mature alligator with twenty babies next to her. In any case, it works, and if you seek out a 'gator hole in winter, you will probably see there all kinds of birds—spoonbills, egrets, ibises, herons, storks, gallinules, coots.

Extremely vocal when born, alligators become extremely vocal when mating time approaches. With their mouth closed and their head arched up out of the water, they vibrate their throat. They can do this so strongly that they send ripples through the water around them and transmit for a mile or so a thunderously low, trembling bellow, which they repeat five or six times. Males and females bellow to each other across the swamp, estuary, or lake, and when they find their way to each other they touch gently, in some cases swimming dreamily in a circle with their noses pressed against each other. At that point the female may or may not blow a soft stream of bubbles under the male's neck, but in any case they soon submerge and experience a submarine copulatory tie, three, maybe four minutes long.

You can observe alligators in any number of places

in the Southeast and along the Gulf Coast, as a general rule more easily in the winter when they tend to congregate near water. Threatened almost to extinction twenty years ago, alligators staged a remarkable comeback once we granted them a protected status. With ten alligator farms now in existence to supply the demand for thousand-dollar wallets and boots fit for royal feet, the poaching problem seems almost a moot issue. Presently bulldozers and developers kill more alligators than bullets and machetes.

One should observe certain rules in alligator country. If an alligator is not afraid of you, you should be afraid of it. Before you go swimming in unknown waters deep in the South, scan them for possible alligators. If you happen to encounter a particularly aggressive alligator, report it to the nearest wildlife authority or the police. Though you should exercise caution while around alligators, you needn't cower in fear when near them. Most supervised areas are relatively safe: no one, for example, has ever been killed by an alligator in Everglades National Park, probably because the rangers keep track of alligators and prevent people from feeding them.

Identifying alligators presents virtually no problems. The only possible mistake would be to confuse one for an American crocodile, of which perhaps two hundred exist, all of them in the northeast section of Florida Bay. Crocodiles have narrower snouts than alligators, and appear green instead of black; if in doubt, you can rest fairly well-assured an unidentified crocodilian was an alligator.

DESTINATIONS AND ACCOMMODATIONS

J. N. "DING" DARLING NATIONAL WILDLIFE REFUGE, FLORIDA

J. N. "Ding" Darling National Wildlife Refuge consists of slightly less than 5000 acres on Sanibel Island. A small island off the west coast of Florida, accessible via a causeway, Sanibel is perhaps most famous for the millions of shells that litter its 14 miles of beaches. Intense tourist traffic may have reduced the abundance of shells, yet the area still ranks as one of the world's major shelling sites.

The refuge has miles of trails and roads, including an 8-mile auto route bordered on either side by water, and a large Visitors Center with displays. The canals here are full of alligators, and one can observe them easily, even from a car. In addition to alligators, the refuge hosts almost overwhelming numbers of birds —from roseate spoonbills to bald eagles. Some 267 species of birds have been sighted here, and enormous flocks of any number of species are much more the rule than the exception. Looking across a stretch of marsh, you might well see several hundred white pelicans, a few thousand roseate spoonbills, a flock of storks, scores of great egrets, a squadron of black skimmers, and several species of hawks.

Bald eagles and ospreys are extremely common in the refuge and on Sanibel Island in general. Now and again you might get a look at a swallow-tailed kite. The most common hawk here is the red-shouldered hawk. The bird is not at all shy. It likes to perch low in trees and scream like a bluejay. Screeching at people is something it seems truly to enjoy.

For information, contact J. N. "Ding" Darling National Wildlife Refuge, Drawer B, Sanibel, FL 33957, telephone: (813) 472-1100.

Driving Instructions: Sanibel Island is about 15 miles southwest of Fort Myers, on Route 867.

Castaways
6460 Sanibel-Captiva Road
Sanibel, FL 33957
Telephone: (813) 472-1252
Open all year.

Across the road from the beach, Castaways consists of twenty cottages, some of which overlook the bay. The cottages are either studio rooms or suites, and most have refrigerators. Simply furnished, the cottages have air-conditioning and color cable television, but no telephone. The facilities include a heated pool, and the grounds feature a few picnic tables and grills. Guests have tennis privileges.

Rates: moderate to expensive; MC,V

Ramada
1131 Middle Gulf Drive
Sanibel, FL 33957
Telephone: (813) 472-4123
Open all year.

The Sanibel Ramada has ninety-eight rooms, some of them suites. A few of the rooms have refrigerators, and all of them have color cable television, telephone, and air-conditioning. The facilities include a heated pool, tennis courts, Laundromat, cafe, and bar. Guests have golf privileges.

Rates: expensive; AE,CB,DC,MC,V

HOMESTEAD, FLORIDA

Everglades National Park
PO Box 279
Homestead, FL 33030
Telephone: (305) 247-6211

Everglades National Park consists of just under a million and a half acres—some 21,000 square miles—at the southwestern tip of Florida, including a significant portion of Florida Bay. Strictly speaking, the Everglades is not so much a swamp as an extremely wide and shallow river that drains Lake Okeechobee into the Gulf of Mexico. The Indians called the place "river of grass." The Everglades is a maze of waterways, of expansive rivers of sawgrass broken up here and there by hammocks of cypress and mahogany, of shadowy passageways through thick stands of mangroves, of a 99-mile wilderness canoe route through the interior and a 500-square-mile section of bay littered with islands.

A great place to see alligators, the Everglades is also a great place to see birds. During the dry season of winter, birds tend to hang out at the same places alligators do, near water. At a popular spot, like Anhinga Trail or Shark Valley, alligators and birds all but overrun the place. The Everglades attracts overwhelming numbers of birds, and you cannot go anyplace in the park without feeling their presence. Enormous flocks of white ibis fly overhead at dusk, great blue herons and egrets show up everywhere, anhingas scream like banshees, brown pelicans accost you looking for a handout, tight squadrons of black skimmers zoom by, bald eagles and ospreys turn lazy circles in the sky.

The Everglades is a naturalist's delight, a stunning landscape teeming with life. Among the most celebrated residents of the area is the Florida panther, or mountain lion, which amateur naturalists spot here probably more often than anyplace else in the country. For non-naturalists, Miami is a few hours away by car.

Driving Instructions: From Homestead take Route 27 southwest for about 10 miles; from Naples take Route 41 southeast to Route 29 (about 30 miles), then take 29 south to Everglades City.

Flamingo Inn
Flamingo, FL 33030
Telephone: (813) 695-3101
Open all year.

Overlooking Florida Bay, Flamingo Inn is a 103-room motel-style structure with a glass-enclosed swimming pool and sixteen efficiency cottages. The rooms vary somewhat in appointments, some being "standard" and some "first class," but they all have air-conditioning, television, telephone, and private bath. About half the rooms overlook the bay.

Flamingo Inn is situated in Flamingo, the center of activity in the park, and within a short walk of it one finds a restaurant, gift shop, grocery/convenience store, marina, and staffed Visitors Center.

Rates: inexpensive to expensive; AE,CB,DC,MC,V

OKEFENOKEE NATIONAL WILDLIFE REFUGE, GEORGIA

Okefenokee National Wildlife Refuge embraces approximately 700 square miles of freshwater marsh and islands in southeastern Georgia, right at the northern border of Florida. Myriad waterways, including the Suwannee River, wind through the refuge, making it an ideal place to explore by canoe. The refuge has more than 90 miles of well-marked canoe trails, which take from one to five days to complete. The overall effect of the place is primeval, broody, and mysterious. Black water trails meander through seemingly endless stands of moss-draped cypress, alligators bellow in the night, and surprising flashes of color turn out to be orchids.

The Okefenokee has probably the largest population of alligators in the country. An estimated 10,000 to 15,000 individuals are in attendance. In spring their bellowing approaches the truly boisterous, and in most seasons park naturalists lead nighttime tours into the swamp, which even in darkness seems utterly awake with the noises of alligators and owls. If you happen to attend an owl prowl and pick up a pair of red eyes in the darkness with your flashlight, they belong to an alligator.

In addition to alligators, the Okefenokee is home to a wide variety of wildlife, from bobcats to otters to black bears to sandhill cranes. The birdlife is particularly spectacular and includes an enormous white ibis colony containing an estimated 10,000 nests— which is to say, 20,000 nesting birds. Herons and egrets are everywhere, and at sunset mind-boggling masses of birds fly overhead on the way to their nightly roosts.

Technically, the Okefenokee is not so much a swamp as an unusually extensive peat-filled bog, with a foundation in many places of 15 feet or more of peat. The Seminole Indians called the place "Land of the Trembling Earth," and, indeed, in some areas you can jump up and down and make nearby trees shake.

Nearby natural attractions include Cumberland Island National Seashore, about 30 miles east of Folkston on the Atlantic Coast.

The refuge has three main entrances: 13 miles south of Waycross on Route 177 is Okefenokee Swamp Park; 11 miles south of Folkston on Routes 121/23 is Suwannee Canal Recreation Area; and 18 miles northeast of Fargo on Route 177 is Stephen C. Foster State Park. Stephen C. Foster State Park, situated on an 80-acre island, has cabins available, as well as canoe and boat rentals. For information, contact Stephen C. Foster State Park, Route 1, Fargo, GA 31631, telephone: (912) 637-5274; and Okefenokee National Wildlife Refuge, Route 2, Box 380, Folkston, GA 31537, telephone: (912) 496-3331.

Red Carpet Inn Tahiti
1201 South Second Street
Folkston, GA 31537
Telephone: (912) 496-2514
Open all year.

A modest motel, Red Carpet Tahiti has thirty-seven rooms with private bath, air-conditioning, color cable television, and telephone. The facilities include a snack bar.

Rates: inexpensive; AE,CB,DC,MC,V

1735 House
584 South Fletcher
Amelia Island, FL 32034
Telephone: (904) 261-5878

A little more than an hour from the Folkston entrance to the Okefenokee, 1735 House is a bed and breakfast with five suites located in two structures, one of them a reproduction lighthouse. The luxurious suites are furnished with many antiques, and each suite overlooks the Atlantic Ocean. A continental breakfast and a newspaper are brought to your room each morning.

Rates: moderate to expensive; AE,MC,V

Holiday Inn–Baymeadows
9150 Baymeadows Road
Jacksonville, FL 32202
Telephone: (904) 737-1700
Open all year.

Holiday Inn—Baymeadows is a 250-room structure with color cable television, telephone, a pool, room service, health club privileges, a restaurant, and a bar. Facilities include room service.

Rates: moderate; AE,CB,DC,MC,V

OTHER PLACES TO OBSERVE ALLIGATORS

Arkansas National   *(see "Whooping Cranes")*
  Wildlife Refuge
Box 100
Austwell, TX 77950

Cumberland Island
  National Seashore
Box 806
St. Mary's, GA 31558

Florida Keys National
  Wildlife Refuges
Box 510
Big Pine Key, FL 33043

Lacassine National   *(see "Geese")*
  Wildlife Refuge
Route 1, Box 186
Lake Arthur, LA 70549

Loxahatchee National
  Wildlife Refuge
Route 1, Box 278
Boynton Beach, FL 33437

Lake Woodruff National
  Wildlife Refuge
Box 488
DeLeon Springs, FL 32028

Sabine National Wildlife
  Refuge
MRH 107
Hackberry, LA 70645

Savannah National Wildlife
  Refuges
Georgia Coastal Complex
Box 8487
Savannah, GA 31402

THE MOONBOW

Rainbows generated by the light of the moon, moonbows are extremely rare.

For reasons we haven't figured out yet, only two moonbows appear with any regularity on earth. One of them occurs at Victoria Falls, where the mile-wide Zambezi River plunges 420 feet at the border of Zambia and Zimbabwe, in Africa. The other shows up in southeastern Kentucky, at a point where the 125-foot-wide Cumberland River spills over the edge of a precipice and drops 68 feet.

Nobody has any idea why these are the only two reliable moonbows. Theoretically, the phenomenon should occur at any number of waterfalls, but it does not; and although it seems that some peculiar set of conditions must certainly exist at Victoria Falls and Cumberland Falls, no one has identified them. One imagines, of course, that one of these days someone will feed all sorts of data into a computer and discover the formula for the two reliable moonbows, but until then they will remain a mystery, and that, perhaps, is as it should be. The best we can do now is wonder and speculate.

The moonbow at Cumberland Falls probably exists because of some unique combination of moonlight, mist, and the observer's position. Moonbows form for the same reasons rainbows do, and in order to see either you have to be at the appropriate angle, which with a little luck you can usually figure out. Generally speaking, you want the sun or the moon behind you and an atmosphere full of water droplets in front of you. Then all you have to do is locate the antisolar point and look about 42 degrees above and around it. I haven't come across the term "antilunar point," but the same principle applies. A discussion of the one will clarify the other.

That point in space directly opposite the sun from an observer, the antisolar point gets lower as the sun gets higher. If you were standing on the equator at high noon, the antisolar point would be under your feet. If at eight o'clock in the morning you look at your lengthy shadow, your head represents the position of the antisolar point. When you stand on the observation platform overlooking Cumberland Falls, the moon rises behind you and, although you can't see it, casts your shadow somewhere near the base of the falls, in the foaming whitewater. The turbulence of the falling water generates enormous amounts of mist, which rises in every direction and fills the air with billions of water droplets, just as an afternoon sunshower saturates the air with raindrops.

Rainbows and moonbows form because droplets of water refract and reflect the sunlight or moonlight that strikes them. Water droplets vary in size and shape, but the nature of water is such that they almost invariably form perfect spheres. This is especially the case with the smaller droplets. One of water's qualities is a high degree of surface tension, a strong, cohesive tendency among molecules to attract each other. The result of hydrogen bonds, the surface tension of water explains such things as why a razor blade, five times denser than water, can float. It also explains why we can fill a glass with water up to the brim and beyond.

A very powerful attraction among molecules, the surface tension of water acts like a tight skin that wraps itself around droplets and squeezes them into perfectly spherical shapes. The structural integrity of these little spheres is sufficiently strong to survive a long fall through the atmosphere, and although very large raindrops deform into odd shapes before they hit the ground, small droplets of rain never lose their spherical shape during their drop through the atmosphere. The smallest droplets occur in fog, clouds, and mist.

When a ray of light, whether from the sun or the moon, strikes a spherical droplet of water, part of it gets reflected and part enters the droplet. The part of the light that enters the droplet gets refracted, or bent, as it passes through the air/water interface of the tiny sphere; and because the different wavelengths of light bend differently, the pure white light of the sun or the moon breaks up into its component colors after experiencing this refraction. The spectrum of colors that combine to make white light— red, orange, yellow, green, blue, indigo, and violet— has different refractive indexes. Red, with the longest wavelength, bends least when refracted; violet, with the shortest, bends most.

So a spectrum of colors enters the water droplet and, in no time flat, reaches the other side of the sphere. Some of the light passes through. Some of it, however, gets reflected, bouncing off the rear wall of the sphere at the same angle it struck. The result is that what entered the droplet as white light travels through it as a spectrum, bounces off the rear wall of it, and emerges out the front again as a spectrum of colors.

In a classic rainbow arch, the outer band of color is red and the inner band violet, for the simple reason that violet bends more readily than red. Visualize a circle that represents a spherical water droplet seen in cross section, from the side. Then imagine a series of straight lines, rays of light, coming from the left and hitting the side of the circle. The rays that strike the circle at its widest point don't really bend much, and as a rule pass right through the circle and out the other side, or else reflect directly back in a straight line. The rays that strike the circle at an oblique angle, however, bend significantly, refracting into their different wavelengths in an orderly fashion.

As a ray enters the top left part of the sphere and separates into colors because of refraction, the violet wavelength will bend more dramatically than the red and, consequently, strike the right end of the circle farther down than the red wavelength. The violet wavelength will also reflect at a greater angle and emerge out the front of the water droplet, the left side, farther down than the red. As a result, the rainbow you see has a red band of color on top and a violet band on bottom.

The moonbow at Cumberland Falls exhibits its most intense reds and violets only on the clearest of winter nights, when zero humidity and the cold clear light of the moon, on its three fullest nights in December, January, and February, touches the droplets of mist. A breeze stirring up the mists enhances the moonbow, which during winter occurs from mid- to late evening, somewhere between nine and eleven o'clock. In winter the moonbow is sharper and more colorful than in summer, but it is also smaller in arch, roughly 20 as opposed to 30 feet long. Summer moonbows range from faint, dullish arcs to an even fainter, white glow, and they appear in the early morning, around one or two o'clock.

The sudden, ominous, apparition-like arching of the moonbow from the base of Cumberland Falls draws people from all over. On nights when the conditions seem favorable, people from as far away as Cincinnati, Ohio, drive 225 miles to try to catch the moonbow. And if the full moon happens to fall on a clear weekend night, a large crowd can assemble on the observation platform, particularly in summer.

DESTINATIONS AND ACCOMMODATIONS

Cumberland Falls State Park Resort
Corbin, KY 40701
Telephone: (606) 528-4121

Cumberland Falls and its moonbow are situated in Cumberland Falls State Park Resort, an 1800-acre heavily wooded preserve situated in the 527,000-acre Daniel Boone National Forest. The park and the surrounding area are wooded primarily with oak and hickory, several species of pine, and, in the understory, magnolia and dogwood. The park itself has 26 miles of trails, and the surrounding National Forest many more. The Daniel Boone National Forest contains several areas of unique geological formations, including Red River Gorge, where there are at least twenty natural stone arches; and Natural Arch Scenic Area, which has a natural stone arch 90 feet long and 70 feet high.

Cumberland Falls State Park Resort has an Olympic-size swimming pool, tennis courts, horseback riding facilities, and numerous special activities: a popular New Year's Eve party and a special Valentine's Day weekend are held here. Naturalists lead interpretative walks, and park personnel arrange photography workshops. Square dancing is a major summertime activity.

DuPont Lodge
Cumberland Falls State Park Resort
Corbin, KY 40701
Telephone: (800) 633-2093 (in state)
(800) 325-0063 (out of state)

The DuPont Lodge at Cumberland Falls State Park is a log building with a dining room, grocery store, coffee shop, and facilities for meetings and banquets. It is situated immediately beside the Cumberland River, and the restaurant as well as most of the fifty-four guest rooms overlook it. The lodge also offers accommodations in forty-five cottages, about half of which have kitchen facilities. All the rooms and cottages have color television and telephone.

Rates: moderate; AE,DC,MC,V

WHALES

And I am convinced that from the heads
of all ponderous profound beings, such as
Plato, Pyrrho, the devil, Jupiter, Dante,
and so on, there always goes up a certain
semi-visible steam, while in the act of
thinking deep thoughts. . . .
   And how nobly it raises our conceit of
the mighty, misty monster, to behold him
solemnly sailing through a calm tropical
sea; his vast, mild head overhung by a
canopy of vapor, and that vapor—as you
will sometimes see it—glorified by a
rainbow, as if Heaven itself had put its seal
upon his thoughts.

—HERMAN MELVILLE, *Moby Dick*

Members of the order Cetacea, the forty-nine species
of whales, dolphins, and porpoises native to North
American coastal waters vary in length from 4 to 90-
some feet, in weight from 150 to 250,000 pounds, in
coloration from black to white to blue to sinuous and/
or mottled combinations thereof, in diet from microscopic phytoplankton drifting with the currents to giant

bioluminescent squid, in ecological status from seemingly stable to seriously doomed, and in brain size from 100 to 600 percent that of humans.

The blue whale, the largest creature that ever lived, has a brain six times the size of a human's; killer whales outweigh us in gray matter four to one; and even bottlenose dolphins, those popular, perennially smiling seaquaria attractions, have a brain half again as large as our own. What, one wonders, do they do with all those brains? Melville's hypothesis that they use them to ponder deep thoughts is probably as valid as any other theory to date. For indeed, the cetaceans have adapted so felicitously to their universe that the mundane problems we terrestrials must deal with never so much as enter their cavernous minds.

Extraterrestrials in no uncertain terms, the cetaceans live in an environment unimaginably more stable than ours, in a vertical landscape where even the concept of weather is moot, food abundant, upward mobility a flick of the flukes. Their brain is in most cases larger and in all cases more complex than our own, with four major sections instead of three and a higher ratio of abstract function to motor control neurons. For all its sophistication, the cetacean brain hasn't had to deal with the mind-boggling contingencies of life on the surface of the planet. It has no concern for volcanoes and glaciers that cover the place with fire or ice, nor for the major hassles of food, shelter, and clothing. For some cetaceans, eating requires little more than swimming in a circle below a school of fish while exhaling a stream of bubbles that corrals them, and then simply surfacing with an open mouth through the enbubbled feast above. For other species, the daily feast takes place among tens or scores of family members and hundreds of friends, none of which ever got caught in the rain or lacked the appropriate outfit. The cetacean brain hasn't had, as it were, to suffer the slings and arrows of atmospheric fortune, albeit of harpoons they have had their share.

Several cetacean species exist now as the rear guard of their kind, effortlessly gliding through vast oceans pitiably barren for them. The northern right whale, a 50-foot-long animal equal in weight to the Statue of Liberty, used to exist in such abundance that early Massachusetts colonists claimed in their diaries that one could almost walk across Cape Cod Bay using the whales as a bridge. Fewer than 300 individuals prevail, out of an estimated pre-whaling population of over 100,000. If the species manages to escape extinction, a miracle will have come to pass.

They were called right whales because they were the right whales to hunt: they yielded generous amounts of oil, they swam so slowly you could easily overtake them in a primitive boat, and they didn't flee from approaching vessels. They float when dead. Primitive whalers decimated them long before the advent of sophisticated whaling apparatus, such as steam engines and explosive harpoons, which opened up new marketing vistas to late nineteenth-century entrepreneurs. Every whale became the right whale.

In Chapter Eighty-one of *Moby Dick*, Melville makes fun of a whaling captain who gives chase to a fin whale, which species he peremptorily classifies as "uncapturable . . . because of its incredible power of swimming." At the expense of this foolish captain, named Derick, Melville goes on about the human tendency for wild-goose chases: "Oh! many are the Fin-Backs, and many are the Dericks, my friend." Observed to swim at 20 miles per hour fin whales were, in the days when only the power of wind or muscle moved boats through the water, subject to Melville's dictum—there was no way to catch one. Times change. Modern whale fisheries decimated the fin whale, only a fraction of their original population remains, and decimated as well the also previously uncatchable blue whale.

Even though they realized nothing short of realistic catch quotas could preserve the valuable stock of blue whales, commercial whaling entrepreneurs hunted the species to virtual extinction, lowering themselves, at the eleventh hour, to taking sexually immature individuals. To perpetuate a species, each mating pair must have at least three offspring. Perusing the average length of blue whales taken over the years— during the 1931 Antarctic season, 31,000 were taken—you can't help but notice that their body size decreases progressively. In the final years of the blue whale harvest, it becomes obvious that even the virgins were game.

The Japanese are perhaps the most guilty of killing large whales in great numbers. International pressure was finally brought to bear, the effect being a diminution of Japanese whaling activities in one place while they formed joint companies with smaller Chilean and Panamanian whaling interests in another.

On closer shores, indigenous American peoples in northern Alaska have claimed that the hunting of the bowhead whale represents the central ritual of their culture. The claim was upheld by a district court judge in San Francisco who proclaimed that the hunt should go on because the preservation of a culture supersedes the preservation of a species. Surely we should all be thankful for being members of a culture rather than a species. That the endangered culture in question long ago traded in oars for outboard engines and harpoons for Winchester 300 magnums seems to have had little effect on the well-intended decision.

Is it ethically valid for us to tell indigenous peoples whose lands we have usurped what species native to their territories they may or may not kill? What came first, the species or the culture?

Cetaceans evolved some 40 million years ago, in all probability from an ancestor that inhabited the shallow estuaries and seas that covered the better part of the continents during the Oligocene epoch of geologic time. In those days competition for food and space was fierce, and so it behooved the cetaceans' ancestors to take to the water where competition was almost nil and space what you made it. Terrestrially disastrous phenomena like glaciers represented comparatively minor concerns—they were unthreatening clouds concentrated solely at the peripheries of the horizon, the edges of the sea. As time went by, the cetaceans adjusted more fully to life in the water: their nostrils moved from the front to the top of their head, their hind legs disappeared entirely, their genitals and ears receded into slits in their incredibly smooth body, and their front limbs evolved into hydrodynamic stabilizers, flippers, which may also function as a thermoregulation apparatus.

Adapting to their marine environment, the cetaceans developed highly specialized biological mechanisms that enable them to frolic for years in water sufficiently cold to kill a human in minutes, and to dive to depths that would kill a human in seconds. They have a thick outside layer of blubber that insulates them from the cold as well as increases their buoyancy. It permits some species to store enough fat to spend an entire winter without eating.

To ensure that the blood pumped to the extremities

of their body does not cool down too much by the time it makes the return trip to their heart, their arteries and veins run parallel to each other so that the warm arterial blood on the way out heats up the cool venal blood on the way in.

Cetaceans' ribs are not connected to their breastbones, affording some species the ability to collapse their lungs completely. Thus oxygen and carbon dioxide are exchanged about six times faster than in humans. With each breath, cetaceans achieve an exchange rate of 90 percent, whereas humans transfer only about 15 percent of their lungs' contents. Consequently, the cetaceans can suffuse themselves with enough oxygen to go for prolonged periods of time without breathing—in the case of the sperm whale for as long as two hours.

They have in their system as well an unusually rich supply of myoglobin. This protein binds to and stores oxygen in their muscles, so that the hemoglobin circulating in the blood can dedicate itself to nourishing the brain and heart during deep and extended dives below the air.

More streamlined than the most high-tech of projectiles, some species of cetacean move more quickly through water than mathematical models of their theoretical hull speed would permit. Theoretical hull speed represents the maximum velocity at which a particular body can move through a fluid medium, and anyone who's crewed aboard a well-trimmed sailboat will relate to the concept. At a certain point—say, when a wind far faster than a boat's theoretical hull speed coincides with the direction it happens to be proceeding in, and prevailing currents similarly propel it—the entire vessel vibrates with an ominous hum. It is as though obscure but powerful Newtonian forces are about to tear the boat apart. The halyards buzz like high-voltage cicadas, the hull sends pins and needles up through your feet, and the owner of the boat, more likely than not slightly behind in insurance payments, rushes to trim the sails. To some that hum is frightening, to others exhilarating.

To the United States Navy, a funder of cetacean research, the hum of maxed-out theoretical hull speeds represents a challenge: if dolphins can move through water at such speed, why can't torpedoes and submarines? Funded by the Navy among others, research has revealed that, in addition to achieving an almost perfect laminar flow, some dolphins literally shed their skin as they swim—sloughing off, as it were, a microscopic envelope they slide through like a sheath, almost frictionlessly. When taking a shower, humans shed dirt and dead cells; to do as much, dolphins need only accelerate. And accelerate they do. Some researchers report dolphins attaining speeds of 40 miles per hour and reaching escape velocities strong enough to propel them clear out of the water in graceful arcs three times their height. What's a theoretical hull speed to them?

Cetaceans have an unusually poor sense of smell, doubtless because they'd drown if they sniffed, even though the design of their esophagus allows them to breathe and swallow at the same time. In all their lives cetaceans never once take a drink of water. Some species have limited eyesight, even unto blindness, while others see quite well. All species have, apparently, a keen sense of hearing, which makes available to them a repertoire of vocalizations that the human ear finds baffling.

The most hauntingly beautiful songs of all time are surely those sung by male humpback whales, who lay neutrally buoyant at an angle of 45 degrees to the zenith, and, with their flippers straight out, declaim sometimes for hours the timelessness of love. Afterward, with 7-foot penises that deliver 15 gallons of semen upon ejaculation, the successful males mate.

Their song is the longest, most complex in the animal kingdom, and it seems to have about it the rudimentary elements of a culture, a shared, universal experience. Whether their bizarre songs intend to cajole nubile females into tasting the delights of procreation or to discourage competing males from entering their territory, no one knows. It seems clear, however, that all the humpbacks of a particular population sing the same song, in concert subtly improvising upon it during the course of the mating season.

Curiously enough, all the sexually mature males of a specific stock begin singing each mating season the precise song they seem to have agreed upon at the end of the previous season, and exactly how they remember that song and how or why they universally improvise upon it, and to what end, will probably always remain a mystery. Could it be they're passing something on? Whatever it means, the song of the humpbacks surely represents that most atavistically powerful of cultural traditions—that is, myth. Humans, too, embody myths in song, and that we fail utterly to comprehend the eerily beautiful myth of the humpbacks in no way diminishes its potency. Only ponderous profound beings can make a myth.

The vocalizations of other cetacean species also baffle us, for their enormous brain has adapted to life in a medium through which sound travels five times faster than through air, and where the difference between daylight and darkness sometimes measures 6 feet. Many species depend more on hearing than on sight, sensing the world about them with an incredibly sophisticated sonar, or echolocation, system. The sounds they emit bounce back to them off objects in the water or on its surface, in some cases with such accuracy that their mind's eye registers an image not only of shape but also of mass. Some species of dolphins literally perform sonograms on objects, easily distinguishing between hollow and solid forms of the same shape, which task a human can accomplish only with ultrasound technology, X rays, or other nuclear imaging systems. Scientists believe, furthermore, that the sperm whale emits subsonic sounds of sufficiently thunderous power to stun its prey, which are as a general rule, 1- to 30-foot-long squid that illumine themselves in the absolute darkness with a light-emitting enzyme, luciferase, named for Lucifer.

Blue and fin whales emit the lowest sounds in the animal kingdom, broadcasting who knows what at frequencies below 100 hertz, a wavelength far below the threshold of human hearing. Sounds so low in frequency, like the distant rumble of thunder, can travel enormous distances under the right conditions, and under about 3000 feet of water where—variables of temperature, pressure, and salinity create a low-velocity sound channel—the right conditions exist. Sounds emitted not too far above or below this channel sort of gravitate toward it until it traps them, carrying them much farther than they could otherwise have gone. Accordingly, sparse populations of blue and fin whales might be able, simply by moaning into vast conduits of high-density water, to reach out and touch someone, and subsequently to perpetuate a few and far between species.

Cold, high-density water carries life as surely as sound, for at temperatures down to about 39 degrees

Fahrenheit water contracts before expanding again as ice, thereby enabling vital nutrient gases, in particular oxygen and carbon dioxide, to become soluble. The ocean's quantity of living matter, its biomass, reaches its highest concentrations in cold, high-latitude water, where negligible temperature differences between the surface and the depths facilitate a thorough mixing, a rising and falling, of water layers. Water saturated with oxygen and carbon dioxide rises to a surface thick as soup with green plants waiting for its nutrients, and so the food chain begins. Though beautifully clear, tropical waters retain sufficient solar heat to create steep thermoclines, drastic changes in temperature that prohibit the upwelling of deep, cold, nutrient-rich water.

Sharply defined at the equator, the ocean's thermocline disappears at the poles. The decreased visibility in northern sections of the Atlantic and Pacific is due primarily to high populations of phytoplankton, tiny aquatic plants. The presence of these gives the water its characteristic color by dispersing light in such a way that only the wavelengths of green and yellow get reflected. The ethereally clear blue water of the tropics exhibits a more generalized, less interfered with, reflection of light, rather like that of the sky. In terms of biological fecundity, tropical waters resemble a barren desert, clear as a bell but for the most part empty; whereas high-latitude waters recall a dense jungle teeming with life.

You can see whales at the equator and near the poles, and, if you know where to look and when, just about everyplace in between. Seeing whales requires far less effort than most people imagine. Organized whale-watching excursions visit everyplace from the tepid lagoons of the Sea of Cortez to the chilling pack ice floes of Baffin Bay. To accommodate those of us whose time or budget proscribes journeys to such exotic climes, a significant industry of whale-watching facilities has sprung up along both coasts of the continent. People in Boston and New York City, San Diego and Seattle, San Francisco and Miami, regularly see whales.

Of course, they have to go out of their way to do so, but not terribly much. I have left Manhattan at 5 A.M., watched a rainbow materialize in the deafening spout of a nearby fin whale, and returned to town in time for dinner at eight. In Vancouver I have left after brunch to watch killer whales breaching and got back to my hotel in time to shower before a fashionably late supper. From dunes on Cape Cod and the coast of Oregon, picnicking and toting binoculars, I have sat, watching whales swim by.

I have also watched the most unanimated of people transformed utterly by the sight of a whale, turned instantly from a bored-looking adult enduring the afternoon to an astonished-looking child, wide-eyed and overwhelmed by the immensity of life, the mystery, the grace. People become silent in the presence of whales, reverently so, as though to give them a chance to speak if they would. When large whales get close the sound of their exhalations overpower even the drone of idling diesel engines. And if their spout rises at an appropriate angle to the sun you'll see a rainbow appear for a melting second and think, surely, of Melville and the world of deep thoughts.

Identifying cetaceans requires, primarily, a knowledge of what you're most likely looking at, what's most likely there. You are not going to see beluga whales in the Gulf of Mexico, nor need you lose any sleep about having to identify a gray whale in the Gulf of Maine. Some cetaceans make brief appearances, breaking the surface only slightly, and only for a second, before disappearing; others breach, leaping clear out of the water, time after time, begging to be identified. Some whales have names, and a few have biographies—painstakingly assembled by researchers using photographic identification techniques. Either out of curiosity or for the sheer fun of it, some cetaceans approach boats so closely that whale watchers, at once exhilarated and terrified, get to pet them.

There is no reason to fear any cetacean species. Even the formidable killer whale, the largest predator on the planet, has never been known to attack a human, and over the years reports have come in of dolphins rescuing struggling swimmers by lifting them to the surface. Fun-loving, affectionate, and intelligent, the cetaceans harbor no ill feelings toward humans, who have persecuted them. While whale watching, one should reserve one's fear for the safety of the whales, which for all their acres of brain do not necessarily understand propellers or the frequently careless folks who operate them.

None of the whale-watching vessels described below ever leaves port for an excursion without a serious naturalist aboard, and for the sake of these larger-brained-than-us, more gentle mammals, one should never patronize a commercial whale-watching operation without thoughtfully assessing its sensitivity to cetacean welfare. I have heard reliable accounts of crazed, dangerously uninformed captains chasing terrified whales and their calves for an hour, gunning their engines within 50 feet of the animals.

In 1984 the National Marine Fisheries Service established a set of guidelines that the captains of whale-watching vessels should follow, if need be at the insistence of passengers. Prospective whale watchers should keep these simple, commonsense rules in mind and openly express indignation to any captain who ignores them:

1. Vessels within a quarter mile of a whale should avoid excessive speed and sudden changes in direction.
2. Vessels within a hundred yards (the length of a football field) should not approach a whale at more than idle speed or bear down on them head-on: approach stationary whales from the side, cruise parallel to moving ones. If, at this distance, several vessels attempt to approach a whale, the captains should not surround the animal nor obstruct its path.
3. Vessels within a hundred feet of a whale should make no attempt to approach the animal more closely: at this range the vessel's engines should be put in neutral and kept there until the animal moves farther away. (Note: If at this range the animal dives, the vessel's propellers should not be reengaged until it appears on the surface again, farther away.)

To appreciate a whale-watching excursion one need only show up. Although some whale watchers tote along all manner of specialized equipment, others will appear entirely empty-handed, and in high-heeled shoes. On a beautiful, clear, calm day it does not matter terribly much what you wear on a whale-watching boat, but if the weather turns and the seas get rough you can easily expose yourself to serious discomfort by wearing unsuitable clothing. I recommend sneakers or rubber-soled shoes with good traction, and a heavy sweater or windbreaker you can easily put on and take off.

Bear in mind that even on a windless, sunny, 70-degree day a boat moving 20 miles per hour generates, for all intents and purposes, a 20-mile-per-hour wind, which makes 70 degrees feel like 50. People with sensitive skin or who haven't spent recent time in the sun should surely consider sunscreen lotion before spending several hours on the open water. The effective wind generated by a moving boat cools off the skin so well that many people never realize how badly they're being burned, until later. I always apply a skin moisturizer before and after a boat journey, in sunny or cloudy weather.

I also always wear sunglasses (polarized, if possible) to avoid the kind of eyestrain vast expanses of sky and shimmering water generate, not to mention unexpected blasts of salt spray. Seasickness debilitates the most physically fit of humans, and to avoid this most unpleasant of syndromes one should eat sensibly before and during any boating excursion. Eat lightly before boarding a boat: avoid coffee, alcohol, and greasy and heavy foods. Foods like tea, cold cereal, and toast tend not to upset the stomach, which erupts with uncommon violence during a seasickness episode. Physiologically, seasickness represents a disagreement between the eyes and the inner ear, which can perceive motion so differently as to involve the stomach in the dispute. In my experience the syndrome occurs in direct relation to the roughness of the water and its consequent effect on the motion of the boat. If you begin to feel ill, stay outside on deck, preferably near the stern, where motion is least. Keep your eyes on the horizon, breathe deeply, and try to distract yourself. For reasons unexplained, people seemingly hopelessly lost in seasickness suddenly revive when a whale shows up.

Whales usually show up at all of the locations detailed below, with sufficient regularity that those who go seeking usually find.

IDENTIFYING CETACEANS

The easiest way to identify a whale is to listen as someone else identifies it. Naturalists on whale-watching excursions tend not only to identify but also to lecture on the cetaceans that appear. But if you're walking a favorite beach at dusk and notice for a fleeting second, out of the corner of your eye, a pair of fins breaking the surface in the darkening light, no such identification or lecture will be forthcoming. Learning to identify cetaceans on your own requires experience, but even the complete novice can venture an educated guess based on a process of geographical elimination and a familiarity with the field marks and behavior characteristics of the most easily distinguished and/or common species.

In no way a substitute for a comprehensive field guide to cetaceans, the following comments and species descriptions intend to sketch briefly the basic differences among cetaceans and the salient characteristics of a very few.

THE ORDER CETACEA

The order Cetacea divides itself into two suborders, the mysticeti and the odontoceti, the "mustached" and the "toothed."

As very few whales have hairs and those that do have very few, by "mustached" one should understand something other than those coifs of hair on the upper lip of some humans or those dark slashes of feather between the eyes and beak of certain falcons. The mustaches of the mysticeti (Greek for "mustached") are, rather, a series of elongated vertical plates, called baleen, that hang from their upper jaw. Soup strainers in their own right, these rows of baleen plates look like vertical Levolor blinds with fringes on the inside. They function as a sieve, allowing water to pass through while trapping food. When viewed under the right conditions—say, when a lunge-feeding humpback breaks the surface, his jaw distended, his mouth wide open, water and fish and foam flying every which way, hysterical herring gulls hovering inches from his jaws—baleen can indeed look like a mustache.

In what must certainly qualify as one of evolution's strangest twists of fate, the mustaches of the planet's most powerful animals became the stuff of ladies' corsets. Until the advent of plastic, baleen was the material of choice among those who manufactured and wore foundation garments—a grim fate for a mustache, that.

Baleen whales feed by filling their mouth with enormous amounts of water, in some cases with as much as 70 tons, and then forcing it out through their baleen, which traps their food. The mysticeti diet varies from tiny organisms scarcely two steps up on the food chain to herring and other relatively large schooling fish. It is interesting to note that although carnivores tend to take larger prey as they themselves increase in size, the largest carnivore that ever lived, the blue whale, feeds largely on krill, tiny shrimplike crustaceans just over an inch long. During their feeding season, blue whales consume about 3 or 4 tons of krill a day.

All but one species of baleen whales divide their

time between feeding and breeding, allocating half a year for each activity. They literally stuff their face all spring and summer, and then cruise through winter in the tropics with no food other than their fat stores. The suborder mysticeti embraces ten species.

The suborder odontoceti (Greek for "toothed") contains some sixty-five species, which differ as a group from the mysticeti in two principal ways: they have teeth instead of baleen, and one blowhole instead of two. Although as a general rule baleen whales are larger than toothed whales, there are exceptions, such as the killer whale and the sperm whale, both of which are larger than the minke whale.

THE MYSTICETI

The Gray Whale

The pride of California and the rest of the West Coast, gray whales are among the superstars of the whale-watching movement. They are easily observed, relatively numerous, acrobatic, and friendly. The species was hunted to virtual extinction, recovered, was hunted to virtual extinction again, and again recovered. It seems the current California stock population, estimated at about 15,000, approximates the pre-whaling population. The species does not exist on the East Coast, possibly because whalers totally exterminated it.

They achieve lengths of 45 feet and weigh as much as 70,000 pounds. Primarily gray, these whales exhibit extensive yellow or yellow-orange blotches, which give them a heavily mottled, encrusted appearance. Barnacles, or whale lice, create this mottled effect. When observed below the surface, they look like ancient torpedoes made of ashen gray and white marble, sometimes tinged a pale shade of blue because of the water.

When they breach (leap clear out of the water) or spyhop (stick their heads above the surface for a look at the airy universe), their barnacle-encrusted body is unmistakable. They have small flippers and lack a dorsal fin, presenting instead a hump followed by a series of six to twelve knobs, or knuckles.

Gray whales migrate some 5000 miles—the longest migration of any mammal—from breeding and calving grounds off Baja California to feeding grounds in the Bering, Chukchi, and Beaufort seas, following the receding pack ice far above the Arctic Circle. They occasionally approach boats so closely as to allow themselves to be touched and were once known as devilfish because females protect their young so fiercely they will attack a boat. Indeed, in 1983 a gray whale did exactly that; it attacked a small boat, two of whose passengers died, one of them apparently from a heart attack during the incident. Such incidents are so rare as to be completely insignificant, but they make a point about mother and child.

Gray whales have small, bushy spouts that rise perhaps ten feet on a windless day. As a rule they tend to blow about every fifteen to thirty seconds, generally exhaling four or five times before diving for five or so minutes. If you watch them swim from a lookout on land, you will note the very regular rhythms of their breath.

During migration gray whales hug the coast, with the result that one can observe them from just about any point along the Pacific shore, especially from November through March. From late December through April, gray whales frolic, mate, and give birth in the lagoons of Baja California, the destination of several exciting whale-watching excursions.

The Humpback Whale

The most acrobatic of large whales, humpbacks almost never fail to put on a show for whale watchers, who, in turn, almost never fail to shriek with excitement when the whales first appear. Even the most experienced and jaded of whale watchers cannot help smiling at the antics of the humpbacks. Their bizarre behavior has generated all manner of explanatory theory, but the fact remains that we do not really know why they do the things they do. They frequently leap clear out of the water, most often emerging headfirst and then twisting in midair so that they crash back into the sea on their enormous backs. They frequently lobtail, raising their flukes high into the air only to sweep them suddenly down on the surface, creating a thunderous crack. Often they raise one of their extremely long flippers, which can exceed 15 feet in length and then slap the surface with it several times. Sometimes they simply lie quietly on the surface with one or both flippers extended straight up. For some reason, the extended flipper of a humpback whale always makes me think of the Lady of the Lake, whose arm suddenly appeared to catch Excalibur, the sword of the once and future king.

Humpbacks occur on both coasts of the continent, and observers view them with regularity in locations as diverse as Cape Cod, Hawaii, the Gulf of Alaska, and the Caribbean Sea. They are, as whales go, relatively easy to identify, in large part because they readily approach boats and make a far more than adequate display of their field marks, which are individually distinctive. Researchers using photographic identification techniques, primarily photos of flukes, have assembled biographies of several thousand humpbacks, and it is not uncommon to hear an experienced whale watcher exclaim: "There's Salt and her new calf."

Though usually 38 to 50 feet long, humpbacks can grow to lengths of 60 feet. They can weigh 80,000 pounds. Black or gray above, humpbacks flash a lot of white below: their belly and throat exhibit varying amounts of white, their flippers are white below and usually above as well, and the patterns of white on the underside of their butterfly-shaped flukes are unique to each individual. Because they descend at a steep angle, they raise their flukes high in the air when they dive, boldly displaying their unique pattern of coloration.

Most have small dorsal fins about one-third up the body from their flukes, and their name, humpback, derives from a small hump the fin seems to rest on and a series of knobs trailing backward from the fin. A series of softball-size knobs, each containing a hair, project from their heads. Their thick, bushy spout rises approximately 10 feet. Their most imperious field mark is their extremely long, thin, white flippers, which underwater in northern latitudes look like ghostly green wings.

The Fin Whale

Long, sleek, swift, and mysterious, fin whales are the most common large cetacean in the western North Atlantic, where they appear with regularity from Long Island to the Maritime Provinces of Canada. Second in size only to the blue whale, the fin whale approaches 90 feet in length. They can swim 20 miles per hour and break the surface only slightly with a long, fluid, roller coaster–like movement—their 20-foot-tall spout followed by a long expanse of back and, a second or two later, a short, two-foot-tall dorsal fin. They tend to blow about five times before diving for as many minutes, and they do not raise their flukes before they dive. Like all whales, when they sound they leave behind massive "footprints," powerful upsurges of water that form smooth circles, even on choppy seas.

The top of their long, slender body is dark silver gray to black, their underside white. Fin whales exhibit more white on their right side than on their left—an asymmetry particularly striking in that their lower right jaw, including the baleen, is white while their lower left jaw and baleen is dark gray or black. It seems that finbacks exploit their asymmetrical coloration by swimming clockwise around their prey and startling them into forming compact, easily taken groups. Under ideal viewing conditions they exhibit a palish gray to white chevron (three chevrons constitute a sergeant's stripes) that begins behind their blowhole and spreads back.

Under less than ideal viewing conditions you probably will not see much of a fin whale at all, although if you are lucky you might see as many as forty of them swimming in circles at the surface through an unusually rich school of fish. We don't know very much about finbacks. Their breeding and calving grounds, if as a group they share one, have not been discovered. Some researchers hypothesize that they feed at high latitudes and breed at low ones, like grays or humpbacks. Others imagine that they mate and calve at the very edge of the pack ice. And some conjecture that, like eagles, they mate for life.

The Blue Whale

The largest animal of all time, the blue whale attains a length of over a hundred feet and a weight of over

300,000 pounds. Current population estimates suggest that perhaps 15,000 blue whales still exist in the world's oceans, and though the figure sounds promising, it could easily be an overestimate. Ninety to 95 percent of the blue whale population was exterminated by whaling interests, and it remains to be seen whether or not the species will recover from such devastation.

Their most salient field mark is their enormous size, which never fails to impress those who see one for the first, or the hundredth, time. They exhibit a spout that rises 20 feet on a still day, and because of their length, as many as four seconds might elapse before their tiny 8- to 12-inch dorsal fin appears. Though they tend to raise their flukes before diving, they raise them only slightly because they descend at a gradual angle.

Pale blue gray mottled with light gray on their backs, blue whales sometimes present a yellow underside, the result of diatom infestation, and they were once known as sulphur bottoms. Their long flippers are whitish underneath, and their baleen is black. They appear with regularity in the Gulf of St. Lawrence.

The Right Whale

Hunted to the very edge of extinction, right whales seemed doomed as a species. Protected since 1937, their populations do not seem to be recovering. Uncertain whether due to a low birth or a high mortality rate, researchers estimate a North Atlantic population of perhaps just 250 animals; North Pacific figures are only slightly higher. These meager numbers represent approximately six one-hundredths of one percent of the right whales' pre-whaling population. It appears their numbers may well have fallen below that critical mass a species needs in order to prevail. Consider yourself lucky if you see a right whale, and bless it as it goes.

Right whales are ponderously fat, dark, roly-poly creatures with no dorsal fin at all. Their backs appear flat and smooth, and their widely separated blowhole produces a short, bushy, distinctly V-shaped spout. The right whale's huge head takes up a full quarter of its body, and its lower jaw is particularly massive. They look, indeed, as though they have no upper jaw, or have just swallowed it. Their lower jaw reminds me of pelicans, or a highly exaggerated Dick Tracy.

Baleen plate 8 feet long hang from their upper jaw into their capacious lower one, creating an enormous filter that enables them to feed on copopeds, tenth-of-an-inch-long organisms that weigh one two-hundred-thousandth of a pound. Though they feed on such small fare, they achieve lengths of 60 feet; they can weigh 50 tons. They eat simply by swimming through fields of copopeds with their mouths open, thereby allowing water to flow freely through their mouths and out through their enormous baleen plates, which gather clumps of copopeds.

White or yellow pinkish callosites mottle their head and lower jaw in individually distinctive patterns. For all their bulk, right whales regularly leap clear out of the water, and observers have witnessed as many as a dozen of them rolling over and over playfully, the males with erections, in the lower Bay of Fundy, which is the most reliable place to see them. They are also common in Cape Cod Bay in winter and spring.

Their most salient field marks are their stout, bushy, V-shaped spout and their fat, finless back.

THE ODONTOCETI

The Killer Whale

Sleek, beautiful, boldly patterned animals, killer whales (actually dolphins) are the ocean's top predator. They travel in groups, or pods, of as many as thirty individuals. Most of them relatives, they stay together for many years, most often in a particular location. Their diet includes just about everything—herring, tuna, birds, seals, other dolphins, large baleen whales—and they hunt in a highly organized fashion, like wolves or lions, particularly when they take prey far larger than themselves. They apparently have a weakness for the huge tongues of baleen whales, which they eat, leaving the rest of the animal as carrion. Many large baleen whales exhibit scars from killer whale attacks.

They achieve a length of 30 feet and a weight of 16,000 pounds. Mature males present enormous, 6-foot-tall dorsal fins that are absolutely unmistakable, although females and immature males present more curved, smaller dorsal fins, like other dolphins. Killer whales are black above, with a faint gray "saddle" behind their dorsal fin and a conspicuous white oval patch above and behind each eye. Their throat and belly are white, and a bold white bar juts on to their black sides immediately behind their dorsal fin. Their flippers are oval, paddle-shaped affairs.

Previously creatures of universal dread, killer whales, by performing startling feats at oceanaria, have earned a reputation as gentle, playful, intelligent, and affectionate animals. Their dazzling antics have endeared them to the hearts of millions, and although a few reports have drifted in of killer whales attacking and sinking small boats, I know of no incident of a killer whale attacking a human swimmer. Just to be on the safe side, never stick your tongue out at a killer whale. People who object to the deadly connotation of the whales' name call them orcas, which means the same thing, after the scientific nomenclature, *Orcinus orca*.

The most reliable place to see them is in the Pacific Northwest, from Seattle to the Gulf of Alaska.

The Sperm Whale
The largest-brained animal of all time, the sperm whale, probably via some fathomless act of cerebral projection, became with *Moby Dick* the central symbol of American art. And that, doubtless, is as it should be. "Better a mighty, misty, enigmatic monster than a mere mortal," I always say. The fittingness of the sperm whale seems poignantly apt when one considers that even the persecuted blacks of William Faulkner's South managed, in his words, to endure. The sperm whale might not, especially in the Pacific.

Obsessed as latter-day Ahabs, the Japanese continue to take sperm whales. They do so in defiance of an international moratorium and the gratuitous pressures exerted on them by the United States to cease and desist. Long before the Japanese took to harpoons, Yankee whalers did their number on the sperm whales. And for good reason—money. In addition to yielding copious amounts of oil, sperm whales also yield some thousand gallons of spermaceti, a highly purified form of liquid, oily wax perfect for making candles. Ambergris, a rarefied substance used to prolong the odor of perfume, forms in their stomach around indigestible clumps of squid beaks.

The sperm whale's huge head, which takes up almost half its length, contains the spermaceti organ, a huge reservoir of purified oil our forefathers mistook for sperm, hence the creature's name. The precise function of spermaceti remains uncertain. It might serve as a buoyancy device that the whales liquefy or congeal by regulating their temperature through some fancy blood/water flow system. It might absorb gases so efficiently that even the implacable pressures two miles beneath the surface cannot squeeze nitrogen into solution in the blood. It might serve, by altering shape, as an acoustic lens in the sperm whale's echo-location system, which has adapted to functioning in a universe utterly bereft of light. It probably serves all three functions, and more.

By focusing the sounds they emit, sperm whales may produce sonic booms that overwhelm their prey. At the depths these whales routinely feed, 80 percent of the resident organisms are bioluminescent, capable of transmuting phosphorus into light with a net loss of less than one percent of their available energy. Some theories suggest that sperm whales exploit bio-luminescence by chewing its avatars and illuminating their teeth and gums so as to attract others. Sperm whales emit a series of monotonous clicks, which form "codas" distinctive to each individual, and sound, to human ears, like a banging hammer.

Although you will probably never see a sperm whale other than during a transatlantic crossing or during some boat ride beyond the continental shelf, you should—for the sake of the great American myth—know how to identify one. The stylized whales one sees on bumper stickers and T-shirts are sperm whales. They have an enormous, square head, and, to use Melville's words, "boom-like lower jaws." Their single blowhole projects a bushy spout 6 feet tall at a distinctly oblique angle to the left—an angle that renders them easily identifiable even at a great distance. They raise their flukes high in the air as they dive at a steep angle, descend as deep as two miles and for as long as two hours. They surface in almost the same spot they sound, probably because their dives involve almost no horizontal movement.

The Beluga Whale

Also called white whales, belugas are unmistakable— they look like ghosts. Mature whales, which grow as long as 13 feet, are completely white and lack a dorsal fin; immature whales are uniformly dark. Although they tend to inhabit circumpolar habitats thick with pack ice, they frequently stray far south of their usual haunts. In 1985 a beluga spent the summer in the New Haven, Connecticut, harbor. In spring and summer, congregations of thousands of them appear in the estuary of the Churchill River at Hudson Bay, and they are a common sight for whale watchers in the Gulf of St. Lawrence.

Belugas made the front pages in March 1985 when the Soviets released films of a successful attempt, called Operation Belhuka, to free 3000 belugas trapped by pack ice 12 feet thick in a narrow strait. Literally piled atop one another, obviously weak and hungry, the whales groped for air at a small hole in the ice. The Soviet icebreaker *Moskva* plowed through 15 miles of thick ice to open an escape channel for the whales, but its crew could not then persuade the belugas to follow the ship to safety. Whereupon a Soviet sailor suggested hooking up a pair of loudspeakers and luring the whales with music. Popular and military tunes failed to impress the belugas, but when a classical selection came on, they began to frolic around the ship, which led them merrily to the open sea. What, one wonders, was the music that did the trick? *The Nutcracker Suite*? Rachmaninoff.

Because of their high-pitched squeaks and whistles, which sometimes pass through the hulls of boats or air, belugas are sometimes called sea canaries. They can apparently resolve extremely fine detail with their sonar. And for purposes that we assume have to do with navigation, the vertebrae in their neck are not attached, an adaptation that enables them to crane their head every which way.

DESTINATIONS AND ACCOMMODATIONS

BAJA CALIFORNIA, MEXICO

Special Expeditions
720 Fifth Avenue
New York, NY 10019
Telephone: (212) 765-7740

Special Expeditions operates two-week, naturalist-led excursions to Baja California. The trips, which depart from San Diego, are aboard the 143-foot *Pacific Northwest Explorer*, a fully air-conditioned one-class ship, of United States registry. The cruises are accompanied by experienced and credentialed naturalists, who not infrequently find themselves and half a dozen passengers in an inflatable boat inches away from a gray whale. Gray whales mate and raise their young in the waters off Baja California, which plays host as well to a plethora of other species. After a day of exploring in motorized, inflatable boats, naturalists conduct a recap session in the lounge before dinner.

The *Pacific Northwest Explorer* has thirty-nine cabins, all of which are outside and have private baths. Rates for the trips, which the company likes to call "voyages

to a strange and beautiful planet," include everything
but drinks and telephone calls. The trips leave every
two weeks, from mid-January to late March.

Rates: $3000 to $4500.

LOS ANGELES, CALIFORNIA

Cabrillo Whalewatch
3720 Stephen White Drive
San Pedro, CA 90731
Telephone: (213) 832-2676 (weekdays 8:30 A.M. to 1:30 P.M.)
** or (213) 548-7562**

Cosponsored by the Cabrillo Marine Museum and the
American Cetacean Society, Cabrillo Whalewatch operates 2½-hour whale-watching tours from the day
after Christmas to mid-April. Tours go out seven days
a week, and some 59,000 people a year go out on
them. Cabrillo Whalewatch functions as a central
booking agency that handles fourteen boats that leave
from four locations: you call Cabrillo Whalewatch and
they refer you to a boat with which you then make a
reservation. The idea for the service originated when
someone realized that most of the large, commercial
sport-fishing boats in the Los Angeles area were not
very busy during the gray whale migration season.
The concept since has generated business for otherwise idle commercial fishing boats as well as the huge,
500-passenger Catalina cruise boats.

Most of the boats have galleys and serve food and
drink, and each is accompanied by a naturalist during
the tour. Depending on where the whales are, the
boats go out 6 or 7 miles into the ocean, and in addition to gray whales Pacific white-sided dolphins are
frequently sighted, and very occasionally a killer, fin,
or pilot whale shows up.

Rates: *Rates vary according to boat, but generally average $8 to $9.*

Driving Instructions: Call for specific driving instructions: cruises leave from four different locations.

SAN FRANCISCO/OAKLAND, CALIFORNIA

The only person I ever met who did not like San Francisco lived there anyway because he loved, above all, the wild fury of the Pacific surf, the redwood forest at noon, and ballet. A city whose cultural charms need no rehearsing here, San Francisco enjoys a marvelous geographical location that many of its visitors never take advantage of. The Golden Gate National Recreation Area embraces more than 70,000 acres of scenic shoreline, a virgin redwood forest waits for you at the Muir Woods National Monument 17 miles out of town, a forty-five-minute drive will get you to the Point Reyes National Seashore, from where you can look for migrating gray whales, and 20 miles west of town blue whales may well be feeding around the Farallon Islands. Hawk Hill, which overlooks the mouth of San Francisco Bay, is the most prolific concentration point of raptor migration on the Pacific flyway. From San Francisco, Yosemite National Park is within weekend range, as is Big Sur and the Mendocino Highlands.

The Whale Center
3929 Piedmont Avenue
Oakland, CA 94611
Telephone: (415) 654-6621

A nonprofit whale conservation organization, The Whale Center lobbies on behalf of cetaceans, sends observers to the International Whaling Commission meetings, and was a vigorous supporter of the Farallon Islands National Wildlife Refuge, a marine sanctuary 30 miles off the coast of San Francisco. In 57-foot boats, the center leads whale-watching journeys either to the Farallon Islands area or along the coast. The trips to the Farallon Islands last about eight hours, those along the coast about three, and each trip is accompanied by at least two naturalists. Facilities on the boats include heads but no galleys, so bring your own food and drink.

The Farallon Islands are the largest seabird rookery in the continental United States, with a population at times of 200,000 birds—murres, petrels, all three cormorants, puffins, auklets, and, among others, 40 percent of the world's western gulls. Cetacean species regularly sighted include blue and humpback whales, Pacific white-sided dolphins, and harbor porpoises; minke, sei, and killer whales occasionally appear; and, rarely, a sperm whale bobs to the surface. The three-hour trips along the coast focus on the gray whale migration, which runs, roughly, from December through May, with peaks in January and March.

The center also offers one- and two-hour flights to see whales, and organizes naturalist-led trips to Alaska and Baja California.

Rates: three-hour trip, $26; eight-hour trip, $44; one-hour flight, $65; two-hour flight, $130.

Driving Instructions: Call for specific driving instructions: some cruises leave from the dock in Sausalito, others from the dock in Half Moon Bay.

American Family Inn/Bed & Breakfast San Francisco
PO Box 349
San Francisco, CA 94101
Telephone: (415) 931-3083

Bed and Breakfast International
151 Ardmore Road
Kensington, CA 94707
Telephone: (415) 525-4569

B&B reservation services match guests and hosts, and
these two services offer unique accommodations in
this unique part of the country. The places to stay
vary from simple to luxurious, and the prices range
accordingly.

The Willows Bed & Breakfast Inn
710 Fourteenth Street
San Francisco, CA 94114
Telephone: (415) 431-4770

Elegantly appointed, the Willows is an eleven-room
inn named after the bent-willow furnishings that were
created for it. A continental breakfast on a tray with
flowers and the morning paper are brought to your
room each morning. The rooms share baths.

Rates: moderate to expensive; AE,MC,V

The Bed and Breakfast Inn
4 Carlton Court
San Francisco, CA 94123
Telephone: (415) 921-9784

The Bed and Breakfast Inn consists of ten rooms in
three renovated Victorian townhouses. The decor
consists primarily of antiques, the grounds include a
lovely garden, and breakfast, on china, arrives at your
door each morning.

Rates: moderate to expensive; NCC

NORTHEAST HARBOR/BAR HARBOR, MAINE

Bar Harbor and Northeast Harbor are both located
on Mount Desert Island, one of the more spectacular
pieces of North Atlantic real estate. Acadia National

Park takes up more than half of the island. It contains spruce-covered granite bluffs rising right out of the ocean, a fjord, numerous lakes and streams, and a hundred plus miles of manicured trails. It is also the home of Cadillac Mountain, at 1530 feet the highest point, as well as the first to catch the sunrise, on the eastern coast of the United States. Though the better part of Acadia National Park is located on Mount Desert Island, smaller sections exist on Little Moose, Cranberry, and Baker islands, on the Schoodic Peninsula, and on Isle au Haut, a remote, ruggedly beautiful island off the coast of Deer Isle.

For those looking for other than natural attractions, Bar Harbor has all manner of diversions: art galleries are everywhere, and antiquing and shopping are major pastimes. The town, quite crowded in high summer, has countless restaurants.

The *Bluenose*, the ferry that makes a six-hour crossing to Yarmouth, Nova Scotia (see "Bay of Fundy"), leaves from Bar Harbor.

Maine Whalewatch
Captain Bob Bowman
PO Box 78
Northeast Harbor, ME 04662
Telephone: (207) 276-5803

Captain Bob Bowman, a naturalist who has worked for the Manomet Bird Observatory and done seabird and marine mammal studies for the University of Rhode Island, conducts whale-watching excursions from Thursday through Sunday during the months of June through September. Captain Bowman also has long been associated with the College of the Atlantic. During May, leaving from Rockland, Maine, rather than from Northeast Harbor, he conducts puffin-watching excursions.

The nine-hour excursions leave at 8:30 A.M. aboard the *Island Queen*, a 42-foot, diesel-powered boat originally built to carry mail between the Cranberry Isles and the mainland. Fully equipped for year-round service, the *Island Queen* has sophisticated navigation and radio equipment and a heated cabin in case the weather turns blustery. The boat has no food available, so passengers are advised, indeed encouraged, to bring along whatever food and drink they anticipate needing during a nine-hour cruise—the vessel has ample storage for coolers.

On the way to the prime whaling areas, the *Island Queen* passes numerous small islands nested upon by all manner of birds—ospreys, bald eagles, eiders, cormorants, black guillemots—and by the time the day is over passengers have usually gone all the way to Seal Island, a whaling hot spot just south of Isle au Haut. Birders will appreciate Captain Bowman's knowledge of pelagic birds, and everyone appreciates the cetaceans that appear—harbor porpoises, Atlantic white-sided dolphins, finbacks, minkes, humpbacks, an occasional right.

Rates: $25 (children under 5 free).

Driving Instructions: From Bar Harbor take Route 3 to its end (about twenty minutes), and turn left on to Route 198. Make the first left, which brings you right to the Northeast Harbor Marina.

Bar Harbor Whale and Bird Watch
West Street
Bar Harbor, ME 04609
Telephone: (207) 288-9794 or 288-9776

Bar Harbor Whale and Bird Watch operates whale-watching excursions from June 1 through October

15. The five-hour cruises are on board a 120-foot boat that can handle 350 passengers, 150 of whom can be seated in the heated interior cabin. The facilities on board include a full galley with hot lunches, snacks, and hot and cold beverages. Beer and mixed drinks are also available.

This whale-watching operation began in 1986 and, like the Maine Whalewatch, sights whales about 98 percent of the time. Every excursion is accompanied by a naturalist who narrates the journey, pointing out and identifying pelagic birds as well as cetaceans.

The Bar Harbor Whale and Bird Watch is a less intimate, shorter excursion than the Maine Whalewatch, but it is definitely more appropriate for people who prefer a shorter experience on a larger boat with more facilities. The upper Gulf of Maine is an incredibly fecund marine environment, where pelagic birds fly fast and low toward the spouts of whales. Any boat that takes you out on the water will almost certainly encounter cetaceans.

One should always make reservations for a whale-watching excursion.

The Inn on High
15 High Street
Bar Harbor, ME 04609
Telephone: (207) 288-3137

A small bed and breakfast, The Inn on High is a 1902 gambrel-roofed structure with three guest rooms, one of them a suite with a fireplace and a bath big enough for two. The house is furnished with many antiques, and all the rooms have color television. Rates include breakfast.

Rates: moderate to expensive; AE,MC,V

Stratford House Inn
45 Mount Desert Street
Bar Harbor, ME 04609
Telephone: (207) 288-5189

Furnished primarily with antiques, Stratford House Inn has ten guest rooms, each of which comes with a mahogany four-poster, brass, or seven-foot-tall cherry bed. Several of the rooms have fireplaces, and every ground floor room but the library is paneled in oak and has exposed beams in the ceiling. Rates include breakfast.

Rates: moderate to expensive; AE,MC,V

Golden Anchor Inn
West Street
Bar Harbor, ME 04609
Telephone: (207) 288-5033

A motel on the ocean, Golden Anchor Inn has its own dock, from where the Bar Harbor Bird and Whale-watch boat departs. The eighty-eight rooms, some of which have balconies, have color television and telephone, and rates include golf privileges. The facilities include a pool and snack bar (in season).

Rates: expensive; AE,DC,MC,V

Kimball Terrace Inn
Huntington Road
Northeast Harbor, ME 04662
Telephone: (207) 276-3383

A seventy-room motel that overlooks the incredibly picturesque Northeast Harbor harbor, Kimball Terrace Inn has a pool with poolside service, room service, a tennis court, golf privileges, and a restaurant.

Rates: moderate; AE,MC,V

Asticou Inn
Route 3
Northeast Harbor, ME 04662
Telephone: (207) 276-3344

A 1902 structure added to over the years, Asticou Inn has sixty-eight guest rooms, fifty-one of them in the main building and seventeen of them in a half-dozen cottages. Situated on landscaped grounds at the head of the harbor, the inn has a restaurant, bar, room service, tennis courts, and golf privileges. Rates include breakfast and dinner.

Rates: expensive; NCC

Bed and Breakfast Down East, Ltd.
PO Box 547, Macomber Mill Road
Eastbrook, ME 04634
Telephone: (207) 565-3517

Bed and Breakfast Directory of Maine
32 Colonial Village
Falmouth, ME 04105
Telephone: (207) 781-4528

Maine has two resident B&B reservation services, which match host homes and potential guests. The accommodations available vary from simple lodgings in a private home to elaborate suites in fancy inns, and the prices vary accordingly.

BOSTON, MASSACHUSEETTS

New England Aquarium
Central Wharf
Boston, MA 02110
Telephone: (617) 973-5277

The New England Aquarium, a nonprofit institution with some dazzling displays, operates a whale-watching vessel that goes out every day from May 1 through October 14. Fully air-conditioned and heated, the 96-foot boat encounters whales 98 percent of the time, and the policy here is such that if you happen to be on board when no whales are sighted you get your next trip out for free. The facilities on board include a galley serving chowder, sandwiches, snacks, and hot and cold beverages; beer, wine, and mixed drinks are also available. Marine biologists accompany every journey, lecturing en route and providing a running commentary when whales show up. The trips go out about 27 miles to Stellwagen Bank, and humpback, finback, and minke whales are the most often sighted.

Rates: $20 adults; $17 senior citizens; $16 children 5 to 15 (children under 5 not permitted).

Driving Instructions: Going north on the expressway, Routes 3 and 93, exit at Atlantic Avenue and follow the fish signs; or take the Blue Line subway to the Aquarium Station; or walk three blocks from Faneuil Hall or Government Center.

Bed & Breakfast Bay Colony, Ltd.
PO Box 166
Boston, MA 02157
Telephone: (617) 449-5302

New England Bed & Breakfast
1045 Centre Street
Newton Centre, MA 02159
Telephone: (617) 244-2112

Bed & Breakfast Agency—Boston Waterfront,
    Faneuil Hall; and Greater Boston
47 Commercial Wharf
Boston, MA 02110
Telephone: (617) 720-3540

Boston has numerous B&B reservation services, which match guests and hosts. The accommodations vary from simple to opulent, and are priced accordingly. In a major urban center like Boston, B&B reservation services tend to be far less expensive than good hotels and motels.

Copley Plaza
138 St. James Avenue
Boston, MA 02116
Telephone: (617) 267-5300 or 1-800-225-7654

A large, lovely, full-service hotel, Copley Plaza has 391 rooms, a shopping arcade, two good restaurants, and a prime location—it is in the reflection of I. M. Pei's Hancock Building, my favorite skyscraper.

Rates: expensive; AE,CB,DC,MC,V

GLOUCESTER, MASSACHUSETTS

A picturesque fishing village, Gloucester has numerous small museums and historic structures that, usually, testify to the village's history as a fishing port, which it still is. The coast here is ruggedly beautiful, and visitors would do well to tool up to Rockport, another interesting village perhaps 5 miles north.

Whale Safaris
Gateway Marina, Rust Island
Gloucester, MA 01930
Telephone: (617) 281-1047

From April through October, Whale Safaris operates two whale-watching boats that have a sighting record of 98 percent. Naturalists involved in research accompany each journey, lecturing and pointing things out as the trip progresses. Each of the boats, one of them

56 and the other 75 feet long, has a galley offering sandwiches, snacks, and hot and cold beverages; beer, wine, and mixed drinks are also available. Humpbacks and finbacks are the whales most frequently sighted.

Rates: $18 adults; $14 senior citizens; $12 children.

Driving Instructions: Take Route 128 to Exit 12—you cannot miss it.

Captain's Lodge
237 Eastern Avenue
Gloucester, MA 01930
Telephone: (617) 281-2420

Captain's Lodge is a thirty-five-room motel that features color cable television, telephone, and heated pool. A few of the rooms have efficiency kitchenette units, and the facilities include a cafe open from roughly 7 A.M. to noon.

Rates: moderate; AE,CB,DC,MC,V

Williams Guest House
136 Bass Avenue
Gloucester, MA 01930
Telephone: (617) 283-4931

A Colonial Revival structure next to the beach at Good Harbor, Williams Guest House has seven rooms, five of them with private bath. Rates here include a continental breakfast. A cottage that sleeps four is also available.

Rates: inexpensive to moderate; NCC

Seafarer Guest House
86 Marmion Way
Rockport, MA 01966
Telephone: (617) 546-6248

Quaint and comfortable, the Seafarer is an 1893 gambrel-roofed structure overlooking the water. Each of the eight rooms (some of which have efficiency kitchenettes) has something of a view.

Rates: inexpensive to moderate; NCC

PLYMOUTH, MASSACHUSETTS

A little less than halfway between the base of Cape Cod and Boston, Plymouth is a coastal town of about 7000 people, most of whom did not come over on the *Mayflower*. The *Mayflower II*, a 90-foot replica of the boat that carried the Pilgrims here, rides at anchor at the State Pier on Water Street. That huge boulder dragged here by the glaciers, Plymouth Rock, is still in attendance, as are any number of historic structures. Drenched with history and the beauty of the Atlantic Coast, Plymouth boasts a plethora of museums, numerous good restaurants, and any number of things to do. Offshore, there are whales.

Captain John Boats
117 Standish Avenue
Plymouth, MA 02360
Telephone: (617) 746-2643

A fleet of three 80-foot vessels, Captain John Boats go out looking for whales from April through October, and they sight cetaceans 98 percent of the time. Every whale-watching journey is accompanied by naturalists, who perform ongoing research as they narrate the journeys, and the facilities aboard the boats include a galley with snack food and a bar that serves beer and mixed drinks. Humpbacks and finbacks are the most common whales sighted, and to the surprise and delight of everybody, more and more right whales seem to be showing up.

The Captain John Boats go out for 4½-hour excursions, during which the naturalists often show films on board.

Rates: $15 adults; $13 senior citizens; $11 children.

Driving Instructions: From Route 3 take 44 East (Essex Avenue) to the waterfront: the boats leave from the town wharf.

Around Plymouth Bay Bed & Breakfast
PO Box 6211
Plymouth, MA 02360
Telephone: (617) 747-5075

Be Our Guest Bed & Breakfast, Ltd.
PO Box 1333
Plymouth, MA 02360
Telephone: (617) 545-6680

Plymouth has two resident B&B reservation services, which match up guests and host homes in the immediate area. The accommodations vary from simple to opulent, and are priced accordingly.

Colonial House Inn
207 Sandwich Street
Plymouth, MA 02360
Telephone: (617) 746-2087

Overlooking the bay, Colonial House Inn has six rooms with private bath, air-conditioning, and television. The facilities include a pool

Rates: moderate; NCC

Pilgrim Sands
150 Warren Avenue
Plymouth, MA 02360
Telephone: (617) 747-0900

Two miles south of town, Pilgrim Sands is a motel with sixty-two rooms, two swimming pools, and a restaurant. Rates include a continental breakfast.

Rates: moderate to expensive; AE,CB,DC,MC,V

PROVINCETOWN, MASSACHUSETTS

The Dolphin Fleet
Captain Al Avellar
MacMillan Pier
Provincetown, MA 02657
Telephone: (617) 255-3857

A splendid marriage of commerce and research, The Dolphin Fleet/Center for Coastal Studies whale-watching excursions has been, and will doubtless continue to be, something of a model for the whale-watching industry. Naturalists from the Center for Coastal Studies accompany every Dolphin Fleet excursion, providing a continuous narrative for the passengers as they conduct research.

The Dolphin Fleet consists of three 100-foot boats, which go out looking for whales from mid-June through mid-September. The boats, which encounter whales 99.7 percent of the time, feature full galleys offering hot lunches, snacks, and hot and cold beverages. Beer and mixed drinks are also available. Each of the boats has modern bathrooms and a large, indoor, heated cabin in case the weather gets nasty.

Departure times for the excursions, which last about four hours, vary, but they always go out in the mornings, afternoons, and early evenings. A typical day, for example, might include departures at the following times: 8:30 A.M., 9:30 A.M., 12:15 P.M., 1:15 P.M., 1:45 P.M., 5:00 P.M., 5:30 P.M., and 6:00 P.M. Despite

the large number of excursions the Dolphin Fleet offers, reservations are almost always a must. The early-
evening cruises can prove particularly delightful, but
remember to bring along something warm to wear.

The Center for Coastal Studies was founded in 1976
and has operated since as an independent scientific
field station. The center's work is nationally recog-
nized, and it cooperates and shares information with
such organizations as the College of the Atlantic, Woods
Hole Oceanographic Institution, National Weather
Service, University of Rhode Island, and Cape Cod
Museum of Natural History. The center's activities
include an active and important Cetacean Research
Program, a Coastal Biology Department, and a Physical Oceanography Program.

One of the center's coups has been Provincetown's
highly successful Trash Fish Banquet, where one can
sample such fare as goosefish à l'orange. The banquet
is the direct result of the center's Underutilized Fish
Project, which has focused the attention of the local
fishery on trash fish, perfectly good fish that used to
be thrown away. Similar programs have sprung up
all over the country.

Rates: Adults $13; $11 senior citizens and children under 6.

Driving Instructions: The Dolphin Fleet boats depart from
the main dock, smack in the middle of Provincetown
(I recommend walking, rather than driving, there).

Asheton House
3 Cook Street
Provincetown, MA 02657
Telephone: (617) 487-9966

A comfortable bed and breakfast, Asheton House has
eight rooms, some of them with water views and all

of them sprinkled liberally with antiques. The accommodations here also include a three-room apartment complete with a kitchen and washer/dryer. Most of the guest rooms share baths, as well as a central "breakfast" area, where guests can fetch themselves coffee, tea, or juice. The accommodations are in two nineteenth-century houses that are a short walk from the Provincetown wharf.

Rates: inexpensive to moderate; NCC

Bed & Breakfast Cape Cod
PO Box 341
West Hyannisport, MA 02672
Telephone: (617) 755-2772

Houseguests Cape Cod
PO Box 8-AR
Dennis, MA 02638
Telephone: (617) 398-0787

Cape Cod has two resident B&B reservation services, which connect guests and host homes, in many cases with admirable efficiency. The accommodations represented by each of these reservation services range from inexpensive lodgings in private homes to expensive suites in fancy inns. Reservation services often come up with unique lodging opportunities; advance reservations are a must.

Holiday Inn
Route 6A
Provincetown, MA 02657
Telephone: (617) 487-1711
Open March through November.

The Provincetown Holiday Inn has 139 rooms, all of them with color cable television and telephone. The facilities here include a pool with poolside service, restaurant, and bar with live entertainment. There is a beach across the street.

Rates: moderate to expensive (lower after Labor Day); AE,CB,DC,MC,V

MONTAUK, NEW YORK

Situated at the extreme eastern end of the south fork of Long Island, the Montauk area offers numerous natural attractions. If you get up too late to catch the whale-watching boat you can console yourself by walking for miles on unspoiled stretches of Atlantic beaches, backed up by dunes thick with beach grass, holly, and black and white oak. The town of Montauk is sandwiched between two state parks—Hither Hills State Park and Montauk State Park—whose habitats range from dunes to moors to forests to high, rocky bluffs fronting the ocean. Nearby natural areas include Morton National Wildlife Refuge in Sag Harbor, Merrill Lake in East Hampton, Sagg Swamp in Bridgehampton, Mashomack Preserve on Shelter Island, and Orient Point Beach State Park, at the extreme tip of Long Island's north fork (all these areas are within an hour's drive of the town of Montauk).

For those interested in other than natural distractions, the Montauk area has all the trappings of a fashionable resort—countless restaurants and shops, numerous museums and historic houses, golf courses, discotheques, and theaters. Although Don Quixote never slept there, the town of East Hampton has the highest concentration of windmills in the United States.

Okeanos Ocean Research Foundation
Box 776
Hampton Bays, NY 11946
Telephone: (516) 728-4522

A nonprofit, educationally oriented organization, Okeanos Ocean Research Foundation conducts whale-watching excursions from May through September. During May and June the weekday trips include large groups of schoolchildren; the weekend trips are geared for adults and families. If you do not object to the shrieks and silences of a hundred teenagers seeing a whale in the wild for the first time, you can reserve a place on the weekday cruises during May and June. July through September excursions geared to adults and families leave every morning of the week.

The excursions are on board a 1986, 90-foot research vessel that leaves the Montauk dock at 10 A.M. and returns, approximately, at 2:30 P.M. Naturalists accompany every journey, lecturing and doing research at the same time. The prime species seen and discussed is the finback whale, the second largest creature ever to have lived. The foundation's researchers are compiling data on the finback whales in the area, of which at least two hundred seem to be resident all year. Part of the research includes photographic studies of the finback's individually distinctive chevron patterns; another line of study involves rangefinder studies of the whales (correlating the exact distance of a whale with the elapsed time between the appearance of its spout and its dorsal fin yields data about size and behavior). Okeanos researchers have also learned to distinguish the sex of finback whales based on bumps on the male's nostrils.

The *Finback II* has a complete galley that serves breakfast, lunch, and snacks; hot and cold beverages, including beer, are available. Passengers on the Okeanos excursions see whales about 95 percent of the time, and although the average number of whales, the vast majority of them finbacks, sighted per excursion is six, the record for 1985 was forty. Minke whales are also sighted with regularity, and very occasionally a humpback bursts into view.

Rates: $25 per adult; $15 for children under 13.

Driving Instructions: Take Montauk Highway, 27A, into the Montauk Business District and turn left at the traffic circle with the flagpole on to Flamingo Avenue; proceed to the Montauk Fishing Fleet, which is on the right, and look for Viking Dock, on the left.

Gurney's Inn, Resort & Spa
Old Montauk Highway
Montauk, NY 11946
Telephone: (516) 668-2345
Open all year.

Situated immediately on the ocean, Gurney's is a full-service inn with 125 rooms. The facilities include more than 300 yards of beach, several spas with whirlpool baths, an indoor pool, tennis courts, a restaurant, bar, beauty shop, airport and railroad pickup, a resident physician, and, well, you name it. Several rooms have balconies, some have refrigerators, and all have cable television and telephone.

Rates: expensive; MAP; AE,DC,MC,V

Hedges House
74 James Lane, PO Box 1553
East Hampton, NY 11937
Telephone: (516) 324-7100
Open April through January.

Listed in the National Register of Historic Places, Hedges House is a lovely country inn that happens to contain an unusually fine restaurant. Lovingly restored and maintained, the inn has fourteen bed-rooms, all of them furnished with antiques. The public rooms are also furnished with antiques, and guests here can walk either to the beach or the village. Rates include breakfast.

Rates: moderate to expensive; AE,CB,DC,MC,VC

The Bowditch House
166 North Ferry Road
Shelter Island, NY 11965
Telephone: (516) 749-0075 or 887-1898
Open Memorial Day through mid-October.

Built in 1854, The Bowditch House is a bed and breakfast situated about an hour from the Montauk area. Furnished with antiques, the house is perhaps ten minutes from the Nature Conservancy's marvel-ous Mashomack Preserve. The preserve embraces roughly a third of Shelter Island, a beautiful and quiet spot between Long Island's north and south forks. The rates include a hearty breakfast.

Rates: moderate; NCC

Hampton Bed and Breakfast
PO Box 378
East Moriches, NY 11940
Telephone: (516) 878-8197

Alternate Lodging, Inc.
Box 1782
East Hampton, NY 11937
Telephone: (516) 324-9449

B&B reservation services match guests and hosts, and offer a wide range of lodging possibilities, from simple and inexpensive to elaborate and pricey.

TADOUSSAC, QUEBEC

A town of fewer than a thousand people, Tadoussac is situated immediately at the confluence of the Saguenay and St. Lawrence rivers, about 150 miles northeast of Quebec City. The area is known for its population of whales, in particular for its populations of belugas and blues. Belugas breed and raise their young in the mouth and estuary of the Saguenay River, which is not only famous for its white whales but also for its fjord. Although it does not extend all the way to the St. Lawrence, the Saguenay "fjord" has sheer cliffs that average 800 and rise as high as 1500 feet right out of the water. Parc Saguenay, which extends upriver, on both sides, for 65 miles is wild and ruggedly beautiful, almost surreally so during foliage season. Park rangers have to trap problem bears now and then, and peregrine falcons ply the air currents swirling in the canyon. The way to see the Saguenay is by boat, and numerous charters in town are available, including one from Hôtel Tadoussac, below.

Société Linnéenne Saint-Laurent
1675 Ave du Parc
St. Foy, Québec GW1 4F3
CANADA
Telephone: (418) 235-4343 or 653-8186

Based in Quebec City, Société Linnéenne Saint-Laurent is a nonprofit organization devoted to the conservation and explanation of Quebec's natural heritage, which includes a considerable number of whales. From late June through October, the society operates a 74-foot whale-watching boat that goes out three times a day looking for whales—finbacks, minkes, belugas, and blues. Accompanied by naturalists, the cruises leave from the dock in Tadoussac and proceed down the St. Lawrence River. The boat has complete facilities, including a simple kitchen and bar.

Minke and finback whales are always sighted, belugas frequently appear, and now and then a blue, pilot, or humpback shows up.

Rates: $30 per person; children under 12 free.

Driving Instructions: The cruises leave from the Tadoussac town dock.

Mingan Island Cetacean Study, Inc.
Box 518
Meriden, CT 06450

or
Station de Recherche des Îles Mingan
C.P. 159
Sept-Îles, Québec G4r 4K3
CANADA

An intrepid research organization, Mingan Island Cetacean Study offers several different types of whale-watching cruises, the shortest of them lasting for a week. The most luxurious journeys are aboard a 62-foot motor yacht, which sports such niceties as private cabins and a salon, and other trips are on a 40-foot sloop, on which no more than six passengers depart. Other programs include a ten-day stay in the tiny coastal village of Longue Pointe de Mingan. From there naturalists lead you out in 20-foot inflatable boats powered by 35-horsepower engines and show you such stuff as 100-foot whales.

Rates: $595 to $1750 (Canadian), depending on tour or cruise.

Hôtel Tadoussac
165 Bord de l'Eau
Tadoussac, Québec GO8 2A0
CANADA
Telephone: (418) 235-4421 or 1-800-361-1155

The Hôtel Tadoussac utterly dominates the town of Tadoussac, which seems much too small and quaint for such an enormous structure. The grounds include extensive gardens running down to the river and a nine-hole golf course. The hotel has two boats, one of them a multimasted tall ship, that cruise up the fjord and down the river, looking for whales and stunning vistas and fun. The hotel has 150 rooms, sixty of them overlooking the Saguenay, and a first-rate restaurant. Rates include breakfast and dinner, and whale-watching weekend packages are available.

Rates: expensive; AE,MC,V

Hôtel George
135 Bateau Passeur
Tadoussac, Québec GO8 2A0
CANADA
Telephone: (418) 235-4393

A nineteen-room motel-style structure, the Hôtel George, and all its rooms, overlook the Saguenay River. The rooms have television but no telephones, and the facilities include a restaurant.

Rates: moderate; AE,MC,V

METEOR SHOWERS

If during the early-morning hours of any August 12 you gaze up at the constellation Perseus, you will see, given clear skies, sixty shooting stars in an hour. And if during the hour, say after each brilliant flash in the sky, you glance from Perseus to the constellation Aquarius, you might well see an additional ten to twenty shooting stars. If in the wee hours of any clear December 14 you stare at the constellation Gemini, you will probably see a shooting star every seventy seconds or so; and if you can't get to sleep on a clear October 22, you might as well get out of bed and stare up at the constellation Orion: you will see only at best twenty shooting stars an hour, but who's counting? Just before dawn one October 22, I had the honor of watching a shooting star light up, for a fraction of a second, a gaggle of low-flying, riotously barking snow geese, whose whirring wings I swore blew out the star.

Although as far as I'm concerned, a shooting star by any other name is still a shooting star, shooting stars are, technically, meteors—small fragments of rock or iron that move through interplanetary space in long elliptical orbits around the sun until they collide with our atmosphere and burst into flame. They form when comets, which also travel in long elliptical orbits, partially vaporize and start to shed their surface. Conglomerate masses of ice and rock and iron, comets partially disintegrate each time their orbit swings in a tight arc around the sun, whose intense heat and radiation "sublimes" them—that is, turns their outer layers of ice instantaneously to vapor, which solar winds blow deep into space, forming the comet's tail. Meanwhile, fragments of the comet dislodge and continue journeying along the comet's orbit, gradually spreading out over time until a huge ellipse in interplanetary space fills up with fragments of rock and iron and dust.

Although we don't really know for sure how many times a comet can orbit the sun before falling apart completely, it seems they lose about one percent of their mass each time they have a solar rendezvous—a close encounter of the hottest kind—so we assume they complete about a hundred orbits. In any case, the fate of a comet is to crumble into smaller fragments. As long as these fragments remain in their interplanetary orbit, we call them meteoroids. When they collide with the earth's atmosphere and friction causes them to incandesce, they become, officially, meteors—or what we call in the Bronx shooting stars. They range in size from thousandths of an inch to several yards in diameter, and billions of them, the vast majority far too small to be seen with the naked eye, collide with our atmosphere every day. The dust on the moon is meteoric dust, and the better part of its craters represent past collisions with meteors. They make more craters on places like Mercury and the Moon than on Earth because Earth's atmosphere usually incinerates them before they reach the surface or erodes them after they land.

Those huge ellipses of meteoroids orbiting the sun out there in interplanetary space come from comets both living and dead. Although we can link some of the major annual meteoroid streams to the orbit of specific comets, other streams represent at best the ghost of comets past. We associate the Orionids (October 22), for example, with Halley's Comet, but we have no idea from where the Geminids (December 14) came, or the Quadrantids (January 3), or both the Aquarids (May 4 and July 29). To date, astronomers have plotted the orbits of well over five hundred comets, which in all probability came from a deep-freeze zone well beyond the orbit of Pluto. There, billions of comets exist and probably stretch in a cloud (Oort's Cloud) all the way to the nearest star, Alpha Centauri.

Shooting stars occur with far more regularity than most people realize. Long-term studies of meteor activity suggest that meteors large enough to be visible to the naked eye collide with the atmosphere at the rate of approximately twelve per hour. Conscientious shooting star watchers, however, plan their observation times to coincide with known meteoroid swarms, or streams, which collide with the earth's atmosphere at specific times and result in meteor showers, an increased rate of shooting stars. Some shooting star fans, myself among them, actually plan vacations and business trips around the possibility of a good meteor shower.

The trick is not to get a stiff neck, and to set aside all earthly cares, and to give yourself over to heavenly happenings. I recommend a reclining beach or lawn chair, or, failing one of those, a sand dune configured in the appropriate direction, or a camping mattress, or a log, or a friend. Resign yourself to watching the sky for an hour, and with a little luck you will have an unforgettable experience. An engrossing solitary activity, watching a meteor shower in the company of others constitutes a singular joy, for each time a meteor streaks across the sky so do the excited voices of your companions: "Jaseethatone!"

Although I can summon no scientific data to prove it, I submit that staring up at the stars for extended periods intensifies one's sense of hearing. While watching shooting stars I've heard, far more clearly and intensely than usual, honking geese, wailing loons, the gentle susurrus of halyards rubbing the mast of a small sloop, and an insomniac mockingbird imitating a Caterpillar (of the industrial, earth-moving variety) going in reverse.

The best time to look for shooting stars is the early morning, during the hour or two immediately preceding the twilight of dawn. Similarly, you will have the worst luck during the couple of hours immediately after sunset. The reason for this has to do with your position on the surface of the earth, which spins around its axis once a day and around the sun once a year. Early in the morning, the rotating earth is positioned such that its atmosphere points toward and plows into the meteor stream with which it happens to be intersecting. In the evening, on the other hand, the meteor stream sort of catches up with, you might say backswipes, the atmosphere rather than colliding with it head-on. In the morning you are facing the direction of the earth's motion; in the evening you are, as it were, on the lee side.

Although people interested in observing meteor showers should familiarize themselves with the dates of the major meteor streams listed below, one should bear in mind that 80 percent of all meteors do not belong to a predictable stream. Sporadic meteors, which can occur at any time, appear at maximum rates during June, July, and August; and at minimum rates during February, March, and April. I've seen half a dozen shooting stars on nights when I didn't expect to see any, even though I planned to look for them. The major streams themselves occur over varying ranges of time, from three or four days to as many weeks, so don't give up on a potentially first-rate shooting star outing because you missed the day of peak meteoroid activity.

Last night, having missed the peak of the Perseid shower for two days on either side of it because of intense cloud cover, I stared up at the constellation Perseus for about twenty minutes and saw zero shooting stars. Then I saw a meteor flash out of Cassiopeia, and before I recovered my composure a fireball burst out of Pegasus and blazed across the zenith, making a faint but audible sound that resembled a piece of fabric ripping. It was ten times the brightness of Venus, the only planet capable of casting a shadow, and it left behind a vaporous trail, called a persistent train, that stretched a quarter way across the sky and hung for a full two minutes like a contrail in front of Jupiter. On a night I figured would be no big deal in terms of the Perseid meteor shower, I saw my first fireball.

As rare as unpredictable, fireballs do not usually occur during meteor showers, and it seems that these spectacular phenomena differ from meteors in their origin. Astronomers suspect that fireballs originate in the asteroid belt, where countless millions of asteroids orbit the sun between Mars and Jupiter, rather than from vaporizing comets. Most of the asteroids have nearly circular orbits, but some have elliptical ones. It seems likely that the powerful gravitational field of Jupiter now and then perturbs, or nudges, an asteroid into a path sufficiently elliptical to intersect with the earth's orbit. If you happen to see a fireball, you will immediately recognize it, and you will never forget the sight of it.

OBSERVING THE MAJOR METEOR SHOWERS

With the exception of the Quadrantids, which are named after a star, the most predictable and prolific meteor showers take their name from the constellation out of which they seem to emerge. The stars that form the constellations are, of course, far more distant than the meteors that seem to be zipping around among them—which explains why something the size of a golf ball 60 miles above the earth looks as large as a huge star hundreds of millions of miles away. In any case, the major meteor showers seem to come from a constellation. One should not, however, stare doggedly at the constellation in question, for it represents more a basic location in the sky than anything else. When looking for meteors, one should scan the sky constantly but not frantically, bearing in mind that the meteors will probably appear in the vicinity of the constellation in question.

Most of the meteors you see you will probably see out of the corner of your eye. I suspect that the more relaxedly you can scan the sky the more likely you will be to spot a meteor. Researchers engaged in counting meteors often start hallucinating shooting stars after gazing up at the heavens for more than an hour or two, so bear in mind that stargazing can get to you if you take it too seriously. Relax, give your eyes time to adjust to the dark, and wait for the meteors to happen.

Describing what the constellations look like goes beyond the scope of this book, but a general idea of where to look in the sky should suffice. To estimate what 10 degrees over the horizon represents, extend your arm forward and make a fist: your fist at arm's length spans about 10 degrees of sky, three fists span about 30 degrees, and so on. The zenith, the point in the sky directly above you, represents 90 degrees above the horizon.

The locations given below apply if you happen to be at latitude 40 degrees north, which most field guides to the stars use as a reference point. If you are south of latitude 40 degrees north, the constellations will be somewhat lower in the sky; if you are north of latitude 40 degrees, the constellations will be somewhat higher. Latitude 40 degrees north divides the lower forty-eight United States almost equally in half, passing through such cities as Philadelphia, Boulder, Colorado, and Reno, Nevada; latitude 30 degrees north runs through Jacksonville, Florida, and Houston; latitude 50 degrees north runs through Winnipeg, Manitoba, and Vancouver, British Columbia.

QUADRANTIDS

The Quadrantids appear in the constellation Boötes; the stream lasts from January 1 through January 4, and peaks on January 3. At peak, the shower produces approximately forty-five visible meteors per hour. Look for the constellation Boötes in the northeast, very low over the horizon, perhaps 10 degrees.

ETA AQUARIDS

The Eta Aquarids appear in the constellation Aquarius; the stream lasts from April 21 to May 12, and peaks on May 4. At peak, the shower produces approximately twenty visible meteors per hour. Look for the constellation Aquarius in the east southeast, about 30 degrees above the horizon.

DELTA AQUARIDS

The Delta Aquarids appear in the constellation Aquarius; the stream lasts from July 21 to August 15, and peaks on July 29. At peak, the shower produces approximately fifteen visible meteors per hour. Look for the constellation Aquarius in the south, about 40 degrees above the horizon.

PERSEIDS

The Perseids appear in the constellation Perseus; the stream lasts from July 25 to August 17, and peaks on August 12. At peak, the shower produces approximately sixty visible meteors per hour. Look for the constellation Perseus in the northeast, about 30 degrees above the horizon.

ORIONIDS

The Orionids appear in the constellation Orion; the stream lasts from October 18 to October 26, and peaks on October 22. At peak, the shower produces approximately twenty visible meteors per hour. Look for the constellation Orion in the southeast about 45 degrees above the horizon.

LEONIDS

The Leonids appear in the constellation Leo; the stream lasts from November 14 to November 20, and peaks on November 17. At peak, the shower produces ap-

transform a deer into little more than a memory, a careless scattering of bones on blood-soaked snow, black ravens pecking at the red.

The wolf is a formidable predator, an extremely intelligent, highly socialized animal capable of acting in concert with its colleagues, capable, if you will, of more than itself. Very few predators routinely feed on game ten times their weight, for the simple reason that attacking something that much bigger than oneself involves considerable risk. Tough as they are, 2-pound peregrine falcons do not take on 20-pound swans, nor for that matter do 1000-pound polar bears mess with 5-ton killer whales. A 900-pound moose in reasonable condition could easily kill a 90-pound wolf, but ten 90-pound wolves can make short work indeed of a 900-pound moose, should they decide to kill it. Wolves decide what to kill very carefully, so carefully, in fact, that they tend to increase the productivity and health of the prey populations they feed on, herds of moose or caribou, for example.

Wolves tend not to kill animals that stand their ground, that confront them rather than flee. They also, for obvious reasons, tend not to kill animals that outrun them, as most of their prey species frequently do. Wolves often give up a chase immediately after having begun it, they seldom pursue something for more than a couple of hundred yards, and for reasons no one seems able to explain they sometimes abandon a chase even before it begins, in some cases even if their quarry has no chance whatever of escaping. Wolves tend to kill primarily the old and the young, the animals in less than prime condition—the weak, the lame, the sick. They function as a natural check and balance, pruning out of the prey population the less-than-fit individuals.

Wolves decide what to kill by communicating among themselves and with their prey, who, if strong enough and determined, can dissuade them from attacking. The crucial moment in a particular hunt occurs when the wolves encounter their quarry, when the pursued notices the pursuers—when a pack of wolves and a potential victim make eye contact. Wolves have penetrating stares. Their eyes seem to look right through you, as though their vision extended beyond your retina into some dark corner of your brain, or into your heart, one of their favorite organs. Their eyes have about them the knowingness of a dog's, and they have an enormously expressive face, which they use extensively to communicate among themselves as well, one suspects, as with their prey. One wonders what precisely their eyes communicate when they engage in a staring contest with a prey species. One wonders less how chilling an experience it must be to return the stares of ten wild wolves, their yellow eyes seemingly aglow in the semidarkness, vapor streaming from their noses, their lips half-curled in smiles of murderous glee, or is it fear, or wonder? Researchers have observed a pack of wolves engaged in a two-minute staring contest with a deer 30 yards away, and watched as the wolves silently withdrew, having chosen not to kill for reasons only they could have explained.

Apparently, the encounter between a wolf pack and its prey determines whether or not the wolves will rush the animal, nonchalantly forget about the whole business, or flee in terror from a formidable enemy. One researcher watched an encounter between a pack of wolves and a large moose perhaps 70 yards distant. Not a creature was stirring. Suddenly the moose charged the wolves, which fled by the time it covered half the ground between them. Although we can only imagine what sort of information the mutually staring eyes of two different species exchange, we know that eye contact among wolves themselves transmits such stuff as social order, on which the survival of the pack depends. If an alpha wolf, one of the pack's two leaders, stares intently at a low-ranking individual, in all probability one of his or her offspring, the subordinate animal cringes, its tail between its legs. Subordinate wolves never stare at the alpha animals.

Wolves live and hunt in packs, which range in size from two to thirty animals, averaging approximately ten. The packs exhibit extremely structured hierarchies, inviolable pecking orders presided over, almost always, by the alpha male and the alpha female, the breeding pair. Only one pair in a wolf pack breeds. The rest of the pack consists of second-year wolves, beta animals still sexually immature, and pups or yearlings. The entire pack cares for the young, which nip at their muzzles until they regurgitate some food. In many instances babysitting has been observed, whereby a beta animal will give the alpha female a break from the rigors of raising the pups so she can go out and join the hunt.

During the denning season—late spring, summer, and early fall—the pack stays close to the den. As soon as the newborn achieve sufficient maturity to travel, the pack moves on and begins expanding, or shifting, their territory, which they mark with their urine. When another wolf infringes on their territory, the pack kills, then eats it. When the beta animals in a pack achieve sexual maturity, rivalries develop and the pack splits up. The perennial lone wolf is usually an older animal ostracized by the pack but allowed to follow, at a respectable distance, and feed on the remains of their kills. Though idealized, this description of a wolf pack represents more the rule than the exception.

Among themselves, wolves communicate with far more than their eyes. Sound, touch, and smell all play important roles. The position of a wolf's tail, for example, conveys not only visual but also olfactory information. When an alpha wolf confronts a subordinate animal, the latter averts its eyes, pulls its tail between its legs, droops its ears, and, basically, cowers in fear. The visual elements of this dominance/submission ritual among wolves say it all, but the ceremony goes further and involves the sense of smell. Just as they reserve for themselves the right to stare intently at other members of the pack, so do the alpha wolves have the unique prerogative of unabashedly displaying their anus for inspection. As the submissive wolf cowers with its tail between its legs, the dominant one approaches with its tail raised to the perpendicular. Then they meet front to back and determine, as though the visual evidence didn't suffice, who rules and who follows.

When the alpha wolves mate the entire pack gathers around them excitedly, as though to wish them well and to celebrate the joyous camaraderie of wolfhood. Perhaps to reinforce the strength of the bond between them, copulating wolves remain attached by their genitals for as long as half an hour, during which entire time the male ejaculates continually, first with clear semen, then with cloudy, finally with clear again. We don't know the specific reason, if there is one, for such an extended copulatory tie and the attendant display of good cheer by the other members of the pack, but some research suggests that wolves, if mortality doesn't interfere, mate for life. To care for their helpless young and to take large game, wolves need strong bonds, powerful emotional attachments, to keep them together and acting as one. United they stand.

The enthusiastic rituals that occur when they sense their prey and when their leaders mate occur as well when the pack gets together for a howling session. When one wolf starts howling the others join in, and pack members that might have wandered off from the main group come dashing over hurriedly, their tail wagging, to join the chorus. They point their nose up at the zenith, draw in their lips, and broadcast to the northern sky a sound no one can ever forget— an incredibly sad, long, low, elegiac moan that makes the hairs on the back of your neck stand up. It is a sound that evokes both terror and pity, above all awe—the penultimate sound of the wilderness. Howling sessions last for a relatively short time, from about half a minute to a minute and a half. Although the wolves can howl anytime they please, they tend to do so most regularly at dusk, when they assemble for the hunt.

The exact purpose of the howling session remains unknown, but several possibilities suggest themselves. Surely a group howl reinforces the solidarity of the pack, for it not only gathers them in the same place but also unites them in a single purpose. The possibility exists that wolves might have individually distinctive howls, which would enable them to identify each other even at a considerable distance, for the howl of a wolf can carry 5 miles on a windless night. A howling session could also serve as something of a territorial imperative, a warning to other wolf packs within earshot, and the earshot of a wolf, no doubt, far exceeds that of a human. As educated estimates of average wolf pack territories come in at about 100 square miles, it seems reasonable to conclude that wolves can hear each other at a distance of 20 miles.

More people hear than see wolves, for they respond enthusiastically not only to recordings of wolf howls but also to human imitations of these howls. Though they obviously love howling back at the humans, wolves prefer to stay out of sight of them, and for good reason. Humans habitually kill wolves, as they have throughout most of history, and the animals that remain remain in remote places. Very few wolves prevail in the contiguous United States. Significant populations survive in northern Minnesota and northern Michigan, but that's about it for the lower forty-eight states—except for the elusive red wolves of southern Texas and Louisiana, which are probably wolf/coyote hybrids.

Most people misunderstand wolves, for the simple reason that they symbolize in our culture the Devil himself, evil incarnate. It seems to me that people fear wolves in direct proportion to how little they know about them. Wolves are terrified of people, so much so that researchers have entered their dens and stolen a pup while its parents cowered and whimpered a short distance away. There is no reason to fear a wolf or, for that matter, a large pack of them: attacks on humans have occurred so infrequently as to be statistically insignificant. Although someone from the archives might produce dusty data suggesting otherwise, no one ever gets hurt by wolves. Ironically, many people who fear wolves do not have any fear of bears, which do represent a major danger.

The best way to get an idea of how little danger wolves represent is to try to see them in their natural habitat, where they manage to remain constantly out of sight. They are extremely difficult to observe, and naturalists studying them rely heavily on small aircraft. They have, however, an enormous presence in the areas where they still survive, where you might just see or hear them.

DESTINATIONS AND ACCOMMODATIONS

ALGONQUIN PROVINCIAL PARK, ONTARIO

Algonquin Provincial Park
Ministry of Natural Resources
Box 219
Whitney, Ontario K0J 2M0
CANADA
Telephone: (705) 633-5572

A 3½-hour drive north of Toronto, Algonquin Provincial Park is a 3000-square-mile wilderness riddled with lakes and streams, and wolves and loons. The park has 1500 miles of marked canoe routes, and visitors can pick up an excellent map detailing these as well as the park's twenty-nine canoe-access points and its two backcountry trailheads. The western part of the park is wooded primarily with hardwoods— sugar maples, oaks, and yellow birches—and the drier, eastern sections evidence more softwoods, white and red pine for the most part. The park has probably the highest concentration of wolves on the continent, and loons are everywhere.

The park has a unique program: in August, on Thursdays, park rangers lead as many as 300 cars, circa 1200 people, on public wolf howls. These public wolf howls take place only if the park rangers manage to locate a wolf pack on Tuesday or Wednesday, and if they do posters go up on Thursday morning announcing the event. People from hundreds of miles away call the park Thursday mornings to inquire as to whether or not a public wolf howl is planned; and it is not uncommon for someone to drive 6½ hours to attend one of these events.

Everybody meets at the park amphitheater (kilometer 35.4 on Highway 60, which runs through the park), where naturalists deliver a talk on wolves and instruct everyone in the logistics of the evening. Amazingly enough, 300 or more cars slink down the highway to a location rangers suspect the wolves are using as a rendezvous point, and then upwards of 1200 people get out of their cars and stand there in utter silence. Then a park ranger starts howling, and 60 percent of the time wolves respond, as the hair on the back of 1200 necks stands up. To get some idea of the almost mystical power of such an event, try to imagine 1200 people, including many children, standing in absolute silence along the edge of a highway, waiting to hear, simply, the penultimate sound of the wilderness.

In August wolf pups are beginning to travel with the pack, and perhaps as a result of their burgeoning freedom from the area immediately around the den, they cannot resist acting wolflike and howling in response to the calls of their comrades or a park ranger. Park rangers locate the pack's rendezvous sites by driving around and howling until they get a response, and although some rendezvous sites, which replace the den as a gathering area, are used only for a day or two others are used for months, with the result that the wolves in the park are found more easily than one might imagine. The scientific technique of howling in order to locate wolves, which howl in response, was developed in Algonquin Park.

Algonquin Provincial Park has three lodges within its borders:

Arowhon Pines
Algonquin Park
Huntsville, Ontario POA 1KO
CANADA
Telephone: (705) 633-5661/2
Open May 14 to October 12.

A central lodge with satellite cabins, Arowhon Pines has forty-seven rooms and three suites, some with fireplaces. The central building, a six-sided structure built of white pine, has a dining room with a huge stone fireplace. Five miles down a dirt road, the lodge is situated immediately on Little Joe Lake, where loons call at night. Recreational equipment includes canoes, small sailboats, and windsurfers. No alcohol served; BYOB. Rates include breakfast and dinner.

Rates: expensive; NCC

Bartlett Lodge
Cache Lake
Algonquin Park
Ontario POA 1KO
CANADA
Telephone: (705) 633-5543
Open May 17 to second Monday in October.

Bartlett Lodge consists of twelve cabins, some frame and some log, along the shore of Cache Lake, and a 1908 lodge building with a dining room with fireplace. Some housekeeping units are available, and recreational equipment includes canoes and small boats with motors. The lodge is accessible only by boat. In 1986 the lake had twelve resident loons. No alcohol served; BYOB. Some rates include breakfast and dinner.

Rates: moderate; NCC

Killarney Lodge
Algonquin Park
Ontario POA 1KO
CANADA
Telephone: (705) 633-5551
Open May 9 to October 19.

At once convenient to the highway and remote, Killarney Lodge consists of twenty-seven cabins overlooking Lake of Two Rivers and a main lodge with a dining room featuring a large stone hearth. The cabins, which can accommodate from two to four, have sleeping and sitting areas. Canoes come with the cabins, as do the calls of loons. No alcohol served; BYOB. Rates include three meals.

Rates: expensive; MC,V

OTHER PLACES TO OBSERVE WOLVES

Anahuac National Wildlife *(red wolf)*
  Refuge
Box 278
Anahuac, TX 77514

Denali National Park and *(see "Bears")*
  Preserve
PO Box 9
McKinley Park, AK 99755

Elk Island National Park
Site 4, R.R. 1
Fort Saskatchewan, Alberta T8L 2N7
CANADA

Glacier Bay National Park and   *(see "Glaciers")*
  Preserve
PO Box 1089
Juneau, AK 99826

Glacier National Park   *(see "Bears")*
West Glacier, MT 59936

Isle Royal National Park
87 North Ripley Street
Houghton, MI 49931

Katmai National Park
Box 7
King Salmon, AK 99613

North Cascades National Park
800 State Street
Sedro Woolley, WA 98284

Superior National Forest   *(see "Loons")*
Box 338
Duluth, MN 55801

Voyageurs National Park
PO Box 50
International Falls, MN 56649

Wood Buffalo National Park   *(see "Bison")*
Box 750
Fort Smith, N.W.T. XOE OPO
CANADA

LOONS

> The silence, after a time, is torn apart by a
> congress of loons: ten loons, racing in
> circles on the surface of the water,
> screaming, splashing, squeaking like dogs,
> taxiing on long half-flying runs. For a full
> ten minutes they keep it up—a ritual
> insanity, a rampant dance of madness, a
> convincing demonstration that everyone of
> them is as crazy as a loon.
>
> —JOHN McPHEE, *The Survival of the Bark
>   Canoe*

It is a truth universally acknowledged, as it has been
since time out of mind, that loons are crazed.

To watch one take to the air after an hysterical dash
across the water, its enormous feet and rapidly beating
wings slapping the surface clumsily as the bird screams
bloody murder, makes one laugh out loud at the slap-
stick possibilities of nature. Sometimes, cruising in at
about 60 miles per hour, they crash when landing,
and again one laughs. On land they achieve an awk-
wardness perhaps unique in the natural world—they
cannot walk upright, and with enormous difficulty

push themselves forward with their chest on the ground. A flock of some 150 migrating loons, mistaking it in the rain for a shiny black river, landed on a black top highway in northern Minnesota. Incapable of attaining flight without at least a hundred yards of water to run on, the loons staggered about helplessly on the highway until some wildlife people showed up with trucks and chauffeured them to a lake large enough to accommodate their lunatic sprints into the air.

Their ruby-red eyes seem as though bloodshot with madness, frenetically alert, and their midnight riffs of maniacal laughter seem the sounds of the truly possessed. In addition to their ghoulish-sounding laugh, loons hold forth as well with a yodel, a tremolo, a coo, and an otherworldly wail that primitive peoples mistook for a disembodied spirit howling for salvation from the abyss. I once watched the hair of a sleeping dog stand on end at the call of a loon. Lazy beyond description, the tired old mutt never awoke, but the hair of her ruff stood up and she whimpered in her sleep, like an overtired infant. Loons can sound like laughing devils, haunted wolves, tender lovers, or disembodied spirits with the hiccups.

You don't even have to see a loon to appreciate one. Indeed, if I had to choose, I would rather hear than see them, preferably a whole chorus of them, echoing across the lambent darkness of a northern lake lit only by stars. Perhaps because they make such strange music, loons exhibit a marked curiosity toward the strange music of others, however extravagantly unnatural. Once, on a totally overcast day in the Pacific Northwest, my wife and I went for an unambitious walk that included a half-mile stretch along the shore of Lake Quinault, on which we spotted a loon, 50, maybe

60 yards away. Having just heard an anecdote from a friend who inadvertently attracted five loons by playing a guitar, we decided to whistle a few bars of one of Mozart's Four Horn Concerti, K. 446, in an attempt to interest the loon. Sure enough, the bird came closer as we whistled, obviously intrigued by our performance, which mercifully fell on no human ears but our own.

The bird approached cautiously, tacking to the left, poking its head underwater, and then tacking to the right, coming finally within 20 feet of where we stood. Mozart was probably turning over in his grave. The loon suddenly dove, and we never saw it again. A man to whom I told this tale one-upped me: his teenage son, armed with a huge portable tape player, positioned himself on the deck of a lakeside cottage and broadcast into the night, at high volume, a Pink Floyd recording, "The Dark Side of the Moon." When the man lost his patience and burst on to the deck to demand that his son lower the volume, "at least half a dozen common loons" flushed from right beyond the deck and "took off like banshees" into the dark.

Loons belong to the order Gaviformes, which embraces but one family consisting of only four species. All four reside in North America, and as a group they represent the oldest, most primitive order of birds, with an ancestry going back some 140 million years. The thunder lizards listened to their ancestors' wailing, and every serious field guide or ornithological listing of the class Aves begins with loons (it's enough to make a birdwatcher paranoid). The preceding and following remarks pertain primarily to the common loon, which breeds extensively in Canada and Alaska and as far south as the northern tier of states. The other three species of loon—arctic, red-throated, and yellow-billed—live in the far north, above the tree line, and comparatively little is known about them. I describe all four below.

Referred to as "divers" in the Old World, loons have been caught in fishing lines 200 feet underwater. Even those skeptical scientists who dismiss such a possibility, writing it off as yet another fisherman's exaggeration, concede that the birds routinely dive to depths of a hundred feet. For diving, loons are well-adapted— their incredibly sleek, torpedo shape; their enormous feet, set so far back they can't walk on land; their specialized metabolisms; and their dense, heavy body, which inhibits their takeoffs—all contribute to an uncanny ability to dive. Most birds, by way of contrast, have hollow bones, an adaptation that facilitates flight, whereas loons have solid bones, which enable them to sink more readily. They go down like rocks propelled by flippers.

The loon's metabolic rate slows down when it submerges. Its tissues contain high levels of myoglobin, a protein that binds to and stores oxygen in the muscles, which can consequently function for protracted periods without replenishment. Scientists first isolated the myoglobin molecule in the tissues of a sperm whale, a creature that can dive to depths of two miles and stay there for as many hours. Like sperm whales, loons have brown or dark maroon, rather than pink, muscles and tissues because of high myoglobin concentrations. Their slender wings fold back tightly against their body when they dive, and their red eyes perceive contrasts at depths where everything is blue.

Of all birds capable of flight, common loons have the lowest proportion of wing surface to body weight, doubtless because their adaptations favor diving over flying. Nevertheless, for all their weight and all their difficulty getting into the air, they attain flight speeds of a hundred miles per hour, their sleek shape, presumably, cutting through air as efficiently as it cuts through water. They fly with their neck and head lower than their wings, and their legs stretched straight out behind them. In the water they ride low, like cormorants, with which they can easily be confused at a distance. Cormorants, however, hold their head upward while swimming; common loons hold their head parallel to the surface.

Loons also have an enormous appetite and an elasticity to their neck that enables them to swallow relatively gigantic fish, such as trout as long as 18 inches. I once watched a double-crested cormorant choking to death on a trout no longer than a foot. First hysterically, then deliriously, then hysterically again, the cormorant tried to swallow the huge fish stuck in its throat, in its last ditch effort actually running backward on the water with its neck pointing straight up, the writhing trout flashing silver in the sunlight. A herring gull suddenly swooped down and started to yank the trout out of the cormorant's throat, for an instant lifting the cormorant out of the water. All at once the cormorant splashed rear end first into the water, the herring gull somersaulted backward in the air, and the trout belly-whopped back to safety. A loon could have swallowed such a fish easily.

IDENTIFYING LOONS

Identifying loons poses few problems. Adult birds in breeding plumage are unmistakable: their very sleek shape and dramatic color patterns resemble nothing else in nature, and even people who have never heard them before instantly recognize their calls. In winter loons assume a dull, fairly nondescript plumage and seldom utter any sounds. They spend the cold season along both coasts of the continent, as far south, and probably farther, as Baja California and Key West, Florida. They mate, breed, and raise their young on freshwater lakes north, say, of the forty-fourth parallel, along a line that extends, roughly, across northern Maine, New Hampshire, Vermont, New York, Minnesota, Michigan, North Dakota, Montana, and Washington. Lakes in these latitudes freeze over in winter, so loons head south and for the coast.

Even people who for the life of them couldn't distinguish between a female mallard and a black duck, can easily identify loons in breeding plumage. I once discussed loons with a very serious and dedicated loon watcher who, to my utter surprise, told me he couldn't identify any other waterfowl and could care less. He wasn't into birds, only loons. He developed his interest in loons after he saw one yodeling and called a friend of a friend who knew all about birds. The birder immediately expressed doubt that he could help identify a bird without an adequate description of it, but sure enough, in two seconds flat he identified it as a loon and started asking for driving instructions.

COMMON LOON

More the size of a goose than a duck, the common loon strikes one immediately as an unusually large waterfowl riding unusually low in the water, its long, thick, dagger-like bill perfectly parallel to the surface. Their shape has about it a surreally smooth, sculpted, Brancusi-like quality, and from a distance they often look uniformly black. At closer range, one observes without fail their scarlet red eyes, which in some light look like drops of blood on the bird's black head, and the delicate white necklace that encircles their black neck. A series of thin, white, vertical lines placed closely together, the necklace of the common loon varies in width from perhaps an inch, at the back of the neck, to perhaps a sixteenth of an inch, on the throat. The necklace, which at a distance appears as a solid bar, does not meet at either of its ends: a small break appears at the very front of their throat and the very back of their neck. On their throat, slightly above the break at the tapering ends of the necklace, one can sometimes see something of a semi-necklace, a series of perhaps a dozen small, vertical bars, at most a third inch long, that run across the front of the neck only —as though they were intended to close the primary necklace but somehow got moved up an inch or so.

Under ideal viewing conditions, common loons seem as though dressed in a tuxedo, elegantly turned out indeed. At the base of their black neck, a series of long, thin, sinuous white lines run aft toward their back and turn into a series of tiny white dots on a deep black background. These series of dots curve upward as they move to the rear of the bird, forming an ellipse on the top of the front part of the common loon's back, where neat little rows of tiny white rectangles form something of a herringbone pattern. The breeding plumage of the common loon is absolutely unmistakable.

In winter common loons appear black above and white below, and their bill takes on a bluish white hue. When viewed from the side in winter plumage, the white that runs from under their bill, under their eyes, and down their neck looks rather like a question mark.

The sounds of the common loons have been extensively studied and documented, most notably by Dr.

William Barklow, who recorded the loons' calls on the *Voices of the Loon*, released by the North American Loon Fund and the National Audubon Society. Anyone interested in loons should surely obtain a copy of this recording. Dr. Barklow's research currently includes a study of loons' calls with the purpose of identifying particular individuals, whose sounds, when analyzed by a computer, may well prove to be individually distinctive.

Anyone interested in loons should also read *Loon Magic* by Tom Klein, with photographs by Woody Hagge. The book combines a thorough and lucid text with marvelous illustrations.

RED-THROATED LOON

The smallest of the loons, the red-throated loon is about the size of a brant. It lacks the black-and-white checkerboard pattern of the other three loons in breeding plumage, and it rides in the water with its slender bill pointed slightly upward. Its black bill blends into a pale gray head and neck that in some light appear subtly tinged with a dusty pink; its throat exhibits a brilliant patch of red. The gray neck and red throat end at the top of the chest in a smooth white line in front; on the back of its neck a delicate series of black-and-white stripes runs up the pale gray neck from a rather plain, uniformly dark back.

In winter plumage red-throated loons look primarily dark above and light below, with a light, slender bill. Distinguishing red-throated loons from other Gaviformes requires a sense of their smaller size and an awareness that they hold their bill slightly upward. They winter along both coasts of the continent.

During breeding season red-throated loons emit a

bizarre variety of squeaks and quacks, not nearly as mellifluous as the sounds of the common loon. They breed in the far north, as a rule no farther south than British Columbia and the northern extremes of Canada's Maritime Provinces.

ARCTIC LOON

Dazzlingly beautiful in breeding plumage, the arctic loon mates and raises its young in Alaska and northwestern Canada, venturing no farther south than the southern terminus of Hudson Bay, almost exactly where it enters James Bay. Hudson Bay seems to act as well as the arctic loon's easternmost range, for while they breed west of the bay they seldom appear east of it other than on Baffin Island, way to the north.

Arctic loons in breeding plumage exhibit a marvelous set of field marks that render them unmistakable even at considerable distances. They have a smallish bill, which they hold straight, and their silvery gray, almost to platinum, head seems to glow. Their red eyes look like beads of blood floating on mercury. Four long, white vertical stripes run up the sides of their otherwise black throat, terminating in a smooth line at their white chest. On the sides and toward the back, their white chest exhibits a series of long, fine, vertical lines that end on their sides immediately below their neck. Their black sides and back have large elliptical areas composed of small, white rectangles arranged in neat rows that taper toward the back and front.

Arctic loons in winter plumage appear black above and white below. They resemble common and red-throated loons in winter plumage, but under reasonable conditions one will detect a much sharper contrast between the light and dark parts of the arctic loon.

On their breeding grounds, arctic loons hold forth with a wide variety of squeaks, shrieks, croaks, and quacks.

YELLOW-BILLED LOON

The most northerly of loons, the yellow-billed loon breeds on the tundra in very northern Alaska and northern Canada west of Hudson Bay, in the Beaufort Sea/Arctic Ocean area. Their coloration pattern closely resembles that of the common loon, but their enormous yellow bill, which they hold conspicuously upward, makes them easily identifiable. Their calls, too, resemble the common loon's, although their voice has a louder, more strident quality and they frequently remain silent.

Birds in winter plumage resemble common loons, but their conspicuous yellow bill sets them apart immediately.

DESTINATIONS AND ACCOMMODATIONS

Loons are creatures of the north, of the latitudes where lakes freeze over during winters of long dark nights. Although you can see loons just about anyplace along the coasts in winter, the birds don't really come into their own until spring, when their coloration turns from drab to brilliant and their eerie calls start echoing in the night. Loons prefer remote, isolated lakes, and as a rule they can be found in direct proportion to how isolated and far north a lake happens to be. The problem is that people also prefer remote, isolated lakes, and as development continues it also continues farther and farther north. Loons are extremely sensitive to environmental disturbances, and although they manage to live in some relatively populated areas, they require a lot of wildlife management to do so.

Loons have many friends. Organizations devoted to preserving the population of loons have been active in Maine, New Hampshire, New York, Vermont, Michigan, Minnesota, and Wisconsin. A large part of their effort goes into educating people about the nature of loons, and the nature of how we should behave when in loon country—in a word, respectfully. The loons need room, and whatever else you do when watching, don't approach them too closely, especially if the bird appears excited or is on a nest. Too much excitement causes many loons to abandon their nest, which they protect aggressively against most natural phenomena. They tend, however, to yield to power-boats and humans more intrigued by than afraid of them.

Curiosity can kill loons, so don't exercise too much curiosity and approach them too closely. Many people do exactly that: all of a sudden this bizarre bird starts dancing on the water, and who could help getting a little closer to check it out? If you happen to see a loon standing on the water while violently kicking its feet and uttering tremolos, withdraw quickly because this behavior, the "penguin dance," represents a very desperate territorial display, an anxiety profound enough to endanger the bird's eggs or hatchlings.

- Leave immediately if you see a loon dancing.
- Don't force them from sheltered areas, where they nest, to more open and trafficked water.
- Never approach nesting birds.
- Don't play recordings of their calls to them.

DESTINATIONS AND ACCOMMODATIONS

OTTOWA NATIONAL FOREST, MICHIGAN

Located on Michigan's Upper Peninsula, Ottowa National Forest embraces almost a million acres of mountainous, densely forested terrain. The forest's highlights include the wild, scenic Sturgeon River with its deep, thickly wooded canyon, Potawatomi, and Gorge Falls. Wooded primarily with hemlocks, spruce, yellow birches, maples, and scattered stands of eastern white pines, the forest is rife with streams and lakes. Some of them are so clear you can see a fish 20 feet below you.

The forest has a high population of loons as well as many nesting bald eagles and black bears. The best place to see loons here is in the Sylvania Recreation Area, a 21,000-acre, roadless piece of the forest set aside for hikers and canoers. Canoes are easily rented in the area, and several portage trails, of varying lengths, are well marked.

Other natural attractions in the area include three state parks that encompass, among them, 20 miles of Lake Superior shoreline, three miles of Green Bay shoreline, and the highest point in Michigan—Mt. Curwood, elevation 1,980 feet. Two of these parks are enormous: Porcupine Mountains Wilderness Park consists of 58,000 acres, Van Riper State Park 10,000. Another is somewhat smaller: J. W. Wells State Park, 974 acres. All three have rustic cabins—contact Michigan Department of Natural Resources (517) 373-1270.

Although by winter the loons are long gone, Ottowa National Forest has plenty of winter activities, in particular skiing and snowmobiling.

Ottowa National Forest, US 2 East, Ironwood, MI 49938, (906) 932-1330.

Driving Instructions: The Visitor's Center is located just southwest of Watersmeet, at the junction of routes 2 and 4.

Powdermill Inn
PO Box 666
Ironwood, MI 49938
Telephone: (906) 932-0800

Opposite Powdermill Mountain, a ski area, Powdermill Inn has fifty rooms with color cable television, telephone, and private bath. The facilities include an indoor pool, a whirlpool, a sauna, a restaurant, and a bar. The grounds feature picnic tables and tennis courts.

Rates: inexpensive; MC,V

Towne House Motor Inn
215 South Suffolk Street
Ironwood, MI 49938
Telephone: (906) 932-2101

Towne House Motor Inn has twenty rooms with color cable television, telephone, and private bath. Facilities here include a restaurant and bar, which has entertainment on weekends.

Rates: inexpensive; AE,MC,V

SUPERIOR NATIONAL FOREST, MINNESOTA

Occupying the better part of the northeastern tip of Minnesota, Superior National Forest embraces more than three million acres, a million of which have been set aside as Boundary Waters Canoe Area. Boundary Waters Canoe Area is located along the Canadian border and contains thousands of lakes—and thousands of loons. It adjoins an additional 1800 square miles of watery wilderness across the border—Quetico Provincial Park.

Superior National Forest has the largest population of loons in the contiguous United States. You don't necessarily have to go canoeing to see or hear them, but you might as well. The canoe trails here are many and well marked, and renting canoes and other equipment requires virtually no effort. Experienced canoers can make 235-mile, three-week journeys into this scenic wilderness of rugged shorelines thick with spruce, and rank amateurs can ply the waters for as short a time as they like. The canoe trails here require very little portaging.

In addition to loons, the forest has a high population of black bears, and during the course of your paddles you might well see a moose or a bald eagle. Wolves, though you probably won't see them, also live here.

Superior National Forest also has some unusually scenic roads through wilderness areas. The Gunflint Trail, for example, starts in Grand Marais and curves for 70 miles or so through genuine wilderness, albeit with civilized places to stop.

Potential visitors here should contact the Visitor's Center. The forest personnel are a storehouse of information about where to stay, what outfitters to use, and so forth.

Superior National Forest, Voyageur Visitor Center, Box 149, Ely, MN 55731, (218) 365-6126; or, Forest Supervisor, Superior National Forest, Box 338, Duluth, MN 55801, (218) 727-6692.

Driving Instructions: The forest has several visitor centers and several approaches. The Voyageur Visitor's Center is in Ely—from Duluth take US 53 north to

Virginia; then pick up 169 and go north about 60 miles to Ely.

Bed and Breakfast Registry
PO Box 80474
St. Paul, MN 55108
Telephone: (612) 646-4238

Bed and Breakfast Registry represents bed and breakfast host homes in the Superior National Forest Area (as well as other areas). They have listings in Ely and Grand Marais. Accommodations and rates vary.

Gunflint Lodge
Box 100
Grand Marais, MN 55604
Telephone: (218) 388-2294 or 1-800-328-3325
Closed mid-October through late December.

A rustic inn on the shores of Gunflint Lake, Gunflint Lodge has four suites in a motel-type structure and nineteen cabins, all with private bath. The cabins vary in size from one to four rooms, and most overlook the lake. The suites and cabins have fireplaces. The facilities include a restaurant, a sauna, a small beach, canoes, and a host of organized activities.

Rates: $500–$550 per week, meals included; daily rates available on request; AE,MC,V

NEW HAMPSHIRE LAKES REGION, NEW HAMPSHIRE

In the foothills of the White Mountains, less than 30 miles from the southern border of White Mountain National Forest, the New Hampshire Lakes Region is a popular, and populated, year-round resort. Water sports in summer, skiing in winter, and dramatic foliage displays in autumn attract visitors from all over the Northeast. Always quietly famous, the lakes region received perhaps its greatest jolt of publicity from the movie *On Golden Pond*, which was filmed at Squam Lake.

There are numerous lakes in the area. Two of them, Squam Lake and Lake Winnipesaukee, support healthy populations of loons. Because of the intense conservation efforts of local naturalists, in particular the Loon Preservation Committee in Meredith, New Hampshire, these loons have managed to endure the slings and arrows of a resort area. This naturalist group, the first of many that have focused on protecting loons, looks after the loons on Squam and Winnipesaukee as well as elsewhere in the state. Loon rangers patrol highly popular lakes to make sure thoughtless boaters don't traumatize the birds, and biologists deploy artificial nesting platforms, which have helped endangered loon populations here and elsewhere.

Residents in the lakes region really love their loons, and the pride they take in them generates an enormously refreshing spirit.

The Squam/Winnipesaukee has numerous natural attractions close by, including Mt. Washington, elevation 6288 feet, the highest summit in the Northeast.

New Hampshire Bed and Breakfast
RFD 3, Box 53
Laconia, NH 03246
Telephone: (603) 279-8348

Located in the lakes region, New Hampshire Bed and Breakfast represents bed and breakfast host homes in the area. Accommodations and prices vary.

Cheney House Bed and Breakfast
40 Highland Street
Ashland, NH 03217
Telephone: (603) 968-7968

Cheney House has three rooms with shared bath in an 1895 Victorian house. The house is a mile from the beach at Squam Lake, and the rates include a full breakfast.

Rates: inexpensive to moderate; NCC

LOWVILLE, NEW YORK

Situated in a remote western section of Adirondack State Park, about 20 miles north, as the crow flies, of Old Forge, New York, Stillwater Reservoir has far and away the largest population of loons in New York State. Fifteen miles long, the reservoir varies in width from a half to 5 miles, and on windy days the water here can get quite rough. Access to the reservoir involves an approximately 10-mile drive on Stillwater Road, an unpaved road that runs from Big Moose to Number Four. Approximately 9 miles east of Number Four (a town) and 12 miles northwest of Big Moose is a public boat-launching facility, where canoes and powerboats alike slide into the water. There's also the Stillwater Hotel.

Stillwater Hotel
Dan and Sue Mahoney
PO Box 258M
Lowville, NY 13367
Telephone: (315) 376-6470
Closed April.

A rustic lodge built in the mid-twenties, paneled with knotty pine inside, Stillwater Hotel has seven rooms with private bath, television but no telephone. Some of the rooms have views of the reservoir, and the lodge's restaurant attracts diners from some distance. Dinner here includes fresh-baked breads and desserts, and a nice wine list accompanies such dishes as veal Oscar and shrimp Provençal.

Rates: moderate; AE,MC,V

OTHER PLACES TO OBSERVE LOONS

Though limited during summer to the very northern sections of the northern tier of the lower forty-eight states, loons become increasingly common in Canada. Both Canada and Alaska support large populations of loons, and travelers to wilderness lakes in both areas stand a good chance of coming across loons. In the lower forty-eight they occur in the greatest numbers on remote northern lakes, like those in northern Minnesota and northern Maine.

Algonquin Provincial Park   *(see "Wolves")*
  Ministry of Natural
  Resources
Box 219
Whitney, Ontario KOJ 2MO
CANADA

Allagash Wilderness
  Waterway
Bureau of Parks &
  Recreation
Maine Department of
  Conservation
Statehouse Station 22
Augusta, ME 04333

Isle Royal National Park
87 North Ripley Street
Houghton, MI 49931

Kejimkujik National Park
Box 36
Maitland Bridge
Annapolis County, Nova
  Scotia BOT 1NO
CANADA

(see "The Bay of Fundy")

Moosehorn National Wildlife
  Refuge
Box X
Calais, ME 04619

Quetico Provincial Park
Ministry of Natural
  Resources
Atikokan, Ontario 1CO 807
CANADA

Rice Lake National Wildlife
  Refuge
Route 2
McGregor, MN 55760

Seney National Wildlife
  Refuge
Seney, MI 49883

Sherburne National Wildlife
  Refuge
Route 2
Zimmerman, MN 55398

Tamarac National Wildlife
  Refuge
Rural Route Box 66
Rochert, MN 55678

THE BAY OF FUNDY

Like a giant cradle endlessly rocking, the moon-drawn waters of the world rise and fall—in some places once, in other places twice a day, changing the coastline constantly, bringing things with them, taking things away. As a pageant of natural change, the ebb and flow of the tides has few equals. The transit of heavenly bodies across dark skies and the fairyland transitions of dawn and dusk compel our attention, as do the metamorphoses of the seasons, but not, I think, quite so powerfully as the tides. Perhaps what lures the waters lures us.

Melville stated it plainly: "Yes, as everyone knows, meditation and water are wedded forever." Swinburne put it more poetically: "I will go down to the great sweet mother,/Mother and lover of men, the sea," of whom he asks, "Set free my soul as thy soul is free."

The variables that contribute to the nature of the tides, as well as, surely, the nature of our responses to them, boggle the mind. If the earth had no continents and an ocean of uniform depth covered the place, if no storms raged and no fault blocks shifted —if, in short, we lived in a laboratory instead of on a planet—predicting the tides would pose few problems. Knock wood for the unpredictability of the tides, for where would we be if the border of things never changed, or if tight little squadrons of sanderlings didn't chase receding waves and flee advancing ones? Where would we be if hundreds of thousands of sandpipers didn't stalk the mud flats left behind by the world's largest ebb tide, or if a waterfall and several fast-running rivers didn't turn still as ponds and then froth with colliding water molecules as they reversed their direction of flow?

We would be without the Bay of Fundy.

The body of water that separates Maine and New Brunswick from Nova Scotia, the 170-mile-long Bay of Fundy varies in width from 40 miles to 40 yards, with the result that tides entering the bay get funneled into an increasingly narrow channel and accumulate, finally, in two narrow, shallow basins that have the distinction of possessing the greatest tidal range in the world. Differences of as much as 57 feet have been recorded between low and high water—differences of 50 feet being as common as full and new moons.

The extraordinary tides of the Bay of Fundy make it seem as though the moon were closer, as though its powers were somehow concentrated here, as though, indeed, they emanated from this rugged coastline. There's a Wizard of Oz–like quality about the tides in the upper reaches of the bay. At Hopewell Cape, New Brunswick, a series of tiny islands covered with balsam fir and dwarf black spruce turn, when the tide goes out, into 70-foot-tall columns of red sandstone, surrounded by shorebirds and perched on by hawks. At Reversing Falls Rapids, in St. John, New Brunswick, a series of rapids and whirlpools thunder through a deep, narrow gorge, reversing their direction of flow twice a day because the level of the bay ranges from 14 feet below to 14 feet above the level of the mouth of the St. Johns River. At Truro, Nova Scotia, a tidal bore, a wave generated by the rising tide, runs up the Salmon River; another bore runs up the Petitcodiac River at Moncton, New Brunswick. Immediately after the bore, which is frequently so slight as to deserve its name, an unearthly stillness comes upon both rivers. Then suddenly an enormous inrush of water, like some mad explosion of celestial plumbing, raises the level of the rivers right before your eyes, as the instantaneous melting of all the snow in the Rockies might raise the level of the Colorado River.

At Minas Basin, Nova Scotia, and Mary's Point, New Brunswick, mile-long, low-tide mud flats attract uncountable numbers of migrating shorebirds, which in late summer stop by here to build up fat stores before attempting things like non-stop, 2500-mile flights to South America. Flocks of 20,000 plovers, drumming the air with twice as many wings, burst into flight as though summoned by a sorcerer. Thousands of sandpipers dash around hysterically. Herring gull yodels come from everywhere. And like the Red Sea in slow motion, the tide comes in and the mud flats, wrinkled with millions of bird tracks, disappear.

Like the tides everyplace else, those in the upper reaches of the Bay of Fundy vary in intensity as the moon spins around the earth, which it does every 29½ days during the lunar, or synodic, month. When the sun and the moon form a straight line with the earth in the heavens, their powers of gravitational attraction complement each other, causing the world's waters to bulge at either end of the globe. Waters rise as though swollen, only to fall, hours later, in a seemingly anemic retreat. This powerful combination of gravitational forces occurs twice a lunar month—when the moon lies between the sun and the earth and is invisible, at new moon; and when the moon lies on the opposite side of the earth from the sun and is fully illuminated, at full moon. The tidal range, or vertical distance between high and low water, varies least at quarter moon, when the sun and the moon are in quadrature, or at right angles in relation to the earth, rather than in opposition (full moon) or conjunction (new moon).

Shortly after an apple compelled by mysterious forces crashed onto his cranium, Sir Isaac Newton, the legend goes, began thinking about it and formulated his universal law of gravitational attraction, claiming: "I deduce the motions of the planets, the comets, the moon, and the sea." Newton mathematically proved that every body in the universe exerts a gravitational force on every other body in the universe, and that this attraction is inversely proportional to the square of the distance between the two bodies. Curiously enough, the tide-generating force, though a function of gravitational attraction, departs from Newton's universal law in that it is inversely proportional to the cube, rather than the square, of the distances between the earth and the sun, and the earth and the moon.

And it's a good thing, too, for if the tide-generating force complied with Newton's universal law of gravitational attraction, the sun all by itself would probably generate a tidal range that would make beachfront property of the Appalachian Trail. Though 27 million times more massive than the moon, the sun is 59 million times farther away, which means, arithmetically, that it exerts 27/59ths, or roughly 46 percent, of the moon's gravitational pull.

The unique range of the Fundy tides is also affected by a phenomenon called resonance, whereby waves moving in opposite directions meet and, rather than cancel each other, amplify their powers and rise higher. Because it takes a pulse of tide slightly longer to exit the Bay of Fundy than to enter it, water moving out of the bay resonates with water moving in, thereby raising the ante. These powerful movements of water moving in and out of the bay gave engineers the idea of damming its upper reaches and harnessing all that energy. The engineering principle couldn't be simpler: put up a dam and force all that water to flow through huge hydroelectric turbines, some pointed this way and some pointed that, some positioned high and some positioned low.

As old as the century, the idea of damming the upper bay has fallen in and out of favor as energy needs and sources have fluctuated. After eighty-five years the project is still in committee, but the recent public opposition to nuclear power plants in New England and the mid-Atlantic states has given the idea new life. Indeed, a consortium of utilities based in the Northeast recently agreed to buy electricity from Hydro-Québec, the province-owned power company whose dam on the St. George River in northern Quebec made front-page news in the spring of 1985. The dam's spillway overflowed and drowned 10,000 caribou.

The same power interests that explained the tragic caribou drowning as a freak happenstance of nature hypothesize that a dam across Minas Basin in the Bay of Fundy would have a positive, if any, ecological impact on the area. Power interests in Nova Scotia, the poorest of Canada's provinces, especially like the idea of building a dam. Think of all those jobs.

The idea is, of course, madness. Even the United States Army Corps of Engineers, which usually waxes enthusiastic about enormously ambitious reclamation projects, applied through international channels to block a Fundy tidal power plant unless it had the corps' approval. The corps claims, and I for one believe it, that no one in Canada has a better computer model of tidal action than it does, and that attempting to dam the bay without its advice would be an act of international ecological irresponsibility. Though by no means the champions of sound ecological policy, the Corps of Engineers will in all probability prevent the Fundy tidal project from coming to pass. Think of all those submarines.

At any given moment some four hundred variables influence the tides, and one would be fey to predict how a dam in the upper reaches of the Bay of Fundy would alter them. Such a structure would, everyone seems to agree, raise the level of the entire Gulf of Maine, increasing its tidal range in the process and damaging who knows what. The blades in the turbines would probably wipe out the better part of the North Atlantic shad population, millions of which feed during summer in the upper reaches of the bay, on the other side of the projected turbines. How many fish will make it through the blades? How many will make it back out? How many will we lose, and how quickly? No one knows.

Although it lacks the dramatic tidal range of its upper reaches, the lower Bay of Fundy, whose tides rise and fall a mere 20 feet, is not without its charms. The bay opens into the Gulf of Maine at a point where cold, nutrient-rich water upwelling from the depths collides with similar water carried by the Labrador Current, creating an exceedingly fecund marine environment. Whales and dolphins can seem common as crows, and pelagic seabirds, like petrels and shear-waters, fly fast and low toward the spouts of whales —humpbacks, finbacks, rights, and minkes. Shoals of Atlantic white-sided dolphins bowride in the wakes of ferries from Maine to Nova Scotia. The lower bay embraces the Grand Manan Archipelago, a series of small islands closer to the northern coast of Maine but, in fact, part of Canada.

The western coast of Grand Manan Island has spruce- and fir-covered vertical cliffs that drop as much as 400 feet into deep water. Machias Seal Island boasts the only significant population of Atlantic puffins south of the Gulf of St. Lawrence. And several of the "rocks" in the archipelago play host to hundreds of sun-bathing seals at low tide, or to extensive colonies of birds—storm petrels, black guillemots, eiders, herring gulls, and cormorants. The archipelago also contains Campobello Island, where the summer home of Franklin Delano Roosevelt functions now as a mu-seum surrounded by a park. Those who approach Campobello Island by the ferry from Deer Island cruise past the "Old Sow," the world's second largest whirl-pool, so named because of its snorting, bovine noise.

With 1700 miles of coastline, the Bay of Fundy is a big place with a vast array of natural attractions. Planning a trip here requires a certain amount of focus, a sense of what you want to see. If you want to experience the bay's dramatic tides, try to arrange your trip around a full or new moon, and do yourself the favor of watching at least one half cycle of the tides: find what looks like a good vantage point, plant yourself there for seven hours or so, and simply watch. Although it seems unlikely that the U.S. Congress will adopt my resolution compelling all lawmakers to spend at least seven consecutive hours per annum observing a full half cycle of the tides, I have adopted the practice myself and advocate it strongly as a powerful antidote to the kinds of foibles we urbanites fall heir to. If, like me, you not infrequently find yourself in a shadow even at high noon, you will discover in the rhythm of the waters one of time's most basic common denominators.

Imagine a rugged, rocky coastline littered with scattered stands of spruce and encroached on by a swollen sea into which scores of screaming terns dive frantically for their dinner. Imagine those imperious crags turning into stone pedestals surrounded by mud flats, with tens of thousands of semipalmated plovers dashing about. Then imagine a full moon rising and casting a brilliant bar across the water, as the birds hammer the air and dapple the moon as they fly off to roost for the night. Never mind imagining it, get thee to the Bay of Fundy.

DESTINATIONS AND ACCOMMODATIONS

The following destinations and accommodations sketch but briefly a large and varied area. They focus on the tides of the Bay of Fundy, a natural attraction worth the trip in and of itself. Other natural attractions in the area are noted and cross-referenced to appropriate chapters in this book. Whales and loons, for example, occur in the region, so I suggest opportunities for observing them. A well-timed trip to the bay could include, in a week's time, some first-rate whale and Atlantic puffin watching, an undisturbed view of half a million semipalmated plovers, and a moonlit look at the world's most powerful tides.

GRAND MANAN ISLAND, NEW BRUNSWICK

Marathon Inn
North Head, Grand Manan
PO Box 129
New Brunswick EOG 2MO
CANADA
Telephone: (506) 662-8144
Open late May through mid-October.

An 1871 Victorian structure, painted white and
trimmed black, Marathon Inn has thirty-three guest
rooms, seven of them with private bath. All the rooms
have running water, and several have a view of the
bay. Rates here include breakfast and dinner.

A mecca for naturalists, the Marathon Inn works
with a captain who takes people to Machias Seal Island
for looks at Atlantic puffins and other pelagic birds.
In addition, the inn operates a whale-watching boat,
a 55-foot vessel that goes out from the second week
of August through the third week of September. Right,
humpback, finback, and minke whales are frequently
observed, as are harbor porpoises and diverse species
of pelagic birds.

Rates: moderate; MC,V; whale-watching boat, $66 per day.

The Compass Rose
North Head, Grand Manan
New Brunswick EOG 2MO
CANADA
Telephone: (506) 662-8570
Open June through October.

Two circa 1900 Victorian structures, The Compass
Rose overlooks the bay and has nine guest rooms with
shared bath. The premises include a restaurant.

Rates: inexpensive, including breakfast; MC,V

ST. JOHN, NEW BRUNSWICK

Hilton International
1 Market Square
St. John, New Brunswick E2L 4Z6
CANADA
Telephone: (506) 693-8484
Open all year.

The St. John Hilton has 200 rooms with private bath and color television with cable. The facilities include a pool, restaurant, bar, and various sports activities (golf, tennis, racquetball, health club, etc.).

Rates: expensive; AE,CB,DC,MC,V

Holiday Inn
350 Haymarket Square
St. John, New Brunswick E2L 4Z6
CANADA
Telephone: (506) 657-3610

The Holiday Inn here has 128 air-conditioned rooms with color television and cable. The facilities also include a pool, restaurant, bar, and health club.

Rates: moderate; AE,DC,MC,V

FUNDY NATIONAL PARK, NEW BRUNSWICK

Fundy National Park consists of 130 square miles of varied terrain. Elevations range from sea level to 1200 feet, and the park has numerous streams and about fifteen lakes, two of them with swimming beaches. Northern harriers and rough-legged hawks frequently appear overhead, and the park seems to be enjoying admirable success with its peregrine falcon reintroduction program. Popular activities here include canoeing, fishing, and hiking on some 80 miles of trails. The park has a golf course, tennis courts, and a heated pool filled with water pumped in from the bay. Approximately 8 miles of the park front the Bay of Fundy: sheer rock precipices wooded with red spruce, balsam fir, and yellow birch drop straight down into the water; pockets of sandy beach among the crags litter the coast.

Tide watchers here tend to congregate at Herring Cove, Point Wolfe, and near the park entrance, which overlooks the small fishing village of Alma. Moncton, Mary's Point, and Hopewell are all less than an hour from the park.

Caledonia Highlands Inn and Fundy Park Chalets
Fundy National Park
Alma, New Brunswick EOA 1BO
CANADA
Telephone: (506) 887-2808 or 2930
Open May through October.

Wood-frame structures built in the 1960s, Caledonia Highlands Inn and Fundy Park Chalets are situated on a hill that overlooks the Bay of Fundy, of which each room has a view. The inn is a motel-style building with twenty rooms, and the twenty-four chalets were constructed in the Swiss style. All the rooms have refrigerators, stoves, and utensils, and guests here can obtain first-rate seafood at a small village market and prepare it themselves (make sure to sample the bay scallops and lobsters from here).

Rates: moderate; MC,V

MONCTON, NEW BRUNSWICK

Hotel Beauséjour
750 Main Street
Moncton, New Brunswick E1C 8N8
CANADA
Telephone: (506) 854-4344
Open all year.

Decorated with Acadian themes, Hotel Beauséjour is a luxurious, full-service hotel with 316 rooms, all of them with color cable television and telephone. The facilities include a pool, two restaurants, and a bar.

Rates: expensive: AE,CB,DC,MC,V

Howard Johnson's Motor Lodge
Highway 106, Box 5005
Moncton, New Brunswick E1C 8R7
CANADA
Telephone: (506) 384-1050
Open all year.

A ninety-eight-room structure, Howard Johnson's is located at Magnetic Hill, a popular optical illusion (if, at a certain point on the hill, you put your car in neutral it genuinely seems to proceed uphill). All the rooms here have color cable television and telephone, and a few have private balconies. The facilities include a pool, sauna, cafe, and bar.

Rates: moderate; AE,CB,DC,MC,V

YARMOUTH, NOVA SCOTIA

Situated at the extreme southwestern tip of Nova Scotia, Yarmouth serves as a gateway to the province, particularly for Americans. During summer (May through October) ferries from Portland and Bar Harbor, Maine, cruise across the mouth of the bay and dock at Yarmouth. Passengers frequently observe whales and pelagic birds during the crossing.

The trip from Portland, Maine, to Yarmouth takes about 12 hours; for information and reservations, contact Prince of Fundy Cruises, Portland, ME 04101, telephone: (902) 742-3513; or CN Marine, Box 250, Sydney, Nova Scotia B2A 3M3, CANADA. Telephone: (800) 565-9470.

The trip from Bar Harbor, Maine, to Yarmouth takes about 7 hours; for information and reservations, contact CN Marine (see above).

Another ferry makes the crossing from St. John, New Brunswick, to Digby (about 25 miles north along the coast from Yarmouth), Nova Scotia, in 3½ hours; for information and reservations, contact CN Marine (see above).

Rodd's Grand Hotel
Box 200
Yarmouth, Nova Scotia B5A 4B2
CANADA
Telephone: (902) 742-2446
Open all year.

Rodd's Grand Hotel has 138 rooms, all of them with color cable television and telephone. Amenities include a restaurant, bar, and view of the lighthouse and harbor.

DIGBY, NOVA SCOTIA

Pines Resort Hotel
Box 70, Shore Road
Digby, Nova Scotia BOV 1AO
CANADA
Telephone: (902) 245-2511
Open late May through mid-October.

An imposing stone structure that overlooks the bay, the Pines has eighty-nine guest rooms in the main building and thirty cottages with fireplaces. The grounds encompass 300 acres that include nature trails, a golf course, pool, lighted tennis courts, and other recreation facilities. The luxurious amenities include a restaurant and bar.

Rates: moderate to expensive; AE,MC,V

KEJIMKUJIK NATIONAL PARK, NOVA SCOTIA

Approximately 35 miles west of Digby off Highway 8, Kejimkujik National Park embraces 147 square miles of gently rolling terrain wooded with a mixture of northern and southern (boreal and hardwood) species. Scoured by glaciers, the land has numerous drumlins and eskers, as well as scores of shallow lakes, which cover a good third of the terrain. A series of very well marked canoe trails meander through the park, and visitors here can rent canoes and explore the park's many lakes (there are primitive campsites all along the canoe trails).

Though not a place to observe the Fundy tides, the park boasts an unusually dense population of common loons: just about every lake in the park has a breeding pair (see *"Loons"*). In addition to loons, birders here will probably observe several species of hawks (red-tails, sharp-shins, broad-wings, kestrels, ospreys, goshawks), an array of warblers (magnolia, Blackburnian, black-throated green, common yellowthroat), boreal chickadees, and that giant woodpecker that eludes so many life lists—the pileated woodpecker.

**Park Address: Kejimkujik National Park
Box 36
Maitland Bridge
Annapolis County, Nova Scotia BOT 1NO
CANADA
Telephone: (902) 242-2770.**

TRURO, NOVA SCOTIA

**Tidal Bore Inn
RR 1
Truro, Nova Scotia B2N 5A9
CANADA
Telephone: (902) 895-9241
Open May through October.**

A motel-style structure, the Tidal Bore Inn has forty-eight rooms with color cable television and telephone. Twenty-four of the rooms overlook the bay at that point where the Salmon River empties into it, with the result that guests here can observe the tidal bore (see above) without ever leaving their room. The facilities include a restaurant.

Rates: inexpensive to moderate; AE,MC,V

ELK

Every year the Jackson Hole Boy Scout Troop collects the antlers shed by the elk at the National Elk Refuge in Jackson Hole, Wyoming, and then sells them. In 1974 representatives of the troop held an auction, and more than $19,000 was raised—from Oriental bidders—for the antlers. In 1984, for the 6500 pounds of antlers collected by the troop, $44,000 was paid by a San Francisco firm that then exported them to South Korea and Hong Kong.

The money raised from the sale of the antlers is used to help offset the cost of food for the tremendous number of elk that winter at this refuge. The refuge was established in 1912—but not before land development had usurped much of the elk's traditional wintering grounds. As early as the turn of the century, homesteaders had begun to fence off the range. Ten thousand elk starved to death one winter, and even when the elk found enough food to eat, they were killed for their meat and their canine teeth, which were prized by college fraternities as key fobs. Finally, local and national outrage was loud enough to demand creation of the Jackson Hole National Elk Refuge.

The customers in South Korea and Hong Kong who buy the antlers grind them into a powder, mix them with who knows what, and market the product as an aphrodisiac.

Curiously, or perhaps appropriately, enough, the prodigious antlers of a mature bull elk represent something of an aphrodisiac even among elk themselves, for the condition of a bull elk's antlers reveals his overall physical shape. In many ways, the entire social organization of elk depends on the status symbol of the rutting bull's antlers. During the breeding season, mature male elk start looking for groups of cows. When they find one, they establish a harem, in some cases with as many as thirty cows. The bull's enormous antlers not only attract females but also discourage other males from coming near the harem. They serve as a weapon as surely as a status symbol.

Elk shed their antlers every winter and grow them again during spring and summer. During autumn when the animals enter the rut—a highly excited sexual state—they go into a frenzy, thrashing wildly at saplings and small trees with their antlers. Up until late summer to early autumn, soft, tender hairs called velvet cover the antlers, but as the seasons change so do the antlers. The velvet, which contains a network of blood vessels that nourish the bone of which the antlers are formed, starts falling off, and the rutting bulls rub them against everything in sight in an effort to remove strips of velvet. Indeed, during the rutting season smashed-up saplings and smooth, rubbed parts of trees indicate a visit by a bull elk. In his pre-breeding frenzy, he tries everything to shed his velvet and polish his antlers.

A prime set of antlers, each of them 5 feet long with six tines, or points, weighs between 40 and 50 pounds. When it comes time for a bull to defend his harem, he will fight vigorously with his antlers. Most of the time nobody gets hurt, but now and again bull elk wound each other, or someone who gets in the way, fatally. Occasionally, two bull elk clashing with their antlers get locked together, and if a predator doesn't get to them first, they starve. Fights over harems usually involve only mature elk in prime condition; younger males, with less developed antlers, flee immediately when a prime animal confronts them. When two mature animals in their prime fight, they square off at a distance of about 30 feet and then charge, lowering their antlers. Often it takes three or more collisions before one of the bulls gives up.

In a particular population of elk, only a small percentage of the bulls actually mate. The rigors of attending to and protecting their harems obviously constitute an enormous strain on the animals. Between holding the harem together and challenging every comer, bull elk harem masters have their work cut out for them. They spend the vast majority of the time fighting and policing the harem, eating less than they would like and generally exhausting themselves.

By the end of the rutting season, the harem masters are all but spent, so much so that the mortality rate during winter of mature bulls is three times higher than that of mature cows. The bulls simply use up all their energy. By the end of the rutting season, they're as undernourished as they are tired. This compromised state makes them easier prey for predators, and if they do not manage to restore their strength quickly on the wintering ground, they can die of malnutrition. A bull elk seldom maintains a harem for more than a year or two.

Members of the deer family, elk can weigh from

400 to 1000 pounds. At a quick glance you may mistake them for a black- or white-tailed deer, but you will not mistake them for such for very long. Elk, second in size among deer only to moose, are 400 to 500 percent larger than deer. They stand as tall as 5 feet at the shoulder, and their overall length from their nose to the tip of their tail ranges from 7 to almost 10 feet. Their 5-foot-long antlers spread out 5 feet horizontally, and can appear almost absurdly large. In addition to antlers (females have none), males have a dark brown mane on their throat. Both males and females are light brown to tan above and somewhat darker below. Their most conspicuous field mark is their yellowish to light brown rump patch, which distinguishes them immediately from any other member of the deer family.

During the rutting season, the bulls tend to give away their location by "bugling." An indescribable combination of a bellow, whistle, and several grunts, the bugle of an elk can carry for several miles and ranks, surely, among nature's most haunting sounds. Elk used to roam most of the continent, with populations as far afield as Georgia, but development and hunting eliminated them from most of their range. Population estimates suggest that in the mid-eighteenth century there might have been 10 million elk in the contiguous United States. By the turn of the twentieth century fewer than 70,000 prevailed. About 75 percent of the elk left in the United States live in the Rocky Mountains, another 15 percent live in the Olympic Peninsula and along the coastal areas of Oregon, and the remainder live in isolated patches here and there.

Elk are magnificent animals to watch, and the sight of a half dozen of them galloping across a stream, sending a spray of water everywhere, sticks in the mind. The sight of 10,000 of them, the Rocky Mountains in the background, sticks deeper in the mind. Visitors to the National Elk Refuge usually see somewhere between 8000 and 12,000 elk.

DESTINATIONS AND ACCOMMODATIONS

NATIONAL ELK REFUGE, WYOMING

Situated in Jackson Hole, a 600-square mile valley surrounded by mountains, the National Elk Refuge serves as the wintering ground for the largest congregation of elk in North America. Some 8000 to 12,000 elk migrate from the higher elevations they inhabit during summer and start arriving in the valley in late autumn. By the time the skiing season is in full swing, the vast herd of elk is in attendance. From mid-December through mid-March horse-drawn sleighs take visitors out to see the elk, which look particularly well against a backdrop of snow and rugged mountains.

In addition to elk, the refuge attracts considerable numbers of waterfowl and a healthy population of hawks. Goldeneyes and teal spend the winter here, as do Canada geese, and that large raptor that looks like an osprey hovering over the snow is a rough-legged hawk. Bald and golden eagles also winter here, and some goldens nest in the area. Trumpeter swans live here year-round.

The Jackson Hole area also contains Grand Teton National Park, which is adjacent to the north side of the elk refuge and the south side of Yellowstone National Park, 55 miles distant. Vast expanses of national forestland surround the entire area, and the Snake

River runs right past the refuge. Incredibly scenic, Jackson Hole enjoys unobstructed views of the Grand Tetons, which look as though they simply burst out of the ground, which they did. A fault block system, the Tetons rise as much as 7000 feet above Jackson Hole, which itself is at an elevation of more than 6000 feet.

An extremely popular ski resort, Jackson Hole sees quite a bit of activity during winter, and visitors here needn't worry about any lack of activities or services. Both Grand Teton and Yellowstone national parks are open during winter.

Signal Mountain Lodge
Box 50
Moran, WY 83013
Telephone: (307) 543-2831
Open all year.

Located in Grand Teton National Park, Signal Mountain Lodge has seventy-nine rooms in several types of structures—cabins, motels, and apartments. All the rooms, or cabins, have a private bath; some have a kitchenette, some have a balcony, some have views of Jackson Lake and the Grand Tetons. The facilities also include a grocery store, gas station, snack bar, cocktail lounge, and several shops.

Rates: moderate to expensive; AE,MC,V

OTHER PLACES TO OBSERVE ELK

Banff National Park
Box 900
Banff, Alberta TOL OCO
CANADA

Elk Island National Park
Site 4, R.R. 1
Fort Saskatchewan, Alberta T8L 2N7
CANADA

Jasper National Park
Box 10
Jasper, Alberta TOE 1EO
CANADA

Olympic National Park
600 East Park Avenue
Port Angeles, WA 98362

Prince Albert National Park
Box 100
Val Marie, Saskatchewan SON 2TO
CANADA

Redwood National Park
1111 Second Street
Crescent City, CA 95531

Rocky Mountain National Park
Estes Park, CO 80517

San Luis-Merced National Wildlife Refuge
Box 2176
Los Banos, CA 93635

Yellowstone National Park
National Park Service
Box 168
Yellowstone National Park, WY 82190

NORTHERN LIGHTS

The aurora borealis, or northern lights, have to be seen to be disbelieved.

Sometimes they appear as a bold, yellow-green arc of light bursting out of the horizon and stretching clear across the night sky, and at other times they look like a gigantic, pleated, multicolored curtain of undulating light wiggling furiously away in the darkness—like a celestial swath of phosphorescent silk a hundred miles high. Sometimes enormous snaky bands of white or green or reddish light writhe overhead, only to disperse in a sudden series of lavender and pale lime green, pencil-thin rays that race toward the zenith to form a huge fan across the heavens. And sometimes an arc, or a band, or vaguely shaped cloud just hangs there, rhythmically pulsating in the darkness, like something with a heart.

In ancient Greenland, the elders got together and decided that the aurora represented, obviously, the spirits of the dead playing catch with the head of a walrus. To the ancient Norse, the northern lights symbolized a procession of Valkyrie galloping across the night sky, transporting on their backs the souls of dead warriors to Valhalla. Some groups of Eskimos called the aurora "Keoeeit," a term suggesting a series of torches held aloft by spirits charged with leading the recently departed into heaven, and in the folklore of the northern Hebrides and Scotland, the northern lights stood for a battle. A scarlet aurora that appeared over Ireland in 1854 seemed, to its rather freaked-out observers, the dancing blood of those killed at Balaclava, where in October of that year the Light Brigade made their ill-advised, ill-fated charge, "Into the jaws of Death . . . the mouth of Hell."

As the name implies, the northern lights appear most often in the far north, but they can, and do, show up in the subtropical south—if less often and less dramatically. Visible some three hundred nights of the year from Churchill, Manitoba, and Point Barrow, Alaska, the aurora appears feebly overhead in northern Florida on perhaps four nights a year. Over Duluth, Minnesota, and Quebec City, auroral displays occur on perhaps forty nights a year. One can't really say the farther north the better, as the aurora occurs most frequently along a narrow band that circles the geomagnetic North Pole, passing along the southern coast of Greenland and running through northern Quebec, central Hudson Bay, and along the northern coast of Alaska. Farther north than this the displays occur less frequently.

As a general rule of thumb, however, the farther north you go, the more auroral displays you will see. The reverse holds true in the Southern Hemisphere, where the aurora australis, or southern lights, occur. Satellite photos of the dark side of the earth often depict simultaneous occurrences of the northern and southern lights, which appear on the shadowed globe like flat, fiery berets or burning half-halos at opposite ends of the sphere.

Although all the facts have yet to come in, since the advent of spacecraft and satellites we have learned a great deal about the causes of the aurora. Numerous celestial and terrestrial factors come into play, and the whole process probably turns on grander cycles we but dimly perceive—even though we have managed, by exploding nuclear devices in space, to create artificial auroras that closely resemble the real thing.

The real thing occurs when charged, high-energy particles—mostly electrons—collide with, and in the process excite, atoms and molecules in the upper atmosphere. When a molecule or atom gets excited, it shifts into a higher level of energy, remains there for a hundred-millionth of a second or so, and then returns to its former energy level, emitting light in the process. Indeed, much of what we know about the ingredients of the upper atmosphere we discovered by analyzing the auroral spectrum of light.

The various colors in this spectrum can be traced to specific molecules or atoms. Oxygen molecules, for example, emit red or yellow light after an electron smashes into them, whereas an individual oxygen atom, after such a collision, glows green. When in the upper atmosphere an electron collides with a proton, the excited couple glows red for a ten-thousandth of a second or so and then wanders off as a relatively content hydrogen atom. Hydrogen atoms also form when protons bounce like billiard balls off other molecules in the upper atmosphere and then, at an altitude of about 70 miles up, abscond with an electron from a nitrogen molecule, which over the loss glows purple.

These charged, high-energy electrons, protons, and other particles that collide with molecules in the upper atmosphere come from the sun by way of the solar wind, or solar plasma, a high-speed stream of ionized (electrically charged) gas—95 percent of it hydrogen nuclei—that races toward the earth at slightly more than a million miles an hour. (The gas inside a neon sign is another form of plasma.) Fortunately for us, the earth's magnetic field deflects the solar wind with all its positively and negatively charged ions. But winds will be winds. The force of the solar wind flattens the earth's magnetic field so that it assumes a shape rather like that of a comet, whose elongated tail, due to the force of the solar plasma, always points away from the sun. So does the earth's magnetotail.

Aligned along and strongest near the North and South Poles, the earth's magnetic field affects the atmosphere in direct relation to altitude, its influence increasing with height. Of little significance at altitudes below 40 miles up, the magnetic field becomes an important factor at heights of 40 to 400 miles, where a high percentage of charged particles makes up the ionosphere. Most auroral displays take place within the ionosphere, at altitudes ranging from approximately 65 to 150 miles up. Above the ionosphere, the earth's magnetic field becomes the dominant force in determining the motions of atmospheric particles, which at such altitudes are almost invariably charged. We call this upper layer of the atmosphere, where charged particles swirl in loops around the earth's magnetic lines of force, the magnetosphere. These charged particles are known as the Van Allen radiation belts.

If it weren't for the solar wind, the magnetosphere would be exactly that—a sphere. The force of the solar plasma, however, flattens the part of the magnetosphere facing the sun, and blows the part on the dark side of the earth hundreds of thousands of miles into space. On the side facing the sun, the earth's magnetosphere extends perhaps 40,000 miles into space, whereas the comet-like magnetotail extends, according to data sent back by the International Sun-Earth Explorer 3 satellite, at least 850,000 miles out. As the world spins, so does the magnetosphere, which acts as something of a protective envelope that surrounds the earth and deflects ionized (or charged) particles—gamma rays and X rays, for example.

So here comes the solar wind, a gaseous plasma of electrically charged particles moving at a thousand miles per second, crushing the magnetosphere facing it to the scant depth of 40,000 miles and blowing the part in darkness a million miles downwind. As fast-moving solar particles encounter the magnetosphere it repels them, rather like a speeding automobile repels falling snowflakes, and they rush around it, some of them spilling into the atmosphere along the whirl-pool-like force lines of the magnetic poles and others eddying into space along the elongated lines of the magnetotail, which draws them into its wake just like the vacuum behind the speeding auto pulls along snowflakes.

All this wind and all the turbulence it encounters generate complex patterns of circulation, so that while some charged particles spill into the atmosphere along the force lines of the magnetic poles, others trail along hundreds of thousands of miles beyond it, while still others get trapped by the Van Allen radiation belts.

During an intense auroral display, charged particles from all these circulation patterns bombard the io-nosphere, the strongest of them penetrating to within 40 miles of the earth's surface. We have known for years that the force lines of the earth's magnetic poles pulled ions from the passing solar wind and the cir-culating Van Allen radiation belts into the ionosphere, but we only recently discovered how ions blown out along the peripheries of the magnetotail contribute to the aurora. It seems that rather like the snowflakes drawn into the wake of the speeding automobile, charged particles from the solar wind swirl and eddy at the far end of the magnetotail, where they spin as though in a plasma generator, a dizzying whirligig of electrified gas and magnetic force lines, which increases their energy until it reaches something of a critical mass, a level too intense to exist. The resulting explosion fires a stream of electrons and protons upwind at the dark side of the earth, whose attenuated magnetotail actually serves as a protective sheath, or magnetized conduit, for these high-speed ions, which hurry toward the magnetic poles.

Themselves the product of motion and electricity, the magnetic poles change constantly. (As Heraclitus' student Cratylus observed, "You can't step in the same river even once.") The easiest way to visualize the magnetic axis of the earth is to imagine a huge magnetized rod passing right through the planet and emerging at the poles—covered by ice and water, and therefore, impossible to see—but such is not the case. The inner core of the earth has no stable magnetic charge because nothing remains permanently magnetic at temperatures above about 932 degrees Fahrenheit, a value known as the Curie Point. Even easily magnetized minerals like iron cannot sustain magnetic charges at such temperatures, and at depths of more than 12 to 18 miles below the crust of the earth, such temperatures perenially prevail. The heat from radioactivity deep inside the planet prevents the formation of a permanent magnetic field.

The magnetic poles shift approximately a tenth of a degree a year, which seems pretty slight, just under

7 miles or so, but represents a rather startling rate of change as far as geological events go. Observers in London, for example, noted an 18-degree variation in magnetic north over the last four centuries: in 1580, compass needles pointed 11 degrees east of true north, and in 1980, 7 degrees west of it. Stonehenge, the while, didn't move at all.

This radical shift of magnetic north owes itself to the outer layer of the earth's fluid-iron core, which the heat from residual radioactivity further within the planet stirs into convective motion. These convection currents of fluid iron interact with stray, minuscule magnetic fields and generate electric currents along their lines of force, creating not only the magnetic poles but also a self-generating dynamo that produces as much electrical current as all the power plants humans currently operate. This million amperes of electric current produces, finally, a magnetic field as strong as the sun's, as powerful, if one can imagine such a thing, as a toy magnet.

The surface of the sun, however, experiences intense magnetic storms, which appear to us as sunspots and represent relatively cool, and consequently dark, areas on the solar disc. Tornado-like whorls within the gaseous surface of the sun, sunspots generate magnetic fields 3000 times more intense than normal. Solar flares, enormous atomic eruptions that discharge far higher than normal levels of charged particles, accompany sunspots, the net result being an increase in the intensity of the solar wind. The number of sunspots and solar flares fluctuates according to a well-defined eleven-year cycle; at the minimum point usually fewer than 10 sunspots exist. During maximum periods of sunspot activity, anywhere from 43 to 193 sunspots wreak magnetic havoc on the surface of the sun. At such times, auroral displays occur more frequently, and more dramatically, south of the geomagnetic North Pole.

The next period of maximum sunspot activity will take place around 1990, but during the last three years of the eighties northern lights watchers can expect more frequent, more southerly, more brilliant auroras.

Three years or so before the last period of maximum sunspot activity, a flock of honking Canada geese woke me in the middle of the night, and I threw on a heavy terry cloth robe and stepped outside to maybe catch a glimpse of them. It was late September, at the northern tip of the Gaspé Peninsula, 38 degrees, a half hour before midnight. When I stepped outside and the cool air hit me, it must have anesthetized me as well, for it took a full minute before I realized the sky was ablaze with a heavens-high curtain of rosy yellow light, rippled like a flag in strong wind, moving to the left, sounding, sure enough, like Canada geese.

DESTINATIONS AND ACCOMMODATIONS

See discussion of Churchill, Manitoba, in "Bears."

BISON

Although estimates vary from a low of about 50 million to a high of 125 million plus, experts generally agree that 60 to 70 million buffalo inhabited North America at one time. They roamed the Great Plains in herds so vast that early pioneers calculated the probable number of buffalo according to a formula that factored in how many miles deep the herd was and how long it took to pass a given spot. Frontiersmen coming back from the West talked about "countless," "numberless," "billions" of buffalo, and the literature of the time rings with descriptions of the earth shaking during a buffalo stampede.

By the beginning of the twentieth century, however, the total population of buffalo hovered at about 500 individuals, the seemingly inexhaustible supply of these animals having dried up. No one was particularly surprised at the imminent extinction of the buffalo, for slaughtering them wholesale had been something of a government policy for some time. Buffalo had the misfortune of representing not only a significant economic resource but also a political one. In 1873, Columbus Delano, Secretary of the Interior during the Grant Administration, said: "I would not seriously regret the total disappearance of the buffalo from our western prairies, in its effect upon the Indians." Politicians in those days considered a dead buffalo a discouraged Indian.

The Plains Indians recycled the buffalo all the way down to its spirit, making some use out of every conceivable part of the animal. The buffalo provided them with food, clothing, and shelter, and though they sometimes killed more than they needed, occasionally stampeding thousands off a cliff, they generally respected the animal as though it were a God. They made utensils out of their horns and bones, and they turned their hides into moccasins, robes, tents, boats, coffins, and clothing of all descriptions. They braided their hair into rope, used their ribs as runners on sleds, turned their hooves into glue. When the Indians could not find any wood to burn, a not uncommon contingency of the Great Plains, they burned "buffalo chips," dried pieces of excrement that lasted for years through all kinds of weather and that made a particularly hot fire. When there were tens of millions of buffalo, there were billions of buffalo chips, and although they never represented the fuel of choice, they probably saved quite a few humans from freezing to death.

The Plains Indians' dependency on the buffalo became the foundation of a political policy that sought to encourage westward expansion at the expense of the buffalo—hence, the Indians. This insidious policy by itself might not have worked, but, as it happened, the buffalo yielded to its harvesters all sorts of products. The scant historical records that we have indicate that hundreds of thousands of buffalo hides per year passed through the warehouses of a single company. After the market discovered buffalo hides, it discovered buffalo tongue, a rare delicacy, which hunters would remove from the animal while leaving the rest of it to rot. Each tongue brought in only about twenty-five cents, but a good hunter could make a small fortune if he moved quickly and killed surely. In 1848 one company sold 25,000 tongues. After hides and tongues became firmly established as seriously marketable commodities, someone realized they could market the buffalo's bones as well. They would do for several agricultural and industrial purposes, including the refining of sugar and the manufacture of high-quality bone china.

The government continued to encourage, indeed applaud, the killing of buffalo for whatever reason. As the nineteenth century wore on, the buffalo hunt became one of the more romanticized rituals of the West. Ultimately, it proved more practical than romantic. Westward expansion involved such stuff as building the railroads, and building the railroads required the building of forts so as to ensure the "passivity of the frontier." A buffalo carcass yielded many cash products, but also considerable amounts of meat, which the railroad companies and the military used for food for their workers and soldiers. By the 1870s hunting buffalo had become a national craze, and everybody from professional hunters to wealthy sportsmen to rail passengers took a shot at them.

Killing buffalo became, in short, a glamorous, profitable, and patriotic thing to do. By the 1870s tens of thousands of people were out there doing it. Roughly 2 million buffalo were killed each year, and their bodies apparently littered the Great Plains, especially along the railroad tracks.

During the last half of the nineteenth century, several states started taking action to protect the buffalo, but it seems that the only states able to pass protective legislation were states in which buffalo no longer existed, and the same type of environmental lassitude prevailed in Washington, D.C. Congress finally did pass landmark legislation making it illegal to hunt buffalo in Yellowstone National Park, where a few of the animals remained, and funds were appropriated to restock the herd there. But all such action came after the fact: the buffalo were for all intents and purposes already gone, reduced to a pitiable fraction of their former population. The North American population of buffalo, once 60 million strong, had dwindled to a mere 500.

By 1910 the movement to rescue buffalo from oblivion was under way in the United States, and by the early 1920s Canada followed by establishing Wood Buffalo National Park. Conservation efforts during the twentieth century have succeeded in increasing the number of buffalo on the continent. Today several large herds of the animal exist, all of them on protected lands of one sort or another. Altogether perhaps 30,000 buffalo prevail.

Buffalo were easy to hunt and kill because they had no fear of man, or guns, or trains, or anything else. The largest terrestrial animal in North America, a large male buffalo can weigh upwards of 2000 pounds, stand 6 feet tall at the shoulder, and measure 12 feet in length. They also have 20-inch horns that measure 16 inches in diameter at the base, massive shoulders and chest, and the ability to gallop at 35 miles per hour. Such an enormous creature never feared anything because nothing really represented a threat. A pack of wolves might occasionally take a sick or feeble individual, but would stay clear of a buffalo in its prime. Several buffalo can crush anything that gets in their way, and they never developed a healthy sense of fear.

Like elk, buffalo form harems, and like bull elk, bull buffalo defend their ladies against all comers. During the rutting season, competing males face off, bellow, paw the ground and then charge at each other, smashing their foreheads, rather than their horns, together. After a few such encounters one bull wanders off, and the victor ambles back to his harem of twenty or so cows. Thick-skulled animals indeed, buffalo have apparently been shot in the forehead with high-caliber rifles and been totally unaffected.

Observing buffalo is relatively easy and predictable, but be aware that these animals are large, powerful, and unpredictable, and if you happen to meet one in the wild, give it plenty of room.

DESTINATIONS AND ACCOMMODATIONS

CUSTER STATE PARK, SOUTH DAKOTA

The second largest state park in the contiguous United States, Custer State Park embraces some 73,000 acres in the rugged Black Hills of South Dakota. The park is adjacent to the Black Hills National Forest, to the west, and to Wind Cave National Park, to the south. Mount Rushmore National Monument is immediately north of the park, and Badlands National Park lies about 70 miles to the east.

Custer State Park has the largest herd of buffalo in the nation, estimated at about 1500 animals, as well as very healthy populations of elk, mule, and white-tailed deer, bighorn sheep, pronghorn antelope, and coyotes. Golden eagles nest here as well. In addition to boasting the country's largest herd of buffalo, the park has numerous historic structures, a museum, and a theater (the Black Hills Playhouse). Four man-made lakes provide fishing and swimming, and several trails, for walkers or horseback riders, wind through the park.

On the other side of the fence at the south end of Custer State Park is Wind Cave National Park, which also has a herd of buffalo, though only 350 strong. Wind Caves takes its name from the strong currents of wind that pass in and out of its entrance, depending on barometric pressure. When the barometer falls, winds come rushing out of the cave's small entrances, and when the barometer rises, the wind goes racing into the cave. Wind Cave is the third largest cave system in the United States and the eighth largest in the world. Forty-seven miles of the cave have been mapped, and at various times of the year naturalists lead tours. Above the cave, buffalo roam and eagles cruise over extensive prairie dog towns.

Naturalists in both parks cull excess buffalo from the herds. These buffalo are then sent to other state and national parks interested in starting or increasing a buffalo herd, or they are given to Indians.

For information, contact Custer State Park, Box 70, Custer, SD 57730, telephone: (605) 255-4515; and Wind Cave National Park, Hot Springs, SD 57747, telephone: (605) 745-4600.

Driving Instructions: Custer State Park is about 5 miles east of Custer, off US 16A; Wind Cave National Park is off US 385, roughly 10 miles north of Hot Springs.

Custer State Game Lodge and Cabins
Box 74
Custer, SD 57730
Telephone: (605) 255-4541

Located in Custer State Park, Custer State Game Lodge and Cabins has forty-seven lodge rooms and twenty cabins. Some of the rooms have a telephone, all the rooms and cabins have a private bath, and all the cabins have a kitchen. The lodge has a large lobby with a fireplace, snack bar, and cocktail lounge. The cabins, which vary in size, can hold as many as eight. The lodge offers jeep rides to see the buffalo, several of which are usually grazing right outside the place.

Rates: inexpensive to moderate; NCC

El Rancho Court
640 South 6th Street
Hot Springs, SD 57747
Telephone: (605) 745-3130

Across the road from Fall River, El Rancho Court is a thirty-six-room motel with a heated pool. The rooms have a private bath, color cable television, and telephone. The motel serves free coffee in the morning. It also offers transportation to and from the airport and bus terminal, and a restaurant is across the street.

Rates: inexpensive to moderate; AE,CB,DC,MC,V

Bavarian Inn
Box 152
Custer, SD 57730
Telephone: (605) 673-2775

The Bavarian Inn has fifty-two rooms with color cable television, telephone, and private bath. The facilities include an indoor pool, a whirlpool and a sauna, illuminated tennis courts, and transportation to and from the airport and bus terminals. Some of the rooms have a private balcony or patio, and several suites are available.

Rates: moderate; AE,CB,DC,MC,V

WOOD BUFFALO NATIONAL PARK, CANADA

Canada's largest national park, Wood Buffalo encompasses some 17,000 square miles that straddle the border of Alberta and the Northwest Territories. Formed in 1922 to protect the endangered wood buffalo, a subspecies of bison, the park now has the largest herd of buffalo on the continent. It is also the only herd that roams freely in the wild. The herd currently numbers approximately 4300 animals, a decline from the 12,000 or so that roamed here before the 1974 flood that killed 6000 buffalo. The population has not quite recovered from this disaster, but it continues to maintain itself and to increase each year. Occasionally, herds of fifty to a hundred buffalo walk on to the road through the park, surround somebody's car, and stare into the windows until they get bored or scared (the buffalo, that is).

The park also contains the unique nesting grounds of the whooping crane. All living whooping cranes descended from birds that nested here and wintered in Aransas, Texas. The nesting area is located in an extremely remote section of the park, so don't plan on seeing the cranes and their nests. In June and September upwards of a million waterfowl stop by the park on their way north or south. They visit the Peace/Athabasca Delta, the largest delta in the world, which is in the southeastern section of the park and not easily accessible.

Most of Wood Buffalo, in fact, is inaccessible, and visitors here need to plan well in advance. Guides and outfitters lead trips to most parts of the park, in particular to the Peace/Athabasca Delta, which is a popular canoe destination. Easily accessible, however, are the park personnel, who understand the nature of a wilderness experience and have the time to advise visitors thoroughly. The park's 200-mile road is subject to sudden floods and, periodically, fires, so make sure to check with the rangers about road conditions.

The Wood Buffalo National Park Visitors Center is located in Fort Smith. From Edmonton scheduled flights leave to Fort Smith six times a week; driving here is possible, but a tough, two-day haul. Potential visitors should contact the park rangers well in advance for a visit.

For information, contact Wood Buffalo National Park, Box 750, Fort Smith, Northwest Territories X0E OP0, CANADA, telephone: (403) 872-2349.

Pelican Rapids Inn
PO Box 52
Fort Smith, Northwest Territories X0E OP0
CANADA
Telephone: (403) 872-2789
Open all year.

A two-story frame building, Pelican Rapids Inn has fifty rooms with color cable television, telephone, and private bath. Some of the rooms have a kitchenette, and a few one- or two-bedroom suites are available. The inn is immediately across the street from the park headquarters/visitors center.

Rates: moderate; AE,MC,V

OTHER PLACES TO OBSERVE BISON

Badlands National Park
PO Box 6
Interior, SD 57750

Elk Island National Park
Site 4, R.R. 1
Fort Saskatchewan, Alberta T8L 2N7
CANADA

Fort Niobrara National Wildlife Refuge
Hidden Timber Star Route
Valentine, NB 69201

National Bison Range
Moiese, MT 59824

Sully's Hill National Game Preserve
Fort Totten, ND 58335

Theodore Roosevelt National Park
Medora, ND 58645

Wichita Mountains National Wildlife Refuge
Route 1, Box 448
Indiahoma, OK 73552

Yellowstone National Park
PO Box 168
Yellowstone National Park, WY 82190

BATS

Everybody's got a bat story.

Mine takes place at an elegant dinner party in Washington, D.C., on a sultry, windless Saturday evening in August. By way of celebrating moving into a large, Georgian-style townhouse he'd rented, furnished, for a song, a good friend decided to invite some folks down for dinner and the weekend. He stipulated, however, that everyone dress formally for the meal, and he, a professional chef, promised to cook accordingly. Naturally, the thought of a fancy meal, served in a fancy Georgian townhouse, among friends, was impossible to resist. Everybody showed up. Wine flowed, hors d'oeuvres circulated, and a four-course meal was served on delicate pink china. Somewhere in the middle of coffee, the host repaired to the far end of the room, which was virtually all glass—two wide floor-to-ceiling windows separated by floor-to-ceiling French doors. He played with the latches on the French doors and secured them in the open position, providing everyone at the table with a lovely view of the garden.

Then the bat showed up.

In the blink of an eye, the congenial and relaxed after-dinner mood turned into a scene of utter hysteria. The quiet murmur of a dozen people talking in small groups around the table turned into a cacophony of deafening shrieks. Glass was breaking everywhere. A shoe went flying across the room, smashing into the china closet, a magazine careened into the chandelier, a floor lamp did a somersault over the couch and exploded with a shower of sparks. Frantically trying to get up from the table, someone nearly overturned it, spilling the milk, sugar, and several bowls of ice cream onto the lap of a woman who was screaming nonstop and flailing wildly at the airspace over her head. In a mad dash from the table, two people tripped over each other and fell, screaming, to the floor.

No doubt as terrified as the people, the bat flew about hysterically, maneuvering its way through the crowded room with incredible dexterity, turning on a dime, avoiding everything from flying magazines to lurching, falling humans. Suddenly it hung a sharp left, flew into the hallway, and then headed up to the second floor. The host signaled me and a friend to follow him into the hallway, and when the three of us arrived there he slammed the dining room door behind us. On the other side of the door we could hear the sounds of somebody hyperventilating, and of more glass breaking. The host dashed over to the hall closet and returned with two tennis rackets and an enormous, multicolored golf umbrella, which he gave to me.

We ran up the stairs, where we separated, each of us going into a different room. But before I even cracked open the door to one of the bedrooms, glass shattered behind me. I spun around and spotted the host, who had just smashed a print at the top of the stairs and was chasing the bat back down to the ground floor. The other vigilante with the tennis racket followed closely, and I, discarding the golf umbrella, took up the rear. Halfway down the stairs I heard the unmistakably clumsy sound of two tennis rackets colliding, and an instant later saw the bat flying up the stairs, heading right for my face. My blood ran cold. Having no time to think, I stuck out my hand so as to motion stop, and, amazingly, the bat flew right into my hand. It fell, unconscious, at my feet. Relieved, I bent over to pick the bat up, grasping the tip of each of its wings with a thumb and index finger. But before I could get back up, the stunned bat regained consciousness and startled me so badly I slipped on the stairs and fell backward into a sitting position, still holding the bat.

It was the ugliest, slimiest, most gruesome-looking creature I had ever laid eyes on, and it struck terror into my soul. It emitted an awful, blood-curdling squeal, bared its incredibly white, razor-sharp-looking teeth, and twisted its entire body in an attempt to bite one of my hands, then the other. My hands, sure enough, started sweating, and my heart began to hammer away in my chest. Word of the capture spread quickly into the dining room, and in no time flat eight or nine people, most of them armed, stood at the base of the stairs. "Kill it!" someone yelled. "Be careful, it's rabid!" someone else screamed. "Trap it between the tennis rackets. Crush it!" The pandemonium prevailed until I, terrified of getting hit with a tennis racket in addition to getting bitten by the surely rabid bat, asked everybody to get out of my way and to open the door to the street, which seemed to me then on the other side of the universe. I made it to the open doorway and, taking care to let go of both wings at once, flipped the bat up into the night air.

In the distance, I could see the Washington Monument, and I breathed a deep breath. Back indoors, some semblance of calm had reasserted itself. It had been no more than five minutes from the moment the bat flew through the French doors to the moment I released it, and the damage twelve hysterical people did to the fancy dining room in so short a time was awesome. Fortunately nobody was hurt, not even the bat, and with a needed burst of good humor and camaraderie we set about the task of cleaning up and assessing the damage—which was significant.

The incident stirred my curiosity about bats, and the more I looked into them the more I realized what I had realized so many times before: we fear what we don't understand. The people at that dinner party had no reason to fear that bat, whose greatest desire upon entering that room was exiting it. Bats almost never bite people. Of the four people bitten by a bat in the United States last year, all of them were handling the animal when it bit them. Indeed, if the bat who came to dinner had bitten me, I would have understood. What we should have done at the dinner party was sit quietly until the bat flew out the French doors again, but the fact is that bats—though clean, gentle, and intelligent—terrify people.

Some people, however, are utterly unafraid of bats, and growing numbers of them spend considerable time, energy, and money trying to conserve North America's population of bats, which has declined drastically over the past fifty years. The population of Brazilian free-tailed bats inhabiting Carlsbad Caverns, for example, has fallen during that time from

8 million to 250,000. Formerly the largest colony in the world, the 30 million bats once resident in the Eagle Creek Cave in Arizona plummeted in population to just 30,000 animals in a period of just six years. When *The New York Times* asked Dr. Merlin Tuttle, the director of Bat Conservation International, about the precipitous drop in bat population, he replied simply: "The entire hillside in front of the cave is just littered with empty shotgun shells."

Bat Conservation International recently started marketing bat houses, which look like birdhouses except for the lack of an entrance hole in front. They have open bottoms and adjustable slats so homeowners can customize the homes for local species. You can even peek under the boxes and watch the bats sleeping, upside down, during the day. To the surprise of everybody, orders for the bat houses poured into Bat Conservation International. At one point, hundreds were sold per day. Dr. Tuttle, commenting on the surprising success of the bat houses and chuckling with satisfaction at America's growing acceptance of bats, compared them to the pet rock craze.

Bats have had a checkered history of acceptance and nonacceptance. While some societies have loathed them, others have cherished them. Ancient Macedonians considered it good luck to carry a bat bone on one's person, and ancient Bohemians believed that carrying a bat's right eye in your pocket would render you invisible, hence invulnerable. In ancient India, on the other hand, people believed that a bunch of bats flying about a house was proof positive that someone was about to die; and in parts of central Africa, the Azande believed that bats carried the souls of witches and demons. In Mayan mythology, the Death Bat, which decapitated its victims, ruled over a region of the underworld called Zotziha, a term that combines the Mayan words for bat (*zotz*) and house (*iha*).

In contemporary Mexico, pregnant women make a pilgrimage to a large cave in Veracruz filled with vampire bats, to whom they make offerings as they pray for their children's safe delivery into the world. And in the Chinese language, the words "bat" and "luck" are homonymous, with wordplays commonly made one on the other.

Possibly because many species of bats are declining in numbers or are outright endangered, the bat conservation movement in America seems to be burgeoning. Thousands of people—many of the once-squeamish variety—each year visit Carlsbad Caverns National Park. From a small amphitheater above the mouth of the cavern, visitors watch as hundreds of thousands of bats emerge in a huge, counterclockwise spiral—especially during the morning and evening rush hours. Sometimes they fly out in a continuous stream, and sometimes they burst out in intermittent pulses. At peak times of flight, 10,000 bats per minute exit the cavern, making a terrific roar, rather like whitewater, with their flapping wings and forming a dark moving cloud one can see from a mile away. The Carlsbad Caverns were discovered, in fact, because of the enormous clouds of bats that emerged from their natural entrance.

True bat lovers make an appearance at the cavern entrance a little before dawn, when the bats return to the cave after a night of hunting. From an altitude of about 1000 feet above the entrance, the bats plunge down at speeds upwards of 30 miles per hour. They do this with their wings closed, only to open them, with one of nature's weirdest pops, immediately above the cavern entrance.

Another enormous colony of Brazilian free-tailed bats inhabits Bracken Cave in Texas. When all 20 million of them emerge at dusk, they rise like a huge tornado cloud, thick and dark in the sky. The Bracken Cave, surrounded by private land, is only accessible through Bat Conservation International. The group leads tours to the cave of which it will become guardians in the near future.

If you happen to be in downtown Austin, Texas, in the summer, take a walk to the Congress Avenue Bridge. Three-quarters of a million Brazilian free-tailed bats live in the expansion joints under the bridge, and they come and go like clockwork at dusk and dawn, to the chagrin, doubtless, of the major hotels on either side of the bridge.

Brazilian free-tailed bats are not, by any means, the only bats in North America, but in terms of exposure to the public, they are the celebrities of the bat world. Their North American population exceeds 100 million, and they make a good representative species of bat to talk about, a good particular to suggest the general. They are, like many species of bat, declining significantly in numbers, and although we don't know for sure why their population continues to dwindle, we suspect pesticides have quite a bit to do with it. Pesticides not only eliminate the insects they feed on but also contaminate the bats themselves.

Brazilian free-tailed bats consume somewhere between 30 and 50 percent of their weight each night, which is to say that a quarter million of these half-ounce animals eat, of an evening, upwards of a ton of insects. Biologists worry that a serious decline in the bat population will generate an increase in the number of insects, a problem that could become acute in the Southwest. Researchers at Carlsbad recently started using a combination television camera/computer in order to census the bat population accurately. Voracious consumers of insects, Brazilian free-tailed bats are enormously beneficial to the ecosystem they inhabit. Dr. Milford R. Fletchere of the National Park Service thinks that Brazilian free-tailed bats play such an important role in the ecology of the Southwest that "we'd all be knee deep in mosquitoes and other insects without them."

Although a few individuals remain in the Southwest and hibernate, the vast majority of Brazilian free-tailed bats migrate to Mexico for the winter. During autumn, when they arrive there, the animals mate. Pregnant females return in spring to their summer quarters and form huge nursery colonies. They give birth to a single baby, which they hang from the roof of the cavern alongside the other babies. These hanging baby bats are packed so closely together that their density in Carlsbad Caverns exceeds 250 individuals per square foot, and it seems that if one of them falls to the cavern floor, none of the mother bats makes any attempt to rescue it.

Watched over by a few babysitters, the babies spend evenings by themselves, and when the mothers return at dawn, they nurse any immature bat that manages to get at their nipples. They apparently have no ability to recognize their own offspring. The mature male bats, meanwhile, congregate in their own colony elsewhere in the cavern.

Many species of bat exhibit this type of segregated male/female social organization whereby the two sexes dwell apart, even in the same cave. In order to reproduce, however, the males and females must at one point come together, which tends to be during autumn at the hibernaculum, the cave where they hibernate. The Social or Indiana bat, a common species in the upper Midwest to Northeast, mates only during a two-week period in autumn. During the day, the males and females occupy separate areas of the hibernaculum, but at night the females invade the male portion of the cave and mass copulation ensues. They are called Social bats because they sleep in such closely packed, neatly organized rows that their noses and lips look like pink bands in the dark of the cave.

The mating rituals of bats vary from the imperceptible to the highly ritualized. Some species of hibernating bats begin copulating while awake only to fall into a profound sleep during coitus. Others mate in a nightclub-like atmosphere called a lek. Rare among mammals, a lek is a traditional spot where a congregation of males repair to perform their elaborate mating displays and wait for a female to come breed with them. Nothing other than displaying and mating goes on at a lek, or arena, mating.

Researchers studying Hammer-headed bats in western Africa observed the following phenomenon: about nintey male bats first position themselves in trees along the heavily forested banks of the Ivindo River, in Gabon, which cuts a 100-foot swath through the forest. At dusk the male Hammer-heads begin to "sing," rather in unison, holding forth with froglike croaks at the rate of about a hundred a minute while beating their wings twice as fast.

Then come the females cruising up the river, checking out the males. They hover in front of this one, scoot over to see that one, alight, finally, beside their choice of mate. The male stops singing soon as he mounts the female, and the pair maintains silence for a minute or so, until the female groans loudly a few times and then flies off. The males start their song again a minute after the female leaves. The nature of a lek, which also occurs among some species of grouse and antelope, is such that some of the males—those in the middle of the lek, according to researchers scoring the location of female groans—have more success than others. Better lek, you might say.

Other species of bats breed in harems, like elk, with a single male servicing thirty females. In some cases, the females will change harems every day. Like many other species of bats, Brazilian free-tails have a reproductive strategy that involves some delay in the implantation of the egg in the female's uterus. This adaptation allows them to pass the winter without the burden of carrying and nourishing a fetus. After awakening from hibernation or migrating back to their summer quarters, the stored sperm or fertilized egg implants itself and an embryo develops rapidly. (As a reproductive mechanism, delayed implantation also occurs among bears.)

Promiscuity and polygamy seem to prevail among bats. If one considers that some species cannot even recognize their own offspring, it should come as no surprise that pair bonding does not matter much.

Aside from rodents, bats are the most diverse group of mammals, with over 950 species represented. Thirty-nine species, of four families, reside in North America, and in sheer numbers of individuals bats outnumber humans.

Bats belong to the order Chiroptera, a term derived from the Greek words for hand, *cheir*, and wing, *pteron*. The wings of bats are, actually, their hands. Their wrist and fingers are longer than the entire length of their body, with the result that a 4½-inch-long Brazilian free-tail has a 12-inch wingspread. A membrane covers their extremely elongated fingers, and when they land, they fold up their wings like a fan. They rest and sleep upside down, in which position they give birth, although during a particularly difficult delivery a female might right herself and enlist the help of gravity. Unlike any other mammal, bats enter the world feet first.

Though some species of bat have excellent vision, most North American species, blind as bats, see poorly. They compensate for poor vision, however, by utilizing a highly sophisticated system of echolocation, which resembles sonar. In the late eighteenth century an Italian scientist, Lazzaro Spallanzani, designed and executed all sorts of experiments to determine how bats navigate in complete darkness. Noting that owls cannot function without seeing, Spallanzani blindfolded bats and discovered that with no vision whatever they still managed to locate and catch tiny insects. Then he inserted tubes in the bat's ears and discovered that when he left the tubes open the bats could function, but when he closed them the bats were helpless. Spallanzani concluded the bats somehow saw with their ears.

Two hundred or so years later, Donald R. Griffin, at the time an undergraduate student at Harvard, took some bats over to a laboratory equipped with microphones capable of detecting ultrasonic sound. He discovered, sure enough, that bats do see with their ears. It was Griffin who coined the term "echolocation," and he and many others have done a considerable amount of work in the area. The complexities of echolocation go well beyond the scope of this book, but a quick look at how it works will perhaps suggest, if only slightly, the incredible sophistication of the only flying mammals.

With a highly specialized larynx, bats emit through their nose and mouth a series of high-frequency sounds, well beyond the range of human hearing. (The squeal of the bat I held in my hands at the dinner party was not an echolocation sound, nor are the sounds one hears at a bat roost.) In addition to a specialized larynx that produces these high-pitch sounds, bats also have special muscles in their ears that expand and contract in synchronization with echolocation sounds. Located in the middle ear and attached to the earbone, these muscles contract and prevent the sound of an echolocation call from reaching the bat's inner ear. These muscles then expand so that the inner ear can receive the echo made by the call. In short, these muscles suppress the echolocation calls and accentuate the echoes they produce.

While just cruising around, bats produce relatively few echolocation calls, perhaps five per minute, but when they start zeroing in on an insect they start emitting as many as two hundred calls a minute. The nature of sound waves is such that objects reflect sounds only of wavelengths smaller than their reflective surface. By interpreting the echoes that its calls produce, a bat can determine the size of an object. Their echolocation calls of some species are frequency modulated (these bats are actually called FM bats), beginning usually at a high frequency and suddenly dropping, so that the size of an object can be determined. Because of the varying frequency of the call, a medium-size insect might reflect echoes of a higher frequency and not those of a lower one. The bat can interpret these signals immediately and decide whether or not the object in question is too big to attack.

Though they may be attracted to them, bats do not attack insect-size objects thrown in their path, so it seems that in addition to size their echolocation system makes quite a few other determinations. They also make routine adjustments for variations caused by the Doppler effect, which comes into play when the object reflecting the sound, as well as the bat, is in motion. Such variables could easily baffle all but the most sophisticated navigation system, and one wonders at the kind of neurological complexity required to interpret subtle differences between echoes separated by $\frac{2}{100}$ths of a second.

As there are more bats on the continent than humans, you can see one just about anyplace. On a walk at dusk recently someone commented on the lovely swallows cruising up and down the stream. When I pointed out that the swallows were bats, he literally jumped backward a step. There is no reason to fear bats. Indeed, they need our protection and could do well without our wrath or ignorance. Although it may seem farfetched that colonies of bats so populous as to form dark clouds can disappear or go extinct, they can indeed. Populations of bats everywhere are in decline. The animals are completely protected in the Soviet Union and just about every European country.

They need more protection here, and more friends.

DESTINATIONS AND ACCOMMODATIONS

CARLSBAD CAVERNS NATIONAL PARK, NEW MEXICO

Located in southeastern New Mexico, just across the border from Texas, Carlsbad Caverns National Park embraces approximately 48,000 acres of desert, mountains, and caves. The park preserves some seventy caves, of which Carlsbad is the largest. One of the rooms in the cave has a floor area equal to that of fourteen football fields. All manner of tours into the caverns are available, and they leave continuously all year long. Tours range from 3-mile hikes beginning at the cavern's natural entrance to wheelchair-accessible tours of the big room. The hikes usually end in the big room, from which high-speed elevators carry passengers 750 feet up to the Visitors Center. The facilities in the cavern include the Underground Lunchroom.

The stalactite and stalagmite formations in the caverns have to be seen to be believed. The most scenic areas are highly accessible as well as well-lit, especially those in the 14-acre Big Room.

Above the caverns the park consists of arid, mountainous terrain, with yuccas at the lower elevations and junipers and pines higher up. Several trails wind into the desert and canyons, and the park features both a 7- and a 10-mile scenic auto route. Hikers here should make sure to carry plenty of water and to bear in mind that sudden weather changes can occur at any season.

Spectacular as the caverns are, the real stars of Carlsbad are, of course, the hundreds of thousands of bats that emerge from the cavern at dusk and return at dawn. At the Visitors Center, park naturalists post the exact time of the flight each evening; you would do well to show up a little early. Park naturalists give bat flight talks, at the entrance amphitheater, right before sunset during summer.

Nearby natural attractions of interest include Guadalupe Mountains National Park across the Texas border from Carlsbad: the rugged, 76,000-acre park varies

in elevation from 3650 to 8749 feet, embracing everything from canyons to forested mountains.

For information, contact Carlsbad Caverns National Park, 3225 National Parks Highway, Carlsbad,
NM 88220, telephone: (505) 785-2233.

Driving Instructions: Carlsbad Caverns National Park is
20 miles southwest of Carlsbad, on US 62/180.

Best Western Motel Stevens
Box 580
1829 South Canal Street
Carlsbad, NM 88220
Telephone: (505) 887-2851
Open all year.

The Best Western Motel Stevens has 181 rooms with
color cable television, telephone, and private bath;
several suites are also available. The facilities include
a pool and wading pool, bar with entertainment and
dancing, package store, and very good restaurant. The
restaurant serves a buffet breakfast each morning,
and special buffet dinners include spreads of Mexican
and seafood dishes.

Rates: inexpensive to moderate; AE,CB,DC,MC,V

Holiday Inn
3706 National Parks Highway
Carlsbad, NM 88220
Telephone: (505) 887-2861
Open all year.

The Carlsbad Holiday Inn has 121 rooms with color
cable television, telephone, and private bath. The facilities here include room service, a restaurant, bar
with entertainment and dancing, pool, and Laundromat.

Rates: moderate; AE,CB,DC,MC,V

BRACKEN CAVE, TEXAS

The Bracken Cave in Texas hosts the largest bat colony in the world, with an estimated population of 20 million bats. By summer's end, when the young take to the air and migrants stop by, the cave's population can expand to upwards of 40 million animals. The vast majority of these are Brazilian free-tailed bats. They emerge from the cave in tornado-like clouds easily visible from two miles away. In early August, when the young first learn to fly, all sorts of predators attend the nightly flight: hawks chase young bats across the sky, and raccoons wait for them on the ground.

The Bracken Cave is accessible only through Bat Conservation International, which is in the process of having the cave and surrounding land deeded to it. A highly visible and important organization, Bat Conservation International was founded by Dr. Merlin D. Tuttle (inventor of the Tuttle Trap, an ingenious and humane bat collection device), who leads the tours to Bracken Cave. The tours are open only to members of Bat Conservation International; they include a talk on the history of the bats and their cave, and Dr. Tuttle and BCI staff members bring along bat detectors that enable you to hear the echolocation signals of the bats.

If you are interested in observing the largest bat flight in the world, contact Bat Conservation International for information about membership and tours. Making arrangements far in advance is advisable, for the number of tours and their times vary greatly.

If you decide to go on one of the tours and to stay in Austin, you can witness a large bat flight right in the middle of town. On a good night, three-quarters of a million bats emerge from the Congress Avenue

Bridge, which crosses the Colorado River between Barton Springs Road and West 1st Street. The bats live in the expansion joints under the bridge. On one side is the Hyatt Regency Hotel, on the other the Sheraton Crest Inn.

For information, contact Bat Conservation International, Inc., Brackenridge Field Laboratory, University of Texas, Austin, TX 78712, telephone: (512) 499-0207.

Tours of the Bracken Cave depart from a rendezvous point between Austin and San Antonio (closer to San Antonio). Both cities are represented by Bed and Breakfast Reservation Services as well as by numerous motels and hotels.

Bed & Breakfast Society of Austin
1702 Graywood Cove
Austin, TX 78704
Telephone: (512) 441-2857

Bed and Breakfast Texas Style
4224 W. Red Bird Lane
Dallas, TX 75237
Telephone: (214) 298-8586 or 298-5433

Bed & Breakfast Society of Austin and Bed and Breakfast Texas Style offer a variety of accommodations in B&B host homes. The lodgings range from simple rooms to luxurious suites, and the prices vary accordingly.

OTHER PLACES TO OBSERVE BATS

Blowing Wind Cave
Wheeler National Wildlife Refuge
Box 1643
Decatur, AL 35601

WHOOPING CRANES

Never particularly abundant or widespread, the whooping crane hovered on the edge of the abyss. Or maybe it danced.

Considered extinct by the first two decades of the century, the whooping crane experienced a phoenix-like rebirth when someone discovered a wintering flock of them on the Gulf Coast of Texas, at Aransas, in 1936. Almost immediately the United States Fish and Wildlife Service established a 47,000-acre wildlife refuge for the birds' protection. By 1941, however, the flock numbered just fifteen individuals and the excitement of having rediscovered them turned to despair over having rediscovered their fate—probable extinction. In both the United States and Canada whooping cranes had been protected against hunters since 1917, but they continued to decline in numbers anyway. The situation looked worse and worse, but rigid protection and good public relations (everybody loves whooping cranes) kept the unique flock alive. People couldn't believe how beautifully they danced.

New life came to the birds in 1954. Naturalists in Canada's Wood Buffalo National Park discovered, while fighting a fire, the unique nesting grounds of the

whooping crane—an area that had escaped destruc-
tion over the years probably because of its inaccessi-
bility in the muskeg wilderness, at a latitude of about
60 degrees north. That the only existing flock of
whooping cranes nested and raised their young exclusively at Wood Buffalo and wintered only at Aransas struck terror into the hearts of those concerned
with saving the birds from extinction. An intense hur-
ricane or a bad oil spill in Texas could wipe out the
entire population, as could a forest fire in Wood Buffalo, and everybody knew it.

Even without a natural or man-made disaster, the
sheer distance between the whooping crane's breeding and wintering grounds represented a significant
jeopardy, and still does. Flying the 2500 miles from
the Northwest Territories to the Gulf Coast takes the
birds approximately two weeks, which biologists consider a very long time for so endangered a bird to be
away from home. All species suffer a higher mortality
rate during migration, and the whooping crane is no
exception. In addition to the usual hazards of a long
migration, such as bad storms and barbed wire,
whooping cranes have the further liability of resem-
bling snow geese, a heavily hunted species. They are,
of course, far larger than snow geese and easily distinguished from them, but to an excited hunter a big
white bird with black wingtips means "snow goose."

The discovery of the whooping crane's breeding
grounds generated an intense research and protection
effort by the Canadian government, and as the birds
enjoyed increased protection at both ends of their
range, the flock began to grow. Yet, to ensure the
preservation of the species scientists from both the
United States and Canada agreed to cooperate in establishing a captive population of birds—a backup

flock, as it were. Luckily, the biology of the whooping crane also cooperated in this venture. Because the birds produce two eggs but seldom fledge more than one chick, stealing whooping crane eggs had no impact whatever on the number of birds in the wild. The United States Fish and Wildlife Service was thus equipped to start a captive flock at the Patuxent Wildlife Research Center in Laurel, Maryland.

Managing this captive flock at Patuxent has proved difficult. Even though biologists and animal behaviorists there have managed to induce the whoopers to perform their celebrated mating dance, none of the birds have actually copulated. All the chicks born at Patuxent have resulted from artificial insemination. Disease one year killed eight birds, and although the flock has suffered this and other setbacks, it does seem to be holding steady at a population of about forty individuals. By way of ensuring the flock's genetic diversity, biologists from the Canadian Wildlife Service continue to contribute eggs from the Wood Buffalo nesting grounds. Most of the eggs, however, go to Grays Lake National Wildlife Refuge, in southeastern Idaho, where biologists place them in the nests of greater sandhill cranes, which raise them as their own.

The concept of using sandhill cranes as foster parents for whoopers had been around for some time, but before you can transplant an egg from one nest to another you have to know the whereabouts of both nests. After the discovery of the Wood Buffalo nesting grounds and after the assessment of how many eggs could be taken from the nests, Canadian and United States wildlife officials embarked on a highly experimental cross-fostering project: since sandhill cranes apparently cannot tell the difference between their own eggs and those of a whooper, why not let the abundant sandhill help establish a new flock of whoopers in the wild? Objections to the program were legion, but between Wood Buffalo and Patuxent a steady supply of extra eggs was at hand, and there was nothing else to do with them.

Grays Lake National Wildlife Refuge became the site of the experiment for several reasons, the two most important being its dense population of nesting sandhill cranes and an enlightened biologist who studied them. Situated at an elevation of 6400 feet, Grays Lake is a 22,000-acre freshwater marsh in a valley surrounded by high mountains. The marsh contains very little open water and can aptly be described as choked by bulrushes. To some species, this presents an absolutely ideal habitat. Rails and soras breed everyplace among the bulrushes, a few thousand breeding ducks and geese utilize the open water, and more sandhill cranes breed here than anyplace in the world. The refuge boasts a breeding population of 200 pairs of sandhill cranes. At the beginning of the migration season, in September, Grays Lake serves as a staging area for 3000 to 5000 sandhills, which gather here before flying south.

Grays Lake's resident crane expert, Roderick Drewien, was at the time a graduate student at the University of Idaho. It was he who suggested the refuge as the site for the cross-fostering experiment, and some combination of his credentials and the quality of the habitat convinced the powers that be to give the project a try. Other than a lot of work, there was nothing to lose, and the possibility of success tantalized everyone. If it worked, there would be a second population of wild whoopers, which, unlike their colleagues at Wood Buffalo, would have to expose themselves to the dangers of migration over a distance of only 800 miles. One-third the distance meant one-third the risk.

In 1975 the Grays Lake experiment began. Although it might seem routine, transporting warm eggs from northern Canada to Idaho, or Maryland, requires formidable logistics. Biologists in helicopters land on the muskeg and obtain the eggs, which they place immediately in portable incubators. Then they put the eggs in another portable incubator, which looks rather like an overgrown attaché case that fits, with ten whooping crane eggs in it, under the seat of a commercial airline, or on your lap. A thermometer built into the top of the incubator allows the biologist transporting the eggs to check its temperature during the flight; a barometer indicates the incubator's humidity. Biologists from the Patuxent Wildlife Research Center, which also contributes whooper eggs to the Grays Lake project, use a similar portable incubator to transport the delicate cargo.

The Grays Lake population of foster whooping cranes has yet to produce a breeding pair of birds, but over the past eleven years something of a wild flock has come into existence. Thirty-five to forty whoopers spend the summer at Grays Lake, and in late April through early May visitors there stand an excellent chance of seeing one. One whooper, called by the refuge manager the "public relations bird," almost always gets seen by visitors who take the trouble to climb to an observation point next to the refuge office. Although it's still too early to determine the outcome of this incredible experiment, it holds for many the possibility of keeping the whooper alive and well and living on the planet.

As it happens, the mid-1980s have been, since we've

been watching, the most productive years for whoopers on the Wood Buffalo nesting ground, with 1986 setting the record for eggs produced in a single year. Twenty-eight pairs of whooping cranes nested at Wood Buffalo in 1986, and biologists removed from their nests twenty fertile eggs. Sixteen went to the Grays Lake project, and four to the Patuxent captive flock. If conditions on the nesting grounds continue to be so favorable, the population of foster whoopers at Grays Lake might well achieve the density necessary to produce a breeding pair.

At the beginning of the project, naysayers raised the old specter of heredity versus environment: Would the young whooping cranes learn the migration route of their foster sandhill parents, or would deep genetic programming compel them to head for Wood Buffalo? Would they learn the ways of those who raised them, or would they perish in the biological neither-here-nor-there? No one knows. As it happens, female whooping cranes raised at Grays Lake seem to be having difficulty finding their way back there, and we suspect that several of them have dispersed to sundry drainages in Wyoming and western Montana, obviously somewhat confused. Locating such far afield birds is next to impossible, and naturalists sometimes have no other choice than to assume a higher migratory mortality rate for mature female whoopers.

The Grays Lake experiment, as surely as the captive Patuxent flock, fuels an ongoing debate about whether or not we should manipulate animals and their natural environment. Some conservationists say save the species at all costs; others say let it go—it doesn't pay to fool Mother Nature. Of course, the debate heats up when a particularly spectacular species is involved, like the doomed California condor or the threatened

polar bear. The status of the whooping crane is nei-
ther as dire as the condor's nor as comfortable as the
polar bear's, but it shares with these creatures a mag-
nificence we simply refuse to let go.

Whoopers dance like nothing else. The tallest birds
on the continent, whoopers stand almost 5 feet tall,
and when a mating pair bows to each other they look
like an image from a Chinese woodcut brought to life
by Walt Disney. And then they start leaping into the
air with a buoyant grace that seems almost the work
of some invisible celestial puppeteer. Dancing or still,
they have about them an unmistakable elegance of
carriage, a stately, royal, majestic gait. Mostly pure
white, they dance and fly on 7-foot wings with jet-
black tips; their chins and crowns, where they have
no feathers, are bright red. Whooping cranes got their
name from their extremely loud calls, which can carry
for miles.

Whoopers can be observed fairly easily at the following locations, most easily at Aransas and Bosque
Del Apache.

DESTINATIONS AND ACCOMMODATIONS

BOSQUE DEL APACHE NATIONAL WILDLIFE REFUGE, NEW MEXICO

About 75 miles south of Albuquerque, Bosque Del
Apache National Wildlife Refuge consists of some
57,000 acres of high desert country surrounded by
mountains. The Rio Grande River flows through the
refuge, which is situated at an elevation of 4200 feet.
The Magdalena Mountains border the refuge to the
west, with the 10,783-foot South Baldy peak less than
10 miles distant. A series of impoundments trans-

formed the arid country here into vast expanses of marsh, with the result that significant numbers of waterfowl utilize the area as a wintering ground.

At peak times, approximately November through January, 57,000 snow geese visit Bosque Del Apache, which also winters about 40,000 ducks. The stars of the refuge, however, are the 12,000 sandhill cranes that winter here and the thirty-five or so adapted whoopers they bring with them. The experimental population of whoopers started in 1975 at Grays Lake National Wildlife Refuge in Idaho winters at Bosque Del Apache, and visitors here frequently see the adapted whoopers. The expansive marshes provide expansive views, delivering a level of visibility that makes wildlife observation particularly easy. Perhaps because of this high visibility wildlife at the refuge seems less shy than when at other locations.

Golden eagles are common here year-round, and in winter hawks are all over the place, northern harriers and red-tails in particular. Bald eagles come down from about October to February. Mule deer are especially common, as are coyotes; and now and again someone spots a mountain lion.

The refuge has 20 miles of road for leisurely wildlife observation, as well as several observation towers and photography blinds. With the Rio Grande flowing through it and 10,000-foot mountains rising beside it, Bosque Del Apache offers some stunning views, including thousands of snow geese flying before a backdrop of darkening mountains.

For information, contact Bosque Del Apache National Wildlife Refuge, Box 1246, Socorro, NM 87801, telephone: (505) 835-1828.

Driving Instructions: From Socorro take I-25 south to

Exit 139 (San Antonio), then take Route 380 east to Route 1. Follow Route 1 south for 8 miles.

Best Western Golden Manor
507 North California Street
Socorro, NM 87801
Telephone: (505) 835-0230

Best Western Golden Manor is a forty-room motel in downtown Socorro, which was the largest city in New Mexico as recently as 1880. Each of the rooms has color cable television and telephone, as well as a private bath. The facilities include a restaurant (no bar) that serves a mixture of American and Mexican dishes, and a pool (open summer only).

Rates: inexpensive; AE,CB,DC,MC,V

Elephant Butte Inn
Route 52
PO Box E
Elephant Butte, NM 87935
Telephone: (505) 744-5431

Sixty miles south of Bosque Del Apache, Elephant Butte Inn is a mile from Elephant Butte Lake State Park. The rooms have color television, telephone, and private bath. The facilities include a bar, restaurant, golf course, tennis courts, and pool. Some of the rooms overlook the lake, an impoundment of the Rio Grande, and several suites are available.

Rates: moderate; AE,CB,DC,MC,V

ARANSAS NATIONAL WILDLIFE REFUGE, TEXAS

The 55,000-acre Aransas National Wildlife Refuge occupies the better part of the Blackjack Peninsula, a south-facing piece of land named for its many black-jack oaks. Almost entirely surrounded by water, the peninsula is situated along the intercoastal waterway, protected from the Gulf of Mexico by Matagorda Island. Tidal marshes, long, narrow ponds, and San Antonio and Aransas bays make Aransas a well-watered—and well-visited—place. Aransas has the longest bird list of any refuge in the system; 350 species have been sighted here.

The whooping crane is, of course, the star of the refuge, and people from all over the world travel here to see them. All the whooping cranes now living are descended from the fifteen birds resident at Aransas in 1941. Currently about 150 whoopers exist—eighty or so at Aransas/Wood Buffalo, about thirty in the Idaho/New Mexico flock, and about another forty in captivity. Knowing how important Aransas has been for the survival of the whooping crane makes seeing them here particularly special.

Aransas has miles of trails, an auto route that circles the refuge, and an observation tower from which one can frequently see a pair of whooping cranes. The surest way to see whoopers is to take a ride on one of the many tour boats that visit the refuge. The whoopers arrive here in twos and threes, with the first groups appearing in October. By November the whoopers have all arrived, and they remain here until approximately March.

In addition to whoopers, Aransas hosts all manner of wildlife, from alligators to javelinas to mountain lions, and the area around the refuge is rife with parks and beaches. Padre Island National Seashore is about 30 miles south of Aransas.

For information, contact Aransas National Wildlife

Refuge, Box 100, Austwell, TX 77950, telephone: (512) 286-3559.

Driving Instructions: From Rockport take Route 35 north to 774, turn east and go approximately 8 miles to 2040. The refuge is about 5 miles southeast on 2040.

Sand Dollar Hospitality, Bed and Breakfast
3605 Mendenhall
Corpus Christi, TX 78415
Telephone: (512) 853-1222

Sand Dollar Hospitality represents B&B homes in the Corpus Christi and Padre Island area. The accommodations vary from simple to fancy, and the prices range accordingly.

Best Western Motel
PO Box 310
Fulton, TX 78358
Telephone: (512) 729-8351

Best Western Motel has seventy-two rooms, all of them with color television, air-conditioning, and telephone. Some kitchenette units are available, and the facilities include a Laundromat, restaurant, bar, and pool.

Rates: inexpensive to moderate; AE,CB,DC,MC,V

OTHER PLACES TO OBSERVE WHOOPING CRANES

Grays Lake National Wildlife Refuge   *(summer)*
Wayan, Idaho 83285

Monte Vista National Wildlife   *(spring/fall)*
   Refuge
9383 El Rancho Lane
Box 1148
Alamosa, CO 81101

INDEX

Accipiters, 2, 10, 16, 22, 23
Accipitridaes, 10, 16–25
Alaska Bed & Breakfast
    Association, 52
Alaska brown bears, 59, 66
Alaska Chilkat Bald Eagle Preserve,
    38
Alaska Discovery, 50
Alaska Private Lodgings, 39
Alaskan Hotel, 52
Algonquin Provincial Park,
    Ontario, 199–202
    loons at, 221
    wolves at, 199–202
Allagash Wilderness Waterway,
    Maine, 221
Alligators, 109–24, 289
    danger of, 110–11
    destinations and
        accommodations, 117–24
    history of, 112–13
    observing, 115–24
    poaching, 113–14, 116
    reproduction of, 114–15
Alternate Lodging, Inc., East
    Hampton, NY, 179
American Family Inn/Bed &
    Breakfast San Francisco, 161
American kestrel, 1, 6, 10, 14
American swallow-tailed kite, 10, 21
American wigeon, 93–94
Anahuac National Wildlife Refuge,
    Texas, 202

Antelope, pronghorn, 257
Aplomado falcon, 13
Aquarids, 185, 188–89
Aransas, Texas, 280, 281
Aransas National Wildlife Refuge,
    Texas, 288–90
Arcadia National Park, 162–63
Arctic loon, 206–207, 212–13
Arkansas National Wildlife Refuge,
    123
Around Plymouth Bay Bed &
    Breakfast, 172
Aurora borealis, *see* Northern lights
Avellar, A1, 173

Badlands National Park, South
    Dakota, 262
Baja California, Mexico, 158–59
Bald Eagles, 3, 4, 6, 19, 38, 39, 71,
    98, 117, 164, 217, 258, 287
Baleen whales, *see* Mysticeti
    (mustached) whales
Banff National Park, Alberta:
    elk at, 243
    glaciers at, 53
Bar Harbor, Maine, 162–65
Bar Harbor Whale and Bird
    Watch, 164–65
Barklow, Dr. William, 210–11
Barnacle goose, 86
Bat Conservation International,
    267, 269, 278, 279

Bats, 263–79
  conservation efforts, 266–67,
    275, 278
  destinations and
    accommodations, 275–79
  echolocation by, 273–75, 278
  fear of, 266, 275
  in history, 267–68
  reproduction of, 270–72
Bay of Fundy, 227–37
  destinations and
    accommodations, 230–37
  tides of, 223–28
  wildlife of, 228–29, 230
Bean goose, 87–88
Bear River Migratory Bird Refuge,
  105
Bears, 54–74, 217
  advice if confronted by, 54–56
  bells, 54, 56
  destinations and
    accommodations, 47–74
  hibernating, 62–63
  observing, 63–74
  species of, 57–61
Bed & Breakfast Agency-Boston
    Waterfront, Faneuil Hall, and
    Greater Boston, 168–69
Bed & Breakfast Bay Colony, Ltd.,
  168
Bed & Breakfast Cape Cod, 175
Bed & Breakfast Directory of
    Maine, 167
Bed & Breakfast Down East, Inc.,
    Eastbrook, ME, 167
Bed & Breakfast International,
    Kensington, CA, 162
Bed & Breakfast Registry, St. Paul,
  218
Bed & Breakfast of Southeast
    Pennsylvania, 34
Bed & Breakfast Society of Austin,
  279
Bed and Breakfast Texas Style, 279
Bed & Breakfast USA, Ltd., 31
Beluga whales, 68, 157–58, 180,
  181
Be Our Guest Bed & Breakfast,
    Ltd., 172

Binoculars, xvii
Bison, 253–62
  destinations and
    accommodations, 257–62
  history of, 253–57
  observing, 257–62
  protection of, 256
  size of, 256
Black bears, 56, 57–58, 63–64, 71,
  217
Black guillemots, 164, 229
Black-shouldered kite, 22
Black vultures, 12
Blowing Wind Cave, Alabama, 279
Blue whales, 132, 134, 139, 151–
  52, 161, 181
Bosque del Apache National
    Wildlife Refuge, New Mexico,
    286–88
Boston, Masssachusetts, 167–69
Bottlenose dolphins, 132
Bowhead whale, 134
Bowman, Bob, 163
Bracken Cave, Texas, 269, 278–79
Braddock Bay State Park, 39
Brant goose, 86
Brazilian free-tailed bats, 266–67,
  269, 270, 278
Brigantine National Wildlife
    Refuge, New Jersey, 101–102
Broad-winged hawks, 1, 6, 10, 25
Buffalo, see Bison
Buffalo Lake National Wildlife
    Refuge, Texas, 105
Buteos, 1, 2–3, 6, 10, 16, 22, 24–25,
  232

Cabrillo Whalewatch, 159–60
California condor, 1, 12–13
Campobello Island, 229
Canada goose, 75–76, 78–79, 85–
  87, 242
Canadian Wildlife Service, 282
Cape Cod, 175
Cape Cod Bay, 153
Cape May, New Jersey, 26–29, 102
Cape May Point State Park, 26–28
Captain John Boats, 171–72

Caracaras and falcons, 1, 3, 4–5, 6, 10, 13–16
Carlsbad Caverns National Park, New Mexico, 266–67, 268, 270, 275–77
Chickadees, 236
Chilkat River, 6
Chincoteague National Wildlife Refuge, Virginia, 103–104
Churchill, Manitoba:
bears at, 67–70
northern lights at, 68, 246
Churchill River, 157
CLIMAP (Climate: Long-Range Investigation; Mapping and Prediction) project, 43
CN Marine, 235
Common loon, 204–208, 209–11, 213–22
Congress Avenue Bridge, Austin, 269, 278–79
Cooper's hawk, 23
Cormorants, 164, 208, 229
Coyotes, 258
Crab Orchard National Wildlife Refuge, Illinois, 106
Craighead, Frank, 61
Craighead, John, 61
Credit card information, xviii
Crested caracara, 13
Crocodiles, 112, 113, 116
Cumberland Falls, 125, 126, 128–30
Cumberland Falls Lodge and Cabins, 130
Cumberland Falls State Park Resort, Kentucky, 129–30
Cumberland Island National Seashore, Georgia, 123
Curie Point, 250
Custer State Game Lodge and Cabins, 259
Custer State Park, South Dakota, 257–62

Daypack, xv
DDT, 3–4, 14

Deer:
mule, 287
white-tailed, 257
Delano, Columbus, 253–54
Delta Aquarids, 190
Denali National Park Hotel, 65
Denali National Park and Preserve, Alaska:
bears at, 64–65
wolves at, 202
DeSota National Wildlife Refuge, Iowa, 106
Digby, Nova Scotia, 235–36
Dolphin Fleet, 173–74
Dolphins, 132, 137, 139, 164
Disenchantment Bay, 41
Drewien, Roderick, 283
Ducks, 88–94, 98, 102, 103, 283, 287
Duluth, Minnesota, 246

Eagle Creek Cave, Arizona, 267
Eagle Nest, 36
Eagles, 3, 4, 6, 16, 18–21, 71, 98, 117, 164, 217, 258, 287
Eiders, 164, 229
Elk, 238–44, 257
antlers, 238–40
"bugling" by, 241
size of, 240–41
Elk Island National Park, Alberta:
bison at, 262
northern lights at, 244
wolves at, 202–203
Emperor goose, 87–88
Endangered Species Act of 1972, 4
Equipment, xiv–xvi
Everglades National Park, Florida, 116, 119

Falcons, 1, 3, 4–5, 6, 10, 13–16, 233
Farallon Islands National Wildlife Refuge, 161
Ferruginous hawks, 2–3, 25
Finback whales, 133–34, 139, 150–151, 164, 171, 177–78, 180, 181, 229, 231
Fireballs, 187–88

First-aid kit, xvii
Flashlight, xvi
Fletchere, Dr. Milford R., 270
Florida, northern, 246
Florida panther, 120
Florida Keys National Wildlife
    Refuge, 123
Flyways, waterfowl, 79–82
Fort Niobrara National Wildlife
    Refuge, Nebraska, 262
Franklin, Benjamin, 3
Fundy National Park, New
    Brunswick, 232–33

Geese, 75–76, 78–79, 85–88, 100,
    102, 103, 242, 281, 283, 287
Geminids, 185, 191
Glacier Bay Lodge and Cabins, 48–
    49, 50
Glacier Bay National Park, Alaska:
  bears at, 73
  glaciers at, 47–49
  hawks at, 39
  wolves at, 203
Glacier/Mount Revelstoke National
    Parks, British Columbia:
  bears at, 73
  glaciers at, 53
Glacier National Park, Montana:
  bears at, 61, 70–72
  hawks at, 39
  wolves at, 203
Glacier Park, Inc., 71–72
Glacier Park Lodge, 71
Glaciers, 40–53
  continental, 46
  destinations and
    accommodations, 47–53
  formation of, 40–41
  movement of, 41–42, 44–46
  observing, –53
  study of, 41–44
  valley, 46
Gloucester, Massachusetts, 169–71
Golden eagles, 3, 19–20, 258, 287
Goldeneyes, 242
Grand Manan Archipelago, 229
Grand Manan Island, New
    Brunswick, 229, 231

Grand Teton National Park, 242,
    243
Granite Park and Sperry Chalets,
    71, 72
Gray Line of Alaska, 50, 51
Grays Lake National Wildlife
    Refuge, Idaho, 282–85, 287,
    290
Gray whales, 147–48, 158
Great blue herons, 95, 97
Great egrets, 95, 96
Greater scaup, 93
Greenland, 245, 246
Green-winged teal, 92–93
Griffin, Donald R., 273
Grizzly bears, 56, 58–59, 60, 61,
    63, 71
Gulf of St. Lawrence, 157
Gunflint Lodge, 218
Gyrfalcons, 1, 4–5

Haines, Alaska, 38–39
Halsingland Hotel, 39
Hammer-headed bats, 271
Hampton Bed & Breakfast, East
    Moriches, NY, 179
Harems, bats mating in, 272
Harriers, 2, 10, 16–17, 232
Harvard Glacier, 46
Hawk Mountain Sanctuary, 4, 6,
    32–34
Hawk subfamily, 1, 2–3, 6, 10, 16,
    22–25
Hawks, 1–39, 236, 242, 287
  destinations and
    accommodations, 26–39
  identifying, 10–25
  see also individual types of hawks
Herring gulls, 229
Hiking shoes, xv
Hook Mountain, New York, 6,
    30–31
Hook Mountain State Park, 30–31
Hopewell Cape, New Brunswick,
    224
Horicon National Wildlife Refuge,
    Wisconsin, 106
Houseguests Cape Cod, 175
Hubbard Glacier, 41

Humboldt Bay National Wildlife
  Refuge, California, 106
Humpback whales, 137–38, 149–
  50, 161, 164, 171, 178, 181,
  229, 231
Hydro-Quebec, 227
Hypothermia, xvi

Ice ages, explanation of, 43–44
Indiana bat, 271
Insect repellent, xvi
Isle Royal National Park,
  Minnesota:
  loons at, 221
  wolves at, 203

Jackson Hole, Wyoming, 238,
  242–43
Japanese hunting of sperm whales,
  134, 155
Jasper National Park:
  bears at, 73
  elk at, 244
  glaciers at, 53
Javelinas, 289
J.N. "Ding" Darling National
  Wildlife Refuge, Florida,
  117–18
Johns Hopkins Glacier, 48

Katmai National Park:
  bears at, 73
  wolves at, 203
Kejimkujik National Park, Nova
  Scotia:
  Bay of Fundy, 236–37
  loons at, 222, 236
Kempton, Pennsylvania, 32–33
Kenai Fjords National Park,
  Arkansas, 53
Killer whales, 154–55, 161
Kirwin National Wildlife Refuge,
  Kansas, 106
Kites, 2, 10, 16, 21–22
Kittatinny Ridge, 7, 32
Klamath Basin National Wildlife
  Refuges, California/Oregon,
  97–99
Klein, Tom, 211

Kluane National Park, Yukon
  Territories:
  bears at, 73
  glaciers at, 53
Knik Glacier, 41
Kodiak bear, see Alaskan brown
  bears
Kodiak National Wildlife Refuge,
  Alaska, 65–67
Kootenay National Park, British
  Columbia, 73

Lacassine National Wildlife Refuge,
  Louisiana, 100–101, 123
Lake Barkley State Resort Park,
  Kentucky, 39
Lake Clark National Park, Alaska,
  53
Lake George, 41
Lake Woodruff National Wildlife
  Refuge, Florida, 124
Lek, 271, 272
Leonids, 190–91
Loon Magic (Klein), 211
Loons, 199, 204–22, 230, 236
  destinations and
    accommodations, 215–22
  diving by, 207
  flight by, 204–205, 207–208
  identifying, 208–13
  observing, 213–22
  sounds of, 205, 210–11, 212, 213
Lorenz, Konrad, 86
Los Angeles, California, 159–60
Lowville, New York, 220–21
Loxahatchee National Wildlife
  Refuge, Florida, 124

Machias Seal Island, 229, 231
McKinley Chalets, 65
Maine Whalewatch, 163–64
Malheur National Wildlife Refuge,
  Oregon, 106
Mallards, 89–90
Mary's Point, New Brunswick, 225
Mattumuskeet National Wildlife
  Refuge, North Carolina, 106
Mendenhall Glacier, 47, 50–51

Meteor showers, 183–91
  explanation of, 183–85
  observing, 185–91
Milankovitch, Milutin, 42, 43
Minas Basin, Nova Scotia, 225, 227
Mingan Island Cetacean Study,
  Inc., 181
Mingo National Wildlife Refuge,
  Missouri, 106
Minke whales, 178, 180, 181, 229,
  231
Molatore's, 99–100
Moncton, New Brunswick, 225, 234
Moonbows, 125–30
  destinations and
    accommodations, 129–30
  formation of, 125–28
Montauk, New York, 176–79
Monte Vista National Wildlife
  Refuge, 290
Moose, 217
Moosehorn National Wildlife
  Refuge, Maine, 222
Mountain lion, 120, 287, 289
Mount Revelstoke/Glacier National
  Parks, British Columbia:
  bears at, 73
  glaciers at, 53
Mule, 257
Mule deer, 287
Mute swan, 83, 84–85
Mysticeti (mustached) whales, 68,
  132, 133–34, 137–38, 139,
  145–53, 158, 161, 164, 171,
  177–78, 180–81, 229

National Audubon Society, 211
National Bison Range, Montana,
  262
National Marine Fisheries Service,
  142–43
New England Aquarium, 167–68
New England Bed & Breakfast, 168
New Hampshire Bed and
  Breakfast, 219
New Hampshire Lakes Region,
  218–20
New World Vultures, 10, 11–13
New York Times, 5, 267

North American Loon Fund, 211
North Cascades National Park,
  Washington:
  bears at, 74
  wolves at, 203
Northeast Harbor, Maine, 162–65
Northern harriers, 10, 16–17, 232
National Elk Refuge, Wyoming,
  238, 242–43
Northern lights, 245–52
  causes of the, 247–52
  observing the, 68, 246
Northern pintail, 90–91
Northwest Bed & Breakfast, Inc.,
  37, 99
Nyack, New York, 30–31

Oakland, California, 160–61
Odontoceti ("toothed") whales, 139,
  145, 154–58, 161, 180–81,
  229, 231
Okefenokee National Wildlife
  Refuge, Georgia, 120–22
Okeanos Ocean Research
  Foundation, 176–78
Olympic National Park,
  Washington, 244
Operation Trophy Hunt, 5
Orionids, 185, 190
Ospreys, 2, 3, 4, 10, 16, 17–18,
  117, 164
Ottawa National Forest, Michigan,
  215–16

Pacific Western Airlines, 69
Patuxent Wildlife Research Center,
  282, 283, 284
Peace/Athabasca Delta, 260–61
Pelicans, 98
Peregrine falcons, 2, 3, 4, 13, 14–
  15, 233
Perseids, 187, 190
Petitcodiac River, 225
Petrels, 229
Plains Indians, 254
Plovers, 225, 230
Plymouth, Massachusetts, 171–73
Point Barrow, Alaska, 246
Polar bears, 59–60, 63, 68–69

Poncho, waterproof, xvi
Porpoises, 131, 161, 164, 231
Prince Albert National Park,
    Saskatchewan, 244
Prince of Fundy Cruises, 235
Provincetown, Massachusetts,
    173–76
Puffin, 163, 229, 230, 231

Quadrantids, 188, 189
Quebec City, 246
Queen Victoria, The, 28–29
Quetico Provincial Park, Ontario,
    222
Quivira National Wildlife Refuge,
    Kansas, 106–107

Rails, 283
Rate information, xviii
Red Rock National Wildlife Refuge,
    83, 85
Red-tailed hawk, 2, 10, 24
Red-throated loon, 206–207,
    211–12
Redwood National Park, California,
    244
Reelfort Lake State Park Resort,
    34–35
Respecting the wilderness, xvii–
    xviii
Reversing Falls Rapids, St. John,
    New Brunswick, 224–25
Rice Lake National Wildlife
    Refuge, Minnesota, 222
Right whales, 133, 152–53, 164,
    171, 229, 231
Rockport, Wahington, 36–37
Rocky Mountain National Park,
    Colorado, 244
Ross goose, 86
Rough-legged hawk , 24–25, 232
Russell Lake, Alaska, 41

Sabine National Wildlife Refuge,
    Louisiana, 124
Sacramento National Wildlife
    Refuge, 107
St. George River, 227

St. John, New Brunswick, 232
St. Johns River, 225
Salmon River, 225
Salt Plains National Wildlife
    Refuge, Oklahoma, 107
Sand Dollar Hospitality, Bed and
    Breakfast, 290
Sandhill cranes, 282–83, 285, 287
Sandpipers, 225
San Francisco, California, 160–62
Sanibel Island, 117–18
San Luis National Wildlife Refuge,
    California:
  elk at, 248
  waterfowl at, 107
Savannah National Wildlife Refuge,
    Georgia, 124
Seals, 229
Seney National Wildlife Refuge,
    Michigan, 222
Sharp-shinned hawk, 10, 23
Shearwaters, 229
Sheep, bighorn, 257
Sherburne National Wildlife
    Refuge, Minnesota, 222
Shooting stars, see Meteor showers
Signal Mountain Lodge, 243
Skagit River Bald Eagle Nature
    Area, 36–38
Snail-kites, 2, 21
Snow goose, 85, 86, 87–88, 100,
    102, 103, 281, 287
Snowy egrets, 95, 96
Social bat, 271
Société Linnéenne Saint Laurent,
    180–81
Solar flares, 251
Soras, 283
Spallanzani, Lazzaro, 273
Special Expeditions, 158–59
Sperm whales, 139, 155–57, 161,
    207
Squam Lake, 219
Squaw Creek National Wildlife
    Refuge, Missouri, 39
Station de Recherche de Îles
    Mingan, 181
Stellar's sea eagle, 19
Stillwater Reservoir, 220

Sully's Hill National Game
    Preserve, North Dakota, 262
Sunspots, 251–52
Superior National Forest,
    Minnesota:
  loons at, 216–18
  wolves at, 203, 217
Swallow-tailed kite, 10, 21
Swans, 83–85, 98, 242

Tadoussac, Quebec, 180–82
Tamarac National Wildlife Refuge,
    Minnesota, 222
Teal, 242
Temsco Helicopters, 51
Theodore Roosevelt National Park,
    North Dakota, 262
Tides, *see* Bay of Fundy
Tiptonville, Tennessee, 34–36
Travel Manitoba, 69
Trumpeter swan, 83, 85, 242
Truro, Nova Scotia, 225, 237
Turkey vultures, 11–12
Tuttle, Dr. Merlin, 267, 278

U.S. Army Corps of Engineers,
    227–28
U.S. Department of Agriculture,
    4–5
U.S. Fish and Wildlife Service, 5,
    280, 282
U.S. Navy, 137

Valerie Glacier, 41
Van Allen radiation belts, 248, 249
Variegated Glacier, 42
VIA Rail, 69
Victoria Falls, 125
Voices of the Loon, 211
Voyageurs National Park,
    Minnesota, 203

Warblers, 236
Water and water bottle, xv
Waterfowl, 75–107, 242
  destinations and
    accommodations, 97–107
  identifying, 82–97

migration of, 75–76, 78–82
see also specific types of waterfowl
Waterton-Glacier International
    Peace Park, 71
Whale Center, 160–61
Whales, 68, 131–82, 229, 230
  biology of, 132, 135–37
  destinations and
    accommodations, 158–82
  guidelines for whale-watching
    vessels, 142–43
  identifying, 141–42, 145–58
  observing, 140–41, 158–82
  vocalizations of, 137–39, 156
Whale safaris, 169–70
Wheeler National Wildlife Refuge,
    Alabama, 279
Whistling swans, 83, 84, 98
White River National Wildlife
    Refuge, Arkansas, 107
White-tailed deer, 257
White-tailed eagle, 19
Whooper swan, 83
Whooping cranes, 260, 280–90
  dance of, 286
  destinations and
    accommodations, 286–90
  efforts to conserve, 280, 281–86,
    287
Wind Cave National Park, 258
Winnipesaukee, Lake, 219
Wichita Mountains National
    Wildlife Refuge, Oklahoma,
    262
Wolves, 192–204, 217
  communication among, 196
  destinations and
    accommodations, 199–204
  fear of, 198–99
  hierarchies in pack life, 195–96
  howling by, 197–98, 199–201
  hunting by, 192–95, 197, 256
  mating by, 196, 197
Wood Buffalo National Park,
    North West Territory:
  buffalo at, 256, 260–61
  whooping cranes at, 260, 280–81,
    282, 283, 284–85
  wolves at, 203

Wood duck, 91–92
Woodpeckers, 236
Worthington Glacier, 47
Wrangell-St. Elias National Park
    and Preserve, Alaska, 53

Yarmouth, Nova Scotia, 234–35
Yazoo National Wildlife Refuge,
    Mississippi, 107

Yellow-billed loon, 207, 213
Yellowstone National Park, 242,
    243
    bears at, 60–61, 74
    bison at, 262
    elk at, 244
    trumpeter swan at, 83, 85
Yosemite National Park, California,
    64